Learning Akka

Build fault-tolerant, concurrent, and distributed
applications with Akka

Jason Goodwin

[PACKT] open source*
PUBLISHING community experience distilled

BIRMINGHAM - MUMBAI

Learning Akka

First published: December 2015

Production reference: 1181215

Published by Packt Publishing Ltd.
Livery Place
35 Livery Street
Birmingham B3 2PB, UK.

ISBN 978-1-78439-300-7

www.packtpub.com

Credits

Author
Jason Goodwin

Reviewer
Taylor Jones

Commissioning Editor
Akram Hussain

Acquisition Editor
Nikhil Karkal

Content Development Editor
Dharmesh Parmar

Technical Editor
Gebin George

Copy Editor
Yesha Gangani

Project Coordinator
Nikhil Nair

Proofreader
Safis Editing

Indexer
Tejal Daruwale Soni

Graphics
Jason Monteiro

Production Coordinator
Melwyn Dsa

Cover Work
Melwyn Dsa

About the Author

Jason Goodwin is a developer who is primarily self-taught. His entrepreneurial spirit led him to study business at school, but he started programming when he was 15 and always had a high level of interest in technology. This interest led his career to take a few major changes away from the business side and back into software development. His journey has led him to working on high-scale distributed systems. He likes to create electronic music in his free time.

He was first introduced to an Akka project at a Scala/Akka shop—mDialog—that built video ad insertion software for major publishers. The company was acquired by Google eventually. He has also been an influential technologist in introducing Akka to a major Canadian telco to help them serve their customers with more resilient and responsive software. He has experience of teaching Akka and functional and concurrent programming concepts to small teams there. He is currently working via Adecco at Google.

Acknowledgments

I wish to write a thank-you note here to a few people who have shaped and formed my opinions, and supported me through my own journey.

First, to my wife Kate, thank you for the many, many months of support while I wrote this book and worked on crazy projects. Without your constant support, patience, and care, changing my career to do things that I love to do, and writing this, would not be possible. We made it to the finish line. Time for painting, fixing the house, and Netflix and chill!

To my parents and grandparents, who always told me that I can do anything that I set my mind to: thank you for your advice. You were right.

To my mDialog/Google team, thanks for your reviews and discipline on my journey—I feel lucky to have had the opportunity to work with you all. To Chris especially, thanks for your faith that my interest would be enough to help me grow into a decent engineer, and for always expecting that the team keep it clean.

To Craig and Herb, thanks for the early start. If I wasn't doing bubble sorts, drawing pixelated circles, or converting customer databases when I was 17, I'm not sure I would have been able to find my way to the work that I love to do so much today.

About the Reviewer

Taylor Jones is a full-stack software engineer specializing in Java-based webapp development currently working at Cisco Systems. He enjoys designing and building complex applications with open source technologies and playing with his dog, and is semi-competent at DotA 2.

www.PacktPub.com

Support files, eBooks, discount offers, and more

For support files and downloads related to your book, please visit www.PacktPub.com.

Did you know that Packt offers eBook versions of every book published, with PDF and ePub files available? You can upgrade to the eBook version at www.PacktPub.com and as a print book customer, you are entitled to a discount on the eBook copy. Get in touch with us at service@packtpub.com for more details.

At www.PacktPub.com, you can also read a collection of free technical articles, sign up for a range of free newsletters and receive exclusive discounts and offers on Packt books and eBooks.

https://www2.packtpub.com/books/subscription/packtlib

Do you need instant solutions to your IT questions? PacktLib is Packt's online digital book library. Here, you can search, access, and read Packt's entire library of books.

Why subscribe?

- Fully searchable across every book published by Packt
- Copy and paste, print, and bookmark content
- On demand and accessible via a web browser

Free access for Packt account holders

If you have an account with Packt at www.PacktPub.com, you can use this to access PacktLib today and view 9 entirely free books. Simply use your login credentials for immediate access.

Table of Contents

Preface

This book attempts to give both the introductory reader and the intermediate or advanced reader an understanding of basic distributed computing concepts as well as demonstrates how to use Akka to build fault-tolerant horizontally-scalable distributed applications that communicate over a network. Akka is a powerful toolkit that gives us options to abstract away whether a unit of work is handled on the local machine or a remote machine on the network. Throughout this book, concepts will be introduced to help the reader understand the difficulty of getting systems to talk to each other over the network while introducing the solutions that Akka offers to various problems.

Soaked in these pages is my own journey, my own discovery—and I hope that you will share that with me. I have a fair amount of professional Akka experience working with both Java8 and Scala, but I have learned a lot of the finer details of Akka while writing this book. I feel that this work is a good introduction to how and why to use Akka, and demonstrates how to start building scalable and distributed applications with the Akka toolkit. It does not simply repeat the documentation, but covers many of the important topics and approaches you should understand to successfully approach building systems to handle the scale-related problems we encounter as developers today.

What this book covers

Chapter 1, Starting Life as an Actor: Introduction to the Akka Toolkit and Actor Model.

Chapter 2, Actors and Concurrency: Reactive. Working with Actors and Futures.

Chapter 3, Getting the Message Across: Message Passing Patterns.

Chapter 4, Actor Lifecycle – Handling State and Failure: Actor Lifecycle, Supervision, Stash/ Unstash, Become/ Unbecome, and FMSs.

Chapter 5, *Scaling Up*: Doing work concurrently, Router Groups/Pools, Dispatchers, Handling Blocking I/O, and APIs.

Chapter 6, *Successfully Scaling Out – Clustering*: Clustering, CAP Theorem, and Akka Cluster.

Chapter 7, *Handling Mailbox Problems*: Overwhelmed mailboxes, choosing different mailboxes, Circuit Breakers.

Chapter 8, *Testing and Design*: Specification, Domain Driven Design, and Akka Testkit.

Chapter 9, *A Journey's End*: Other Akka Features. Next steps.

What you need for this book

You will need a PC with access to install tools such as Java JDK8 (for Java development) or Java JDK6 (for Scala development). You will also require sbt (Simple Build Tool) or Typesafe Activator, which contains sbt. Installation is covered in this book.

Who this book is for

This book is intended for beginner to intermediate Java or Scala developers who want to build applications to serve the high-scale user demands in computing today. If you need your applications to handle the ever-growing user bases and datasets with high performance demands, then this book is for you. *Learning Akka* will let you do more for your users with less code and less complexity by building and scaling your networked applications with ease.

Conventions

In this book, you will find a number of text styles that distinguish between different kinds of information. Here are some examples of these styles and an explanation of their meaning.

Code words in text, database table names, folder names, filenames, file extensions, pathnames, dummy URLs, user input, and Twitter handles are shown as follows: "We can include other contexts through the use of the `include` directive."

A block of code is set as follows:

```
// The executor function used by our promise.
// The first argument is the resolver function,
// which is called in 1 second to resolve the promise.
function executor(resolve) {
    setTimeout(resolve, 1000);
}
```

New terms and **important words** are shown in bold. Words that you see on the screen, for example, in menus or dialog boxes, appear in the text like this: "Select the folder and click **Next**."

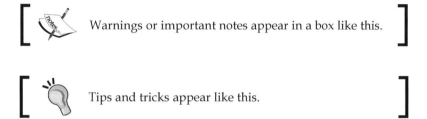

Warnings or important notes appear in a box like this.

Tips and tricks appear like this.

Reader feedback

Feedback from our readers is always welcome. Let us know what you think about this book—what you liked or disliked. Reader feedback is important for us as it helps us develop titles that you will really get the most out of.

To send us general feedback, simply e-mail feedback@packtpub.com, and mention the book's title in the subject of your message.

If there is a topic that you have expertise in and you are interested in either writing or contributing to a book, see our author guide at www.packtpub.com/authors.

Customer support

Now that you are the proud owner of a Packt book, we have a number of things to help you to get the most from your purchase.

Downloading the example code

You can download the example code files from your account at http://www.
packtpub.com for all the Packt Publishing books you have purchased. If you
purchased this book elsewhere, you can visit http://www.packtpub.com/support
and register to have the files e-mailed directly to you.

Downloading the color images of this book

We also provide you with a PDF file that has color images of the screenshots/
diagrams used in this book. The color images will help you better understand the
changes in the output. You can download this file from https://www.packtpub.
com/sites/default/files/downloads/LearningAkka_ColoredImages.pdf

Errata

Although we have taken every care to ensure the accuracy of our content, mistakes
do happen. If you find a mistake in one of our books—maybe a mistake in the text or
the code—we would be grateful if you could report this to us. By doing so, you can
save other readers from frustration and help us improve subsequent versions of this
book. If you find any errata, please report them by visiting http://www.packtpub.
com/submit-errata, selecting your book, clicking on the **Errata Submission Form**
link, and entering the details of your errata. Once your errata are verified, your
submission will be accepted and the errata will be uploaded to our website or added
to any list of existing errata under the Errata section of that title.

To view the previously submitted errata, go to https://www.packtpub.com/books/
content/support and enter the name of the book in the search field. The required
information will appear under the **Errata** section.

Piracy

Piracy of copyrighted material on the Internet is an ongoing problem across all
media. At Packt, we take the protection of our copyright and licenses very seriously.
If you come across any illegal copies of our works in any form on the Internet, please
provide us with the location address or website name immediately so that we can
pursue a remedy.

Please contact us at copyright@packtpub.com with a link to the suspected
pirated material.

We appreciate your help in protecting our authors and our ability to bring you
valuable content.

eBooks, discount offers, and more

Did you know that Packt offers eBook versions of every book published, with PDF and ePub files available? You can upgrade to the eBook version at www.PacktPub. com and as a print book customer, you are entitled to a discount on the eBook copy. Get in touch with us at customercare@packtpub.com for more details.

At www.PacktPub.com, you can also read a collection of free technical articles, sign up for a range of free newsletters, and receive exclusive discounts and offers on Packt books and eBooks.

Questions

If you have a problem with any aspect of this book, you can contact us at questions@packtpub.com, and we will do our best to address the problem.

1
Starting Life as an Actor

This book is primarily intended for intermediate, to senior-level developers wishing to explore Akka and build fault-tolerant, distributed systems in Scala or modern versions of Java.

This book has been written for the engineer who is faced with building applications that are fast, stable, and elastic, meaning they can scale to meet thousands or tens of thousands concurrent users. With more users having access to the Internet with faster devices and networks, today, more than ever, we need our applications to be able to handle many concurrent users working with larger datasets and with higher expectations of application stability and performance.

This book does not assume that you have a deep understanding of concurrency concepts and does try to introduce all of the concepts needed to know how to start a project from scratch, work with concurrency abstractions, and test and build standalone or networked applications using Akka. While this book should give you everything you need in those regards, it's not meant for an absolute beginner and does assume some does assume some programming proficiency.

Here is a quick overview of what you'll need and what you'll get out of this book.

- Requirements:
    - Intermediate Scala or Java experience
    - A computer
    - Internet connectivity
- Recommendations (but you can learn as you go):
    - If using Java, Java8 lambda exposure
    - Git and GitHub experience for assignments

- What you'll learn:
  - ○ Learn to build distributed and concurrent application
  - ○ Learn techniques for building fault-tolerant systems
  - ○ Learn techniques for sharing code between projects and teams
  - ○ Learn several concepts and patterns to aid in distributed system design

What's in this book?

To meet the modern challenges a platform developer may face, this book puts a strong focus not only on Akka but also on distributed and concurrent computing concepts. It is my intention to give you a toolkit to understand the problems you'll face while trying to scale these distributed and concurrent applications.

These pages are not a re-iteration of the Akka documentation. If you want a desk reference or manual, the 460-page Akka documentation will serve that purpose well. This book is not simply a book about Akka, it is a book about building concurrent and distributed systems with Akka.

This book will take you on a journey to show you a new way of working with distributed and concurrent applications. This book will arm you with an understanding of the tools, and then will show you how to use them. It will demonstrate how to build clusters of applications that talk to each other over the network and can have new computing nodes added or removed to be able to scale to meet the needs of your users. We'll learn how to do things like building pools of workers to handle huge jobs at scale to show how it's done. We will talk about important theorems and common approaches in distributed systems and show how they affect our design decisions, and we will discuss problems you will encounter related to network reliability and demonstrate how we can build our applications to be resilient to those problems.

Chapter overview

At the heart of Akka is an implementation of the Actor Model, which is a theoretical model of concurrent computation. In this, chapter we will introduce core concepts in Akka by looking at the history of Akka and the actor model. This will give you insight into what Akka is and help you understand what problems it tries to solve. Then, the goals of this book will be introduced with recurring examples that will be used.

After covering these concepts, the chapter will move into setting up your development environment with the tools you need to start building. We will set up our environment, **Integrated Development Environment (IDE)**, and our first Akka project, including unit testing.

What is Akka

This section will introduce Akka and the actor model. Akka, purportedly named after a mountain in Sweden, is often referred to as a distribution toolkit—a collection of tools that are used to do work across remote computing resources. Akka is a modern implementation of the actor model of concurrency. Akka today could be seen as an evolution of other technologies, borrowing from Erlang's actor model implementation while introducing many new features to aid with building applications that can handle today's high-scale problems.

Actor Model origins

To better understand what Akka is and how it is used, we will take a brief trip through time looking at the Actor model to understand what it is and how it has evolved into a framework for building fault-tolerant distributed systems in Akka today.

The actor model of concurrency was originally a theoretical model of concurrent computation proposed in a paper called *A Universal Modular Actor Formalism for Artificial Intelligence* in 1973. We will look at the actor model's qualities here to understand its benefits in aiding our ability to reason about concurrent computation while protecting against common pitfalls in shared state.

What's an Actor anyway?

First, let's define what an Actor is. In the actor model, an actor is a concurrency primitive; more simply stated, an actor can be thought of as a worker like a process or thread that can do work and take action. It might be helpful to think of an actor as a person in an organization that has a role and responsibility in that organization. Let's say a sushi restaurant. Restaurant staff have to do various pieces of work throughout the day such as preparing dishes for customers.

Actors and Message passing

One of the qualities of an object in object oriented languages is that it can be can be directly invoked–one object can examine or change another object's fields, or invoke its methods. This is fine if a single thread is doing it, but if multiple threads are trying to read and change values at the same time, then synchronization and locks are needed.

Actors differ from objects in that they cannot be directly read, changed, and invoked. Instead, Actors can only communicate with the world outside of them through message passing. Message passing simply means that an actor can be sent a message (object in our case) and can, itself, send messages or reply with a message. While you may draw parallels to passing a parameter to a method, and receiving a return value, message passing is fundamentally different because it happens asynchronously. An actor begins processing a message, and replies to the message, on its own terms when it is ready.

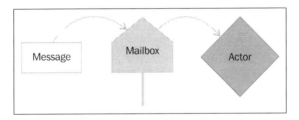

The actor processes messages one at a time, synchronously. The mailbox is essentially a queue of work outstanding for the worker to process. When an actor processes a message, the actor can respond by changing its internal state, creating more actors, or sending more messages to other actors.

The term *Actor System* is often used in implementations to describe a collection of actors and everything related to them including addresses, mailboxes, and configuration.

To reiterate these key concepts:

- **Actor**: A worker concurrency primitive, which synchronously processes messages. Actors can hold state, which can change.
- **Message**: A piece of data used to communicate with processes (for example, Actors).
- **Message-passing**: A software development paradigm where messages are passed to invoke behavior instead of directly invoking the behavior.
- **Mailing address**: Where messages are sent for an actor to process when the actor is free.

- **Mailbox**: The place messages are stored until an actor is able to process the message. This can be viewed as a queue of messages.

- **Actor system**: A collection of actors, their addresses, mailboxes, and configuration, etc.

It might not be obvious yet, but the Actor Model is much easier to reason about than imperative object oriented concurrent applications. Taking a real world example and modeling it in an actor system will help to demonstrate this benefit. Consider a sushi restaurant, We have three actors in this example: a customer, a waiter, and the sushi chef.

Our example starts with the customer telling our waiter their order. The waiter writes it down this onto a piece of paper and places this message in the chef's mailbox (sticks it in the kitchen window). When the chef is free, the chef will pick up the message (order) and start preparing the sushi. The chef will continue to process the message until it's done. When the sushi is prepared, the chef will put this message (plate) in the kitchen window (waiter's mailbox) for the waiter to pick up. The chef can go work on other orders now.

When the waiter has a free minute, the waiter can pick up the food message from the window and deliver it to the customer's mailbox (for example, the table). When the customer is ready, they will process the message by eating the food.

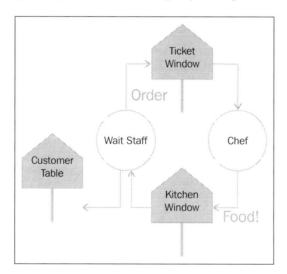

It's easy to reason about the restaurant using the actor model. If you take a moment to imagine more customers coming into the restaurant, you can imagine the waiter taking orders one at a time and handing them off to the chef, the chef processing them, and the waiter delivering food, all concurrently. This is one of the great benefits of the actor model; it's very easy to reason about concurrency when everyone has their own tasks. Modeling real applications with the actor model is not much different than what we have done in this example.

The next benefit to the actor model is elimination of shared state. Because actors process one message at a time, state can be stored inside an actor safely. If you have not worked on concurrent systems this may be harder to see immediately but we can demonstrate it quite easily. If we try to do two operations that read, modify, and write a value at the same time, then one of the operations will be lost unless we carefully employ synchronization and locking. It's a very easy mistake to make.

Let's take a look at a non-atomic increment operation called from two threads at the same time, to see what happens when state is shared across threads. We'll have multiple threads read a value from memory, and then write an incremented value back to memory. This is a *race condition* and can be partly solved by ensuring mutually exclusive access to the value in memory. Let's actually demonstrate this with a Scala example:

If we try to concurrently increment an integer 100000 times with multiple threads, there is a good chance that we will lose some writes.

```
import concurrent.Future
import concurrent.ExecutionContext.Implicits.global
var i, j = 0
(1 to 100000).foreach(_ => Future{i = i + 1})
(1 to 100000).foreach(_ => j = j + 1)
Thread.sleep(1000)
println(s"${i} ${j}")
```

Both i and j are incremented 100000 times using this very simple function — x = x + 1. i is incremented from multiple threads concurrently while j is incremented by only one thread. We wait for a second before printing to ensure all of the updates are done. If you think the output is 100000 100000 you are very wrong.

```
scala> (1 to 100000).foreach(_ => Future{i = i + 1})

scala> (1 to 100000).foreach(_ => j = j + 1)

scala> println(s"${i} ${j}")
71914 100000
```

Shared state is not safe. Values are being read by two threads, and then saved back incremented. Because the same value is read by multiple threads, increment operations are lost along the way. This is a race-condition and is one of the fundamental problems with shared-state concurrency models.

We can demonstrate what may be happening with the race condition more clearly by reasoning about the reads and write operations:

```
[...]
Thread 2 reads value in memory - value read as 9
Thread 2 writes value in memory - value set to 10 (9 + 1)
Thread 1 reads value in memory - value read as 10
Thread 2 reads value in memory - value read as 10
Thread 1 writes value in memory - value set to 11 (10 + 1) !! LOST
INCREMENT !!
Thread 2 writes value in memory - value set to 11 (10 + 1)
Thread 1 reads value in memory - value read as 11
[...]
```

For shared state in memory to work correctly, we have to apply locks and synchronization to stop threads from reading and writing from a value at the same time. This introduces complexity and it's hard to reason about it and to ensure it is done right.

The biggest threat is that often your code will appear correct in testing but it will fail intermittently once you have a bunch of concurrent users working on it. The bugs are easily missed because testing often excludes situations with lots of traffic. Dion Almaer once blogged that most Java applications are so rife with concurrency bugs that they only work by accident. Actors help safeguard against these problems by reducing shared state. If you move state inside an actor, access to that state can be limited only to the actor (effectively only one thread can access that state). If you treat all messages as immutable, then you can effectively eliminate shared state in your actor system and build safer applications.

The concepts in this section represent the core of the actor model. *Chapter 2, Actors and Concurrency* and *Chapter 3, Getting the Message Across*, will cover concurrency, actors, and message passing in greater detail.

The Evolution of supervision and fault tolerance in Erlang

The actor model evolved over time since its introduction in the aforementioned paper. It was a noted influencer in programming language designs (Scheme for example).

There was a note-worthy appearance of the actor model when Ericsson produced an implementation in the 80s in the Erlang programming language for use in embedded TELECOM applications. The concept of fault tolerance through supervision was introduced here. Ericsson, using Erlang and the actor model, produced an often cited appliance, the AXD301. The AXD301 managed to achieve a remarkable nine nine's of availability (99.9999999% uptime). That's about 3.1 seconds of downtime in 100 years. The team working on the AXD claimed to have done this through elimination of shared state (as we have covered) and by introducing a fault-tolerance mechanism in Erlang: Supervision.

Fault-tolerance is gained in the actor model through supervision. Supervision is more or less moving the responsibility of responding to failure outside of the thing that can fail. Practically speaking, this means that an actor can have other child actors that it is responsible for supervising; it monitors the child actor for failures and can take actions regarding the child actor's lifecycle. When an error is encountered in an actor that is running, the default supervision behavior is to restart (effectively recreate) the actor that encountered the failure. This response to failure—the recreating the component that fails—assumes that if an unexpected error is encountered that it could be a result of bad state, and so throwing away and re-creating the failing piece of the application can restore it to working order. It is possible to write custom responses as supervision strategies so almost any action can be taken to restore working order to the application.

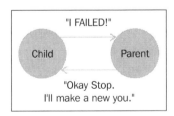

Fault Tolerance in relation to distributed systems will be addressed as a general cross-cutting concern throughout the book with an emphasis on fault tolerance in Akka and distributed systems in *Chapter 4, Actor Lifecycle – Handling State and Failure*.

The Evolution of distribution and location transparency

Business today demands that the capable engineers be able to design systems that can serve traffic to thousands of users concurrently and a single machine is not enough to do that. Further, multi-core processors are becoming more prevalent so distributing across those cores is becoming important to ensure our software can take advantage of the hardware that it runs on.

Akka takes the actor model and continues to evolve it by introducing an important capability for today's engineers: distribution across the network. Akka presents itself as a toolkit for fault-tolerant distribution. That is, Akka is a tool kit for working across the physical boundaries of servers to scale almost indefinitely while maintaining high availability. In recent releases, many of the features added to Akka are related to solving problems related to networked system. Akka clusters was introduced recently which allows an actor system to span multiple machines transparently, and Akka IO and Akka HTTP are now in the core libraries to help us interact with other systems more easily. One of Akka's key contributions to the actor model is the concept of location transparency—that is, an actor's mailing address can actually be a remote location but the location is more or less transparent to the developer so the code produced is more or less identical.

Akka extends on what Erlang did with the actor model and breaks down the physical barriers of the actor system. Akka adds remoting and location transparency, that is, the mailbox of an actor could suddenly be on a remote machine and Akka would abstract away the transmission of the message over the network.

More recently, Akka introduced Cluster. Akka Cluster uses modern approaches similar to what you might see in distributed systems influenced by the Amazon Dynamo paper such as Dynamo, Cassandra, and Riak. With Cluster, an actor system can exist across multiple machines and nodes will gossip and communicate about state to other members to allow an elastic Akka cluster with no single point of failure. The mechanism is similar to Dynamo style databases such as Riak and Cassandra. This is an incredible feature that makes creating elastic, fault-tolerant systems quite simple.

Typesafe , the company that provides technologies like Scala and Akka, are continuing to push forward distributed computing with a plethora of networking tools such as Akka IO and Akka HTTP. Further, Typesafe have been involved in the Reactive Streams proposal and Akka has one of the first implementations for producing non-blocking back-pressure for asynchronous processing.

We will cover many of these items in detail throughout the course of this book. *Chapter 4, Actor Lifecycle – Handling State and Failure* and *Chapter 5, Scaling Up* will cover remoting in greater detail. Cluster will be covered in *Chapter 6, Successfully Scaling Out – Clustering*. Reactive Streams will be covered in *Chapter 7, Handling Mailbox Problems*.

What we will build

We will produce two primary services throughout the book and recommend that you follow along. There is a homework section at the end of every chapter that will give you exercises to help put the material to use— complete the activities before you head on to the next chapter. Post them up to GitHub if you want to share your progress or have a good open-source idea.

We can define two main pieces of software we will focus on developing in the book. One example will be used to demonstrate how to handle state and distribution and the other will be used to demonstrate how to get work done.

Example 1 – handling distributed state

We're going to look at how we would build a scalable distributed in memory database that we will store data in from the other example. To be clear, we will build a highly available key value store similar to Redis or memcached. The database that you build will handle all of the concurrency, clustering, and distribution concerns needed for this to really work. Many of the skills you build will be in learning how to separate and distribute the data and load for our database in a cluster so we can take advantage of the hardware, and scale out to utilize multiple machines, you'll get a real taste of the design challenges and common solutions in real world situations. We're also going to look at how to build a client library to interact with our Akka-based database so anyone on the JVM can use it. It is highly recommended that you build a database like this for yourself, put it on GitHub, and show it off on your resume.

If it sounds like a lot of work—good news, this will all actually be fairly simple to do using the Akka toolkit. We will take you from zero to hero in no time.

Example 2 – getting lots of work done

For an example of doing lots of work at scale in this book, we will produce an article reading an API that will take a blog or news article, rip out the main text body, and store it in our database for later consumption.

For a use case, imagine a mobile device will have a reader on it requesting articles from popular RSS feeds from our service and presenting the main body text in a nice reader experience that can reflow the text to fit the display. Our service will do the extraction of that body text from major RSS feeds so the user has a nice fast experience on the device and never has to wait. If you want to see a real example of this on a device, check out Flipboard for iOS: it is a great example of what a consumer of our service might look like.

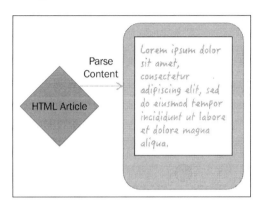

Now that we've covered the content that is in this book, let's get started by setting up your environment, and building an actor!

Setting up your environment

Before we really dig into Akka, we're going to cover setting up your environment and scaffolding a project. You can refer back to this section in later chapters of the book as we will create a few projects along the way.

Choosing a language

The Scala and Java APIs are more or less 1 to 1 for Scala and Java so use whichever language you are comfortable with. If you know both languages, Scala certainly has a more idiomatic API but both are very serviceable choices. An Actor built in Java is accessible from Scala through the Scala actor API and visa versa so there is no need to decide which to build on immediately; do whatever will get you to where you are going faster. Right now your focus is on learning Akka, not a language. You'll be able to pick up the other API later without much effort once you know Akka.

Installing Java – Oracle JDK8

This book will forego all older versions of Java and focus only on Java8. If you are a Java developer but not familiar with Java8 features, you should take some time to familiarize yourself with lambdas and the stream API as covered in this tutorial: `http://www.oracle.com/webfolder/technetwork/tutorials/obe/java/Lambda-QuickStart/index.html`

You'll see lambdas are used heavily in this book. you will benefit from taking the time to get acquainted.

Installing on Windows

Download and install the Windows JDK8 installer (dmg) from Oracle: `http://www.oracle.com/technetwork/java/javase/downloads/index.html`.

Follow the instructions.

Installing on OS X

Download and install the OS X JDK8 installer (dmg) from Oracle: `http://www.oracle.com/technetwork/java/javase/downloads/index.html`

Follow the instructions.

Installing on Linux or Unix (Universal instructions)

There are a couple approaches that can be used for Nix installations. You can use the Universal installer, or try to use a package manager like Yum for **Red Hat Enterprise Linux** (**RHEL**) based distributions or Apt-Get for Debian-based distribution. Instructions for the package manager can vary from distribution to distribution but instructions can be found via Google if desired.

The Universal installer will work on all systems so will be covered here. This is the most basic installation you can get away with. It will install the JDK and enable it for your current user but will not change your system. If you want to change your system's JDK/JRE you can follow the install instructions for your particular distribution. This would be suitable for servers or desktop environments. If you're working on a desktop environment, you can see if there are instructions for your particular distribution if you want it available for other users as the default JDK/JRE.

Download the Linux `tar.gz` JDK distribution from Oracle: `http://www.oracle.com/technetwork/java/javase/downloads/index.html`.

It will likely be in a file named something like `jdk-8u31-linux-x64.tar.gz`
Decompress the `tar.gz` file in an appropriate location such as `/opt`:

```
sudo cp jdk-8u31-linux-x64.tar.gz /opt cd /opt sudo tar -xvf jdk-
8u31-linux-x64.tar.gz
```

You'll want to set your user's Java home to the Java8 folder:

```
echo 'export JAVA_HOME=/opt/jdk1.8.031' >> ~/.profile
```

Also ensure that Java bin is on the path

```
echo 'export PATH=$PATH:/opt/jdk1.8.031' >> ~/.profile
```

Now your IDE and Sbt/Activator can use the JDK to build and run apps we build.

Ensuring Java is configured in your environment

Regardless of the OS you're on, you'll want to ensure that JAVA_HOME is set and also that the Java binary is on the path. You shouldn't need to do this unless you use the universal installer but you should validate in a new terminal that JAVA_HOME is set in the environment, and that the JDK bin folder is on the path.

Installing Scala

If you're using Scala, then you'll want to have Scala and the REPL installed on your system. At the time of writing, the current Scala version (2.11) compiles to Java 1.6 byte-code so we can assume you do not need to install JDK8. There is talk of future versions of Scala requiring JDK8 so this may change.

Scala does not need to be installed on its own. Typesafe Activator contains Scala and all of the tools we will need to work with it; we will install next.

Installing Typesafe Activator

Typesafe Activator installation is a bundle that contains Scala, Akka, Play, **Simple Build Tool** (**SBT**) and some extra features such as project scaffolding and templates.

Windows

Download Typesafe Activator from Typesafe—http://www.typesafe.com/get-started.

Run the installer and follow the onscreen instructions.

Linux/Unix/OS X

Download Typesafe Activator from Typesafe:

- `http://www.typesafe.com/activator/download`
- `http://www.typesafe.com/get-started`

Unzip the file in an appropriate location such as `/opt cd /opt sudo unzip typesafe-activator-1.2.12.zip`

Make the Activator executable: `sudo chmod 755 /opt/activator-1.2.12/activator`

Add the Activator to your path: `echo 'export PATH=$PATH:/opt/activator-1.2.12'`

Log out and back in. Ensure you can run the following on the command line:

`activator --version`

That should display text similar to this: sbt launcher version 0.13.5

OS X

Activator can either be installed with Linux or using `brew`. This section will cover the brew installation:

Open a terminal.

Place the following in your terminal (copied from `http://brew.sh`). This will install the Homebrew OS X Package manager.

```
ruby -e "$(curl -fsSL https://raw.githubusercontent.com/Homebrew/
install/master/install)"
```

Finally, place the following in your terminal and press *Enter*:

`brew install typesafe-activator`

Check that the Activator is available on the command line:

`activator --version`

Creating a new project

We will use the Activator to quickly scaffold projects in this book. We can generate a project from any number of templates. We will only use the basic Java and Scala templates in this book. Feel free to explore other options. Typesafe has many user-submitted Activator templates that will demonstrate various technologies and approaches used together.

To create a new Activator template, in a terminal/command prompt, type:

`activator new`

You will see the following.

Choose from these featured templates or enter a template name:

- minimal-akka-java-seed
- minimal-akka-scala-seed
- minimal-java
- minimal-scala
- play-java
- play-scala

[You can hit *Tab* to view a list of all templates]

Select the minimal-scala or minimal-java project depending on your language preference. You will be prompted to name your application next, call it akkademy-db.

Enter a name for your application (just press *Enter* for minimal-scala) > akkademy-db

To confirm that the project and your environment are set up correctly, change into the folder and run `activator test`

`cd akkademy-db activator test`

You will see output indicating that the project compiled and the test ran. If there are any problems, you may have to head to stack-overflow and sort out your environment before proceeding.

You will see the following success message if all went well:

```
[info] Passed: Total 1, Failed 0, Errors 0, Passed 1 [success] Total
time: 3 s, completed 22-Jan-2015 9:44:21 PM
```

Installing an IDE

We have our environment set up and running now and we can actually start to work on the code. If you want to use a simple text editor, feel free to skip this section. Emacs or Sublime are good choices for text editors and have syntax highlighting and integrations that can provide autocomplete. If you want to get an IDE up and running, we'll cover setting up Eclipse, and IntelliJ here.

Install IntelliJ CE

If you choose to use an IDE, IntelliJ is the recommended IDE. If you're using another IDE, I still strongly recommend you attempt to use IntelliJ. While writing this book, I've worked with many Java developers who transitioned to working with SBT projects and almost all of them switched to IntelliJ and never looked back.

IntelliJ now has built-in SBT support, which makes it a fast IDE to use for your Akka projects; setting up and configuring of the IDE is virtually non-existent—it will just work with the technology we will use in this book.

Steps for getting the project up and running:

1. Download and install IntelliJ CE (free).
2. After installing choose to open a project. Select the `akkademy-db` folder.
3. Select Java 1.8 if you're using Java (or if Scala 2.12 requires it). You can use Java 6 or 7 if using Scala 2.11. Turn on the Auto Import feature. Hit okay.

Eclipse

If using Eclipse, it is recommended that you download Scala-Ide, which contains all of the required plugins to work with our sbt/Akka projects in either Java or Scala. Even if you're only using Java, you may find you want to inspect some Scala along the way.

Installing Eclipse (Scala-Ide)

Download Scala-Ide from `http://scala-ide.org` which is a packaged version of Eclipse with sbt and Scala plugins integrated.

Unzip the file that is downloaded. You can move the unzipped folder to another location if desired such as `/opt (linux)` or `~/Applications (OSX)`.

Run the Eclipse binary. Choose a workspace folder or select the default.

Check that the Java JDK is correctly selected in `Preferences: Java | Compiler`.

Preparing the project for Eclipse

In order to open the project in eclipse, we must first generate an Eclipse project.

First we must add the eclipse sbt plugin to our environment. Open your global sbt plugins file (create it if it's not there), is located in `~/.sbt/{version}/plugins/plugins.sbt` where version is the sbt version. It is 0.13 at the time of writing, so `~/.sbt/0.13/plugins/plugins.sbt`

Include the following in the file, ensuring there is a blank line between each line in the file if there are multiple lines.

```
addSbtPlugin("com.typesafe.sbteclipse" % "sbteclipse-plugin" %
"3.0.0")
```

You may want to ensure this is current by checking the sbteclipse GitHub project: `https://github.com/typesafehub/sbteclipse/`

Once you have the plugin installed, you need to generate the eclipse project: `https://github.com/typesafehub/sbteclipse/`

In the terminal, navigate to the project we created earlier (`akkademy-db`). In the root of the project, run Activator eclipsify to generate the eclipse project structure.

You will see the following success message if all went well:

```
[info] Successfully created Eclipse project files for project(s): [info]
akkademy-db
```

Importing the project into Eclipse

In Eclipse, select **File | Import**.

Choose **General | Existing Projects into Workspace**.

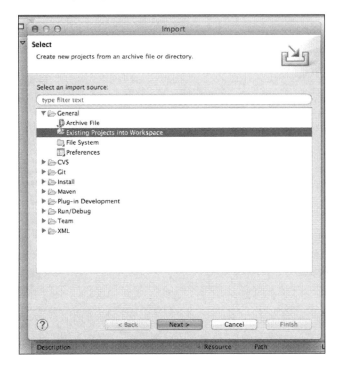

Select the folder and click **Next**.

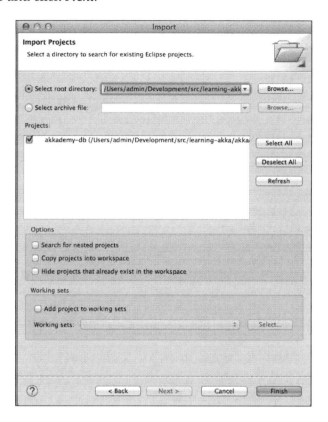

 Note if you change `build.sbt` you will need to re-generate the project and may need to re-import it.

Creating your first Akka application – setting up the SBT project

Now that we have covered setting up your environment and how to create a project, we can proceed with creating some actor code in Akka, and then look at how to validate that code. We will be using **simple build tool(SBT)**, which is the preferred build tool for Scala projects and is also the build tool that Play Framework and Activator use under the hood. It's not complex and we will use it only for managing dependencies and building a testing and running applications, so it should not be an obstacle to learning Akka.

Adding Akka to build.sbt

We will now open the application (either Java or Scala) in our favorite IDE. The scaffolding Activator created is not for an Akka project, so we will need to add the Akka dependencies first. We will add both the Akka core Akka module (akka-actor) and the Akka test-kit, which contains tools to more easily allow us to test the actors.

In the `build.sbt` file, you will see something roughly like this for a Scala project. Note the dependencies are actually Maven dependencies. Any Maven dependencies can easily be added, as we'll cover shortly. The Java and Scala projects will be more or less identical; however the Java project will have a Junit dependency instead of Scalatest:

```
name := """akkademy-db-java"""
version := "1.0"
scalaVersion := "2.11.1"
libraryDependencies ++= Seq(
  "com.typesafe.akka" %% "akka-actor" % "2.3.6",
  "com.typesafe.akka" %% "akka-testkit" % "2.3.6" % "test",
  "junit"             % "junit"            % "4.11" % "test",
  "com.novocode"      % "junit-interface" % "0.10"  % "test"
)
```

To Include Akka, we need to add a new dependency.

Your dependencies should look something like this for Java:

```
libraryDependencies ++= Seq(
  "com.typesafe.akka" % "akka-actor_2.11" % "2.3.6",
  "junit"             % "junit"            % "4.11" % "test",
  "com.novocode"      % "junit-interface" % "0.10"  % "test"
)
```

And something like this for Scala:

```
name := """akkademy-db-scala"""
version := "1.0"
scalaVersion := "2.11.1"
libraryDependencies ++= Seq(
  "com.typesafe.akka" %% "akka-actor" % "2.3.3",
  "com.typesafe.akka" %% "akka-testkit" % "2.3.6" % "test",
  "org.scalatest" %% "scalatest" % "2.1.6" % "test"
)
```

A note on getting the right Scala version with %%

As Scala does not have binary compatibility across major versions, libraries will often be built and published across several versions of Scala. To have SBT try to resolve the dependency built for the correct Scala version for your project, you can change the dependency declared in the `build.sbt` file to use two % symbols after the group ID instead of specifying the Scala version in the artifact id.

For example, in a Scala 2.11 project, these two dependencies are equivalents as shown in the following code:

```
"com.typesafe.akka" % "akka-actor_2.11" % "2.3.3"
"com.typesafe.akka" %% "akka-actor" % "2.3.3"
```

Adding other Dependencies from Maven Central

Any Maven dependencies can be added here—for example from `http://www.mvnrepository.com`. You can see on this link that for any artifact there is an sbt tab that will give you the line to add for the dependency.

Creating your first Actor

In this section, we will create an actor that receives a message and updates its internal state by storing the values from the message into a map. This is the humble beginnings of our distributed database.

Making the Message first

We're going to begin our in-memory database with a `SetRequest` message that will store a key (String) and a value (any Object) in memory. You can think of it as a combination of both an insert and an update in one, or like the `set` operation on a Map.

Remember, our actor has to get the message from his mailbox and check what the instruction is in that message. We use the class/type of the message to determine what the instruction is. The contents of that message type describe the exact details of how to fulfill the contract of the API; in this case we will describe the key as a String and the value as an Object inside the message so that we know what to store.

Messages should always be immutable in order to avoid strange and unexpected behavior, primarily by ensuring you and your team don't do unsafe things across execution contexts/threads. Remember also that these messages may not be simply destined for a local actor but for so another machine. If possible, mark everything `val` (Scala) or `final` (Java) and use immutable collections and types such as those found in Google Guava (Java) or the Scala Standard Library.

Java

Here is our Set message in Java as an immutable object. This is a fairly standard approach to immutable objects in Java. It will be a familiar sight to any skilled Java developer; you should generally prefer immutability in all of your code.

```
package com.akkademy.messages;
public class SetRequest {
    private final String key;
    private final Object value;
    public Set(String key, Object value) {
        this.key = key;
        this.value = value;
    }
    public String getKey() {
        return key;
    }    public Object getValue() {
        return value;
    }
}
```

Scala

In Scala we have a much more succinct way of defining immutable messages — the case class. The case class lets us create an immutable message; values can only be set once in the constructor and then are read from the fields:

```
package com.akkademy.messages
   case class SetRequest(key: String, value: Object)
```

That's it for the messages.

Defining Actor response to the Message

Now that we have the message created, we can create the actor and describe the behavior that the actor will take in response to our message. In our very early example here, we are going to do two things:

1. Log the message.
2. Store the contents of any Set message for later retrieval.

We will build on the example in future chapters to let us retrieve stored messages so that this actor can be used as a thread-safe caching abstraction (and eventually a full-on distributed key-value store).

We'll have a look at the Java8 actor first.

Java – AkkademyDb.java

The following code denotes Actor response to the message in Java:

```java
package com.akkademy;
import akka.actor.AbstractActor;
import akka.event.Logging;
import akka.event.LoggingAdapter;
import akka.japi.pf.ReceiveBuilder;
import com.akkademy.message.SetRequest;
import java.util.HashMap;
import java.util.Map;
public class AkkademyDb extends AbstractActor {
    protected final LoggingAdapter log = Logging.getLogger(context().
system(), this);
    protected final Map<String, Object> map = new HashMap<>();

    private AkkademyDb(){
        receive(ReceiveBuilder.
                        match(SetRequest.class, message -> {
                            log.info("Received set request - key: {}
value: {}", message.getKey(), message.getValue());
                            map.put(message.getKey(), message.
getValue());
                        }).
                        matchAny(o -> log.info("received unknown
message {}", o)).build()
        );
    }
}
```

The actor is a Java class that extends `AbstractActor` (a Java8 Akka Actor API). We create the logger and the map in the class as protected members so we can access them in test cases later in the chapter.

In the constructor we call receive. The receive method takes a `ReceiveBuilder` which has several methods that we call chained together to produce the final `ReceiveBuilder`. With this, we describe how the actor should behave in response to different message types. We define two behaviors here and we will look at them one at a time.

First, we define the behavior to respond to any `SetRequest` messages with:

```java
match(SetRequest.class, message -> {
                        log.info("Received Set request: {}",
message);
                        map.put(message.getKey(), message.
getValue());
                    }).
```

The `ReceiveBuilder` match method in the Java8 API is somewhat similar to a case statement except that we can match on class types. More formally, this is pattern matching.

The match method call, then, says: if the message is of type `SetRequest.class`, take that message, log it, and put a new record in the map using the key and value of that Set message.

Second, we define a catch-all to simply log any unknown message.

```
matchAny(o -> log.info("received unknown message"))
```

Scala – AkkademyDb.scala

Scala is a natural fit as the language has pattern matching as a first-class language construct. We'll have a look at the Scala equivalent code now:

```
package com.akkademy
import akka.actor.Actor
import akka.event.Logging
import scala.collection.mutable.HashMap
import com.akkademy.messages.SetRequest
class AkkademyDb extends Actor {
  val map = new HashMap[String, Object]
  val log = Logging(context.system, this)
  override def receive = {
    case SetRequest(key, value) => {
      log.info("received SetRequest - key: {} value: {}", key, value)
      map.put(key, value)
    }
    case o => log.info("received unknown message: {}", o);
  }
}
```

In the Scala API, we mix in the Actor trait, define the map and logger as we did in Java, and then implement the receive method. The receive method on the Actor super-type returns the Receive which, in the Akka source, is defined as a partial function as follows:

```
type Receive = scala.PartialFunction[scala.Any, scala.Unit]
```

We define the behavior for the response to the `SetRequest` message using pattern matching to produce the partial function. We can extract the key and the value variables for clearer code using pattern matching semantics:

```
case SetRequest(key, value)
```

The behavior is to simply log the request, and then to set the key/value in the map.

```
case SetRequest(key, value) => {
  log.info("received SetRequest - key: {} value: {}", key, value)
  map.put(key, value)
}
```

Finally, we add a catch-all case to simply log unknown messages:

```
case o => log.info("received unknown message: {}", o);
```

That's it for the actor. Now we have to validate we did everything correctly.

Validating the code with unit tests

While books covering frameworks may print to the console or create web pages that are suitable evidence that our code is working, we're going to be using unit tests to validate code and to demonstrate its use. Library code and services often don't have an API that is easy to interact with or to otherwise to observe, testing is generally how these components are validated in almost every project. This is an important skill for any serious developer to have under their belt.

Akka Testkit

Akka provides a test kit that provides almost anything you would ever need to test your actor code. We included the test kit dependencies earlier when we set up our project. For reference, the SBT dependency to place in `build.sbt` is as follows:

```
"com.typesafe.akka" %% "akka-testkit" % "2.3.6" % "test"
```

We're going to use the `TestActorRef` generic here from the testkit instead of a normal `ActorRef` (which we will look at in the next chapter). The `TestActorRef` does two things: it makes the actor's API synchronous so we don't need to think about concurrency in our tests, and it gives us access to the underlying Actor object.

To be clear, Akka hides the actual Actor (`AkkademyDb`) and instead gives a reference to the actor that you send messages to. This encapsulates the actor to enforce message passing as nobody can access the actual object instance.

Next we will look at the source code, and then explain it line by line.

Java

This is the source code for Akka toolkit:

```java
package com.akkademy;
import static org.junit.Assert.assertEquals;
import akka.actor.ActorRef;
import akka.actor.ActorSystem;
import akka.actor.Props;
import akka.testkit.TestActorRef;
import com.akkademy.messages.SetRequest;
import org.junit.Test;
public class AkkademyDbTest {
    ActorSystem system = ActorSystem.create();

    @Test
    public void itShouldPlaceKeyValueFromSetMessageIntoMap() {
        TestActorRef<AkkademyDb> actorRef = TestActorRef.
create(system, Props.create(AkkademyDb.class));
        actorRef.tell(new SetRequest("key", "value"),ActorRef.
noSender());
        AkkademyDb akkademyDb = actorRef.underlyingActor();
        assertEquals(akkademyDb.map.get("key"), "value");
    }
}
```

Scala

The following source code represents interaction with the actor:

```scala
package com.akkademy
import akka.util.Timeout
import org.scalatest.{BeforeAndAfterEach, FunSpecLike, Matchers}
import akka.actor.ActorSystem
import com.akkademy.messages.SetRequest
import akka.testkit.TestActorRef
import scala.concurrent.duration.
class AkkademyDbSpec extends FunSpecLike with Matchers with
BeforeAndAfterEach {
  implicit val system = ActorSystem()
  describe("akkademyDb") {
    describe("given SetRequest"){
      it("should place key/value into map"){
        val actorRef = TestActorRef(new AkkademyDb)
        actorRef ! SetRequest("key", "value")
        val akkademyDb = actorRef.underlyingActor
        akkademyDb.map.get("key") should equal(Some("value"))
      }
```

```
        }
    }
}
```

This is the first time we are looking at interacting with an actor so there is some new code and behavior, some of it is test-specific and some related to interacting with the actor.

We've described an Actor System as a place where actors and their addresses reside, the first thing we need to do before creating the actor is to get a reference to an actor system. We create one as a field in the test:

```
//Java
ActorSystem system = ActorSystem.create();
//Scala
implicit val system = ActorSystem()
```

After creating the actor system, we can now create our actor in the actor system. As mentioned, we're going to use Akka Testkit to create a `TestActorRef` which has a synchronous API, and lets us get at the underlying actor. We create the actor in our actor system here:

```
//Java
TestActorRef<AkkademyDb> actorRef = TestActorRef.create(system, Props.
create(AkkademyDb.class));
//Scala
val actorRef = TestActorRef(new AkkademyDb)
```

We call the Akka Testkit `TestActorRef` create method, passing in the actor system we created (it is implicitly passed in Scala) and a reference to the class. We will look at actor creation in further chapters. Actor instances are hidden away so the act of creating an actor in our actor system returns an `ActorRef` (in this case, a `TestActorRef`) that we can send messages to. The system and class reference is enough for Akka to create this simple actor in our actor system so we have successfully created our first actor.

We communicate with an actor via message-passing. We place a message into an actor's mailbox with 'tell' or '!' in Scala, which is still read as 'tell'. We define that there is nobody to respond to for this message as a parameter of the `tell` method in Java. In Scala, outside of an actor, this is implicit.

```
//Java
actorRef.tell(new SetRequest("key", "value"), ActorRef.noSender());
//Scala
actorRef ! SetRequest("key", "value")
```

Because we are using `TestActorRef`, the call to tell will not continue until the request is processed. This is fine for a look at our first actor but it's important to note that this example does not expose the asynchronous nature of the Actor's API. This is not the usual behavior; tell is an asynchronous operation that returns immediately in normal usage.

Finally, we need to ensure that the behavior is correct by asserting that the actor placed the value into its map. To do this, we get the reference to the underlying Actor instance, and inspect the map by calling `get("key")` and ensuring the value is there.

```
//Java
AkkademyDb akkademyDb = actorRef.underlyingActor();
assertEquals(akkademyDb.map.get("key"), "value");
//Scala
val akkademyDb = actorRef.underlyingActor
akkademyDb.map.get("key") should equal(Some("value"))
```

That's it for the creation of our first simple test case. This basic pattern can be built on for unit testing Actors synchronously. As we go through the book, we will look at more extensive unit-testing examples as well as asynchronous integration testing of our actors.

Running the test

We're almost there! Now that we've built our tests, we can go to the command line and run 'activator' to start the activator cli. Next we can run 'clean' to tidy up any garbage and then 'test' which will fire off the tests. To do this in one step, we can run activator clean test.

You should see something like the following for the Java Junit test:

```
[INFO] [01/12/2015 23:09:24.893] [pool-7-thread-1] [akka://default/
user/$$a] Received Set request: Set{key='key', value=value}
[info] Passed: Total 1, Failed 0, Errors 0, Passed 1
[success] Total time: 7 s, completed 12-Jan-2015 11:09:25 PM
```

And if you're using Scala, then scala-test will give you a bit nicer output:

```
[info] AkkademyDbSpec:
[info] akkademyDb
[info] - should place key/value from Set message into map
[info] Run completed in 1 second, 990 milliseconds.
[info] Total number of tests run: 1
[info] Suites: completed 1, aborted 0
[info] Tests: succeeded 1, failed 0, canceled 0, ignored 0, pending 0
[info] All tests passed.
```

The output will tell you some information about how many tests were run, how many tests failed, and, if there are any errors, it will indicate where the failures occurred so that you can investigate. Once you have a test in place on a behavior, you can be confident that any changes or refactorings you apply did not break the behavior.

Homework

To ensure you have a good grasp on the content, an assignment will be given at the end of each chapter:

- Place the Akka documentation in your Bookmark bar. Also place *Hacker News* there and read it every day.

- Come up with an idea for a service you want to build and provide on the Internet. Preferably the service should involve processing some input and storing it or returning it.

- Create a repository in GitHub for your project. Check your project into GitHub. If you've never worked with Git or GitHub, now is a good time as the source from this book is available there! You can use it to post and display the work you do in this book. Tag your README with LEARNINGAKKAJG so others can search for your project on GitHub to see what you've done.

- Create an actor. Have the actor store the last string that it was sent.

- Write a unit test to confirm the actor will receive a message correctly.

- Write a unit test to confirm the actor behaves correctly if it is sent two messages.

- Push your project to GitHub.

- Check out the book source code from http://www.github.com/jasongoodwin/learning-akka

Summary

We have officially started our journey into building a scalable and distributed applications using Akka. In this chapter, we looked at a brief history of the actor model to understand what Akka is and where it came from. We also learned how to set-up an sbt project for our Akka code. We set up our environment to work with sbt projects and created an actor. Then, we tested the behavior of our actor with a unit test

In the following few chapters, our example application will really start to take shape as we expand it with a client and distribute it across cores and processes.

2
Actors and Concurrency

This chapter will focus on preparing you for the rest of this book by ensuring that you have the necessary background in working with concurrent and asynchronous code. This chapter is incredibly important to get down before you proceed. If you are very comfortable working with Scala futures, Play promises, or Java8 completable futures, you may skim through this chapter. If you have experience with Guava or Spring Listenable Futures, you'll want to learn the differences in the APIs presented here. If you have never worked with a monadic future, you'll want to take your time here.

The chapter will cover the following topics:

- The anatomy of, creation of, and communication with an actor
- The tools and knowledge necessary to deal with asynchronous responses from the Actor API
- Working with Futures—place-holders of results that will be available in the future that can succeed or fail

Reactive system design

A book on Akka would not be complete without a description of the term "Reactive". If you look at books being published or the names of new libraries and frameworks, you may see the word "Reactive" in quite a few of the titles. Akka is also called a **Reactive platform** or more specifically part of the Typesafe Reactive platform. In this context, the term has become more popular, partially thanks to the Reactive Manifesto, which is a document that attempts to distill the qualities required for a web application to successfully grow while meeting the demands of users today.

At this point, the word is practically a piece of developer pop-culture. Of course, then, there are a few out there that may grumble when they hear the word.

This section will briefly introduce the four tenets of the Reactive Manifesto. These are the qualities that we will strive for in our applications so that they will scale and be resilient to failure. We will refer back to these qualities throughout this book. The Reactive Manifesto can be found at `http://www.reactivemanifesto.org/`.

The 4 reactive tenets

The reactive manifesto includes four tenets or design goals—responsiveness, elasticity, resiliency, and event-driven design. The four tenets are outlined in the following with examples of their application.

Responsive

Our applications should respond to requests as fast as possible.

If we have a choice between getting data in a serial manner or in parallel, we should always choose to get the data in parallel in order to get a response back to a user faster. Requests for unrelated data can be made at the same time. When requesting unrelated non-dependent pieces of data, we should evaluate if it's possible to make those requests at the same time.

If there is a potential error situation, we should return a notification of the problem to the user immediately rather than having them wait for the timeout.

Elastic

Our applications should be able to scale under varying workload (especially achieved by adding more computing resources). In order to achieve elasticity, our systems should aim to eliminate bottlenecks.

If we have our in-memory database running on a virtual machine, adding a second machine node could split the queries across the two servers, doubling potential throughput. Adding additional nodes should allow performance to scale in a near-linear manner.

Adding a second in-memory database node could double memory capacity by splitting the data and moving half of it to the new node. Adding nodes should expand capacity in a near-linear manner.

Resilient

Our applications should expect faults to occur and react to them gracefully. If a component of the system fails, it should not cause a lack of availability for requests that do not touch that component. Failure is inevitable — that impact should be isolated to the component that fails. If possible, failure of a component should not cause any impact in behavior by employing replication and redundancy in critical components and data.

Event-driven/message-driven

Using messages instead of method invocation prescribes a way in which we can meet the other three reactive tenets. Message-driven systems move the control over how, when, and where requests are responded, which allows routing and load balancing of the responding component.

An asynchronous message-driven system can more efficiently utilize a system's resources as it only consumes resources like threads when they are actually needed. Messages can be delivered to remote machines as well (location transparency). As messages are queued and delivered outside an actor, it's possible to self-heal a failing system via supervision.

Reactive Tenet Correlation

The following figure shows Reactive Tenet Correlation:

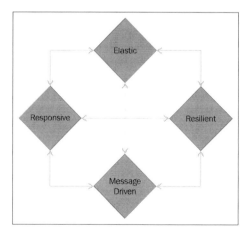

Reactive tenets are not completely independent of one another. Often an approach that is used to meet one of the reactive tenets will aid a system in meeting others. For example, if we note that one of our services is behaving slowly, we may stop sending requests to that service for a short period of time to let it recover while giving users an error message immediately. This improves resiliency of our system by reducing risk of a slow service crashing under load, and also improves the responsiveness of our system by indicating to a user that there is an issue right away.

Anatomy of an Actor

Before we move into a more relevant example, we'll cover the most basic features of an Actor to understand the basic structure and methods. To demonstrate the simplest case possible, for this example we'll build a simple actor that receives a String—"Ping"—and gives a response—"Pong".

Java Actor API

We'll look at the Java implementation first. The Java and Scala APIs are different enough that they each need their own introduction.

```java
public class JavaPongActor extends AbstractActor {
    public PartialFunction receive() {
        return ReceiveBuilder.
                matchEquals("Ping", s ->
                                sender().tell("Pong", ActorRef.
noSender())).
                matchAny(x ->
                        sender().tell(
new Status.Failure(new Exception("unknown message")), self()
)).
                build();
    }
}
```

The preceding code shows the Java `actorAPI`. We'll look at this example in detail.

- `AbstractActor`: First, we extend `AbstractActor` class This is a Java8-specific API that is meant to take advantage of the Java8 lambda features. There is another base Actor API that can be used for Java if you look at the documentation—`UntypedActor`. The `UntypedActor` is an older model for working, which we won't cover in this book. In that API, you get an object and must use `if` statements to match on the object. We will focus on the Java8 specific API as it is more expressive, presenting a way to pattern-match using lambdas.

- `Receive`: The `AbstractActor` class has a method that must be implemented or invoked via the constructor, which is the receive method. It returns a `PartialFunction`, which is from the Scala API. In Java, we don't have any native way of building a Scala `PartialFunction` (a function that does not match all potential inputs), so Akka gives us a Builder abstraction for producing the `PartialFunction` called `ReceiveBuilder` and that we use to produce the return value. Don't worry, you won't need to understand Scala `PartialFunctions` to use Akka!

- `ReceiveBuilder`: We call `ReceiveBuilder` methods, stringing together match cases as needed to describe the response to each type of message we need to handle, and then call `build()` to produce the `PartialFunction` that we need to return.

- `Match`: There are a few `match` functions in the receive builder that are worth noting. We'll show examples of how to match on ping with each:

  - `match(class, function)`: This describes behavior to apply to any unmatched class instance.

    ```
    match(String.class, s -> {if(s.equals("Ping"))
    respondToPing(s);})
    ```

  - `match(class, predicate, function)`: This describes behavior to apply to a message if it is the type of the class and the predicate function is true.

    ```
    match(String.class, s -> s.equals("Ping"), s ->
    respondToPing(s))
    ```

  - `matchEquals(object, function)`: This describes behavior to apply if the call to equals is true for the object supplied.

    ```
    matchEquals("Ping", s -> respondToPing(s))
    ```

  - `matchAny(function)`: This matches any unmatched messages. It's generally a good practice to respond with a failure, or at least log in to aid in troubleshooting during development.

The `match` function will pattern-match from top to bottom, so you can describe specific and then general cases:

```
ReceiveBuilder
    .matchEquals("Ping", s -> System.out.println("It's Ping: " +
s))
    .match(String.class, s -> System.out.println("It's a string: "
+ s))
    .matchAny(x -> System.out.println("It's something else: " +
x))
    .build
```

- `Reply to sender()`: Calling the `sender()` method will allow us to reply to the message. This could be an actor or this could potentially respond to an ask from outside an actor system. The first case is pretty straightforward—the message will go back into the sending actor's inbox. The second case we'll look at in more detail.later

- `Tell()`: `sender()` function gives us an `ActorRef`. In the example, we call `tell()`; providing the sender. `tell()` is the most basic one-way message pattern. The first argument is the message we want to place in the sender's mailbox. The second argument is the sender that actor will see.

  Similar to what we did in *Chapter 1, Starting Life as an Actor* we describe behavior for messages of the String class. We're using a different match method here—we include a predicate for the second argument as we need to check that the string equals Ping. We then describe the behavior—we send a message back to the `sender()` with `tell()`. We send back the String Pong. The `tell` method in Java requires the sender of the message to be identified—`ActorRef.noSender()` is used to indicate there is no reply addresses.

- Replies with `akka.actor.Status.Failure`: To report an error back to the sender, we need to send them a message. If an exception is thrown in the actor, it will trigger the supervisor to be notified (covered in *Chapter 3, Getting the Message Across*), but, in any case, if we want to notify of a failure, we need to send back a failure to the sender. If there is a placeholder 'future' for a response, then this will cause the future to fail. We'll cover this shortly.

This covers the basics of the Java `AbstractActor` API. We'll look at the Scala API next.

Scala Actor API

The following code shows a Scala actor:

```scala
//Scala
class ScalaPongActor extends Actor {
  override def receive: Receive = {
    case "Ping" => sender() ! "Pong"
    case _ => sender() ! Status.Failure(new Exception("unknown
message"))
  }
}
```

We'll look at the actor in detail now:

- `Actor`: To define an actor, we extend the Actor base class. This is the basic Scala actor API. It's simple and a natural fit for Scala's language features.

- `Receive`: Override the receive method in the Actor and return a `PartialFunction`. Note that Receive is the return type on the receive method—it's just a type definition for `scala.PartialFunction[scala.Any, scala.Unit]`. If you're not too familiar with `PartialFunctions` in the Scala API, not to worry—you just need to build some pattern matching cases that return Unit and know that you're free to make your statements non-exhaustive. If you want to see what's going on under the hood with the receive method, you can play with `scala.PartialFunction` on the REPL:

  ```
  scala> val pf: PartialFunction[Any, Unit] = {
    case _: String => println("Got a String")
    }
  pf: PartialFunction[Any,Unit] = <function1>

  scala> pf("hey")
  Got a String
  ```

- `Reply to sender`: In the example actor code, we then access the sender `ActorRef` via the `sender()` method. We can reply to the sender by sending it a message. We send back a "Pong" in this case.

- `tell method (!)`: We send the message to the sender with the tell method that is invoked via the `!` method. You'll note if you read the Java section that the sender must be specified, but here we are omitting any reference to a sender as it's implicit. The tell method `!` has an implicit `ActorRef` parameter in the method signature. It defaults to `noSender` if you're using tell from somewhere outside an actor. The following is the method signature:

  ```
  def !(message: Any)(implicit sender: ActorRef = Actor.noSender):
  Unit
  ```

The Actor has an implicit sender value through `self`, which is used in the actor, so tell will always provide self as the sender.

```
implicit final val self = context.self
```

The sender is implicit so we never have to worry about it, but it's helpful to understand where the values are coming from while comparing the Java and Scala APIs.

- • **Reply with akka.actor.Status.Failure**: The last piece to note is the reply with `akka.actor.Status.Failure` in the case of an unknown message. The actor will never reply with a failure—even if the actor itself fails—so you will always need to ensure you send back a failure if you want to notify anyone who is asking that there was an issue. Sending back a failure will cause a placeholder future to be marked as a failure.

We'll look at the specifics of getting a reply from an actor shortly—first we need to be able to create an actor.

Creating an actor

Actors are not accessed like ordinary objects. You never get an instance of an actor. You do not call methods on actors or directly change their state—you pass them messages. You do not access members of the actor—you request information about its state through message-passing. Using message-passing instead of method invocation enforces encapsulation. Alan Kay, who originally described Object-Oriented programming, actually included message-passing as one of the definitions of object-oriented programming. I'm sure Alan Kay looks at what OO has turned into and shakes his head some days.

> *I made up the term 'object-oriented', and I can tell you I didn't have C++ in mind*
>
> *-- Alan Kay, OOPSLA '97*

Using a message-based approach allows us to encapsulate the instance of an actor quite completely. If we only communicate through messages, then there is never any need to access the actor instance. We only need a mechanism to send the actor messages and to get responses.

In Akka, this reference to an actor is called an `ActorRef`. The `ActorRef` is an un-typed reference that encapsulates the actor behind a layer of abstraction and gives us the mechanisms to interact with the actor.

We've covered the fact that the actor system is where actors exist. It may be obvious that this is also where we create actors and obtain references to them. The `actorOf` method will produce a new actor and return a reference to it:

```
//Java
ActorRef actor = actorSystem.actorOf(Props.create(JavaPongActor.
class));
```

```
//Scala
val actor: ActorRef =
actorSystem.actorOf(Props(classOf[ScalaPongActor]))
```

 Note here that we don't actually create the actor — we don't, for example, call actorOf(new PongActor).

The actors are encapsulated — they should not be accessible. We never want to be able to access the Actor's state from our code. The creation pattern used ensures this; we'll now look at this.

Props

To ensure we encapsulate the actor instance and never gain access to an instance of it, we pass in a Props instance with all of the constructor args. Props lets us pass in the class, and a variable lengle list of arguments:

```
//Java
Props.create(PongActor.class, arg1, arg2, argn);
//Scala
Props(classOf[PongActor], arg1, arg2, argn)
```

If the actor takes constructor arguments, it's recommended that the props is created via a factory method. If we wanted our *Pong* actor to respond with a message other than *Pong*, we might take that as a constructor arg. We can create a factory method to produce the Props instance like so:

```
//Java
public static Props props(String response) {
    return Props.create(this.class, response);
}
//Scala
object ScalaPongActor {
  def props(response: String): Props = {
    Props(classOf[ScalaPongActor], response)
  }
}
```

Then we would create the actor using the props factory method:

```
//Java
ActorRef actor = actorSystem.actorOf(JavaPongActor.props("PongFoo"));
//Scala
val actor: ActorRef = actorSystem.actorOf(ScalaPongActor props
"PongFoo")
```

Creating the props factory method isn't required but moves the concern of creating the Props object into one place so that any changes to the actor's constructor can be isolated to avoid making breaking changes as the code changes over time.

`actorOf` creates an actor and gives you an `ActorRef` for the newly created actor. There is another way to get a reference to an Actor — `actorSelection`.

To understand `actorSelection`, we first need to look at actor paths. Each actor is created with a path that you can see at `ActorRef.path`. It might look something like the following:

- `akka://default/user/BruceWillis`

It's a URI and it can even reference a remote actor with the `akka.tcp` protocol:

- `akka.tcp://my-sys@remotehost:5678/user/CharlieChaplin`

Note that the preceding path states `akka.tcp` as the protocol and specifies the host and port of the remote actor system. If we know the path of an Actor, we can use `actorSelection` to get a reference — an `ActorSelection` — for that Actor, even if it is on a remote machine:

```
ActorSelection selection = system.actorSelection("akka.tcp://
actorSystem@host.jason-goodwin.com:5678/user/KeanuReeves");
```

The `ActorSelection` here is a reference to a remote actor — we can use the `ActorSelection` like the `ActorRef` to communicate over the network. This demonstrates how easy it is to send messages over the wire, and is an example of Akka's location transparency in action. We're able to change an application to communicate with remote services merely by configuring where an actor is located.

To recap this section, we can create an Actor and gain a reference to it by calling `system.actorOf` and pass it a Props instance with the list of `args`. We can also give the actor a name by passing that into the `actorOf` method. Finally, we can look up an existing actor, even on a remote system, by using `actorSelection`.

Next we'll begin to look at how to write asynchronous and event-driven code.

Promises, futures, and event-driven programming models

Before moving on to working with more complex Actor-based applications, we need to understand some basic abstractions for working in an event-driven programming model—Promises and Futures. In *Chapter 1, Starting Life as an Actor* we saw how to send a message to an actor and have it invoke some behavior in response to that event. But, what if we need to get some output from the actor in response to that message? Let's say we need to get a record from our in-memory key-value store?

Blocking versus event-driven APIs

Blocking code is familiar to almost any developer. It's where we start when we begin with IO. When we make a call to a synchronous API, the calling method does not return immediately—the application waits for execution to complete. For example, if you make an HTTP request, you'll get back a response object once the request is completed. Code that waits for IO to complete is called blocking as a thread sits and waits—it is blocked from doing any other work until the IO is complete. We can demonstrate blocking code by showing a query using **Java Database Connectivity (JDBC)**:

```
stmt = conn.createStatement();
String sql = "select name from users where id='123'";
ResultSet rs = stmt.executeQuery(sql);
rs.next()
String name  = rs.getString("name");
```

Here we retrieve a user's name from a database using JDBC. The code looks very simple but there are hidden effects that make this simple code less readable:

- **Latency**: It takes time to go over the network to get the result.
- **Failure**: The request can fail if, for example, the remote service is unavailable. An exception might be thrown for any number of reasons.

When we call executeQuery, the thread that is executing this code has to wait for the database query to complete. In a web application, where many users may be making concurrent requests, the finite limit of the thread pool can be reached. There are a limited number of threads in that thread pool, and if all of them are waiting on IO, then you can't put any more traffic through the server even if you have free compute resources as there are no threads available to use those resources. If you've done any performance tuning on blocking Servlet-based web applications, you may have witnessed the limitations of threadpool. Usually the CPU will be under-utilized when the server is at capacity because all of the threads are just waiting.

This is potentially because the `threadpool` is exhausted, or it may also be because the system is spending time loading and unloading the context of threads that need the free CPU time instead of actually doing work on the CPU. Similarly, there are a limited number of threads in the `threadpool`. So, if all of the threads are waiting, the next calls that come into the server cannot be handled until a thread is freed, causing latency to grow.

So you might ask why we don't simply use an unlimited `threadpool` (create one new thread for every request). Creating a thread has a cost and maintaining many active threads has a cost. When using many threads on a core, the operating system has to context-switch between threads in order to ensure all of the threads are getting CPU time. The CPU has to unload and store the current thread's state, and then load in another thread's context that is waiting for CPU time. If there are 1,000 threads actively working, you can imagine that this may represent a lot of overhead in loading and unloading contexts.

To summarize, there are a few problems with using many threads to handle blocking IO:

- Code does not obviously express failure in the response type
- Code does not obviously express latency in the response type
- Blocking models have throughput limitations due to fixed `threadpool` sizes
- Creating and using many threads has a performance overhead due to context-switching

A non-blocking asynchronous event-driven system can run with only a handful of threads and will not block those threads, only using them when computation is needed. This gives the system better responsiveness at scale and can allow better system resource utilization. Depending on the implementation, there can also be a benefit in making effects such as failure and latency more clearly defined in the types, as we'll see soon.

The downside is that it can take a bit of time to understand how to write code using event-driven paradigms. We'll look at an example of each model to better understand how the two design approaches work.

First, we'll look at a very simple call to a database using blocking IO.

```
//Java
String username = getUsernameFromDatabase(userId);
System.out.println(username);
//Scala
val username = getUsernameFromDatabase(userId)
println(username)
```

The method is invoked and the thread continues into the method, returning once there is a result.

If you were debugging, you could step into the method with the thread and see each line of the method `getUsernameFromDatabase` method called. Once the actual IO is executed, the thread will sleep until the result comes back. Then the thread returns the method, and jumps back out of the method and continues to print the result.

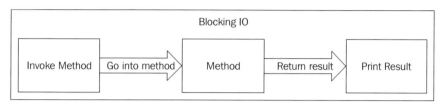

The event-driven equivalent will look different because we have to describe what happens when the completion event occurs, and that code is executed in a different context. To turn our example above into an event-driven equivalent, the code needs to express the print statement as something that happens when the result comes back from the database. It can take some time to adjust to this model, but you only have to learn it once.

To move to an event-driven model, we have to express the result in code differently. We have to use placeholders for values that will eventually be there—a future. The printing of the result is registered as something to do when the completion event occurs. We register some code that we to be invoked when the value the placeholder represents becomes available. The term "event-driven" describes the way that we express code to execute on certain events:

```
//Java
CompletableFuture<String> usernameFuture = getUsernameFromDatabaseAsy
nc(userId);
usernameFuture.thenRun(username ->
    //executed somewhere else
    System.out.println(username)
);
//Scala
val future = getUsernameFromDatabaseAsync(userId)
future.onComplete(username =>
  //executed somewhere else
  println(username)
)
```

From the thread's perspective, the code will call the method and go into the method, and then return with a Future/Completable Future almost immediately. The result is only a placeholder of the value that will eventually be there.

We won't look at the method invocation itself in too much detail—you should understand that the method will return immediately and the database call and result will happen somewhere else, on another thread. There is an `ExecutionContext` that represents the threads where the other work is done, which we'll look at later in this book. (In Akka, you'll see a dispatcher in the `ActorSystem`, which is an `ExecutionContext` implementation.)

Note, there is a critical difference if you're trying to debug async code—you won't see all of the details of the call to the database on the invoking thread, so you can't step through the database call from the invoking thread using a debugger like you can in a blocking model. Similarly, if you look at a stack trace from a failure, you may not necessarily see the original calling code—you'll see references to another stack where the code is being run.

After the method returns the future, we only have the promise of a value that will eventually be there. We don't want to make the thread wait for the result, but we want to take some action when the result becomes available (print it to the console). The way we do work in an event-driven system is to describe the code to run when an event happens. In an actor, we describe the behavior to use when a message is received. Similarly, with a future, we describe the behavior to execute when the future's value becomes available. The methods on a future to register code to run on the successful completion event successfully with then Run (Java8) or on Complete (Scala).

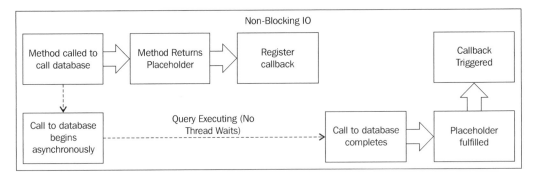

It's important to highlight again—the print statement will not run on the thread that registers the event. It will run somewhere else, on another thread via the `ExecutionContext`. Futures are always created with `ExecutionContext`, so you can choose where to run them.

All of the variables in scope are available to the lambda registered. Methods, however, should be invoked with special care, or simply should not be invoked within the closures, as they won't be invoked in the same lexical scope. We'll look at this gotcha in the next chapter.

Note that futures can fail and should always be bounded by a timeout (required in the Scala API) so they will not hang around forever and will always finish—either successfully or with failure. We'll take a closer look at handling futures now.

Skills check-point

Scala developers should be familiar with using higher order functions/lambdas. It would be helpful for the developer to have some familiarity with the option or try types to ensure the material is fast to understand.

If you're using Java8, it's a good time to check in and see if you're comfortable reading the code examples so far. If you're unclear on the use of lambdas, you should take the time now to go through the Oracle Java8 lambda primer, which can be found at `http://www.oracle.com/webfolder/technetwork/tutorials/obe/java/Lambda-QuickStart/index.html`.

You should get some experience working with them by exploring the Stream API and the Optional type. The Optional type is helpful to learn as it's semantically similar in its use to `CompletableFuture`.

Understanding the following material will be easier if you have some experience to relate the material to first.

Having an Actor respond via a future

We looked at a hypothetical example of an asynchronous database call, where the result of a call to the database completes a future. We'll introduce a real example now by communicating with the example actors that we built earlier in this chapter—the `PongActor`. We'll have a way of communicating with actors from outside the actor system after this so that we can use Akka to build the core of an application or library and use it from plain Java or Scala code.

While the test case here does introduce the asynchronous API, the test cases are still blocking by awaiting the result. This is useful in demonstrating another way of handling Akka in your test cases. We need the test cases to block because, if we don't wait for the result, the test case will always return immediately and, hence, will always pass.

You should build these test cases and use them to explore the future API introduced in the next section to understand it well. By building these examples, you'll always have a sandbox you can return to if you need to further examine how futures work. They are included in the source code for this book as well.

Java example

We'll cover the Java8 examples first. Akka is built in Scala, and, generally, the Scala and Java APIs are one to one. There is a notable exception and that is that all asynchronous methods that return a future will return the Scala `scala.concurrent.Future`.

Working with Scala futures

For the Java examples, we need a way to handle Scala futures — in this book, we'll convert them to the Java8 `CompletableFuture`.

The Play Promise API is also a good choice if you're building a Play application. I personally prefer the semantics used in the Play Promise API over the Java8 `CompletableFuture` API, but the Java8 API may be more readable for those not accustomed to working with asynchronous code yet. It's recommended if your code may be placed into a library that you use the Java8 `CompletableFuture` so you do not have a dependency on Play in your code outside the controller.

To start, we need to add this dependency from the Scala team to your `build.sbt` to be able to convert between Scala and Java8 Futures:

```
"org.scala-lang.modules" %% "scala-java8-compat" % "0.6.0"
```

Test case

The following is the complete test case. Next, we'll look at each element of the APIs in detail:

```
package pong;
//[...imports]
import static scala.compat.java8.FutureConverters.*;
public class PongActorTest {
    ActorSystem system = ActorSystem.create();
    ActorRef actorRef =
            system.actorOf(Props.create(JavaPongActor.class));
```

```
    @Test
    public void shouldReplyToPingWithPong() throws Exception {
        Future sFuture = ask(actorRef, "Ping", 1000);
        final CompletionStage<String> cs = toJava(sFuture);
        final CompletableFuture<String> jFuture =
(CompletableFuture<String>) cs;
        assert(jFuture.get(1000, TimeUnit.MILLISECONDS).
equals("Pong"));
    }
    @Test(expected = ExecutionException.class)
    public void shouldReplyToUnknownMessageWithFailure() throws
Exception {
        Future sFuture = ask(actorRef, "unknown", 1000);
        final CompletionStage<String> cs = toJava(sFuture);
        final CompletableFuture<String> jFuture =
(CompletableFuture<String>) cs;
        jFuture.get(1000, TimeUnit.MILLISECONDS);
    }
}
```

Our Pong Actor test has a test for both the success case and failure case.

Actor creation

We begin by creating an `ActorSystem`, and then an actor in that actor system with `actorOf`, as previously covered:

```
ActorSystem system = ActorSystem.create();
ActorRef actorRef =
system.actorOf(Props.create(JavaPongActor.class));
```

Now, we ask the actor for a response to a message:

```
final Future sFuture = ask(actorRef, "Ping", 1000);
```

This is fairly straightforward—we call the ask method, passing:

- The actor ref to send the message to
- The message we want to send the actor
- The timeout for the future—how long to wait for a result before considering it a failure

This gives us back the placeholder of the response we'll get in the future—a Scala Future. In the actor code, the actor will send a message back to `sender()`, which we will receive as the response to this future.

We can't use the Scala Future from Java8, but we can convert it with the library we imported earlier:

```
final CompletionStage<String> cs = toJava(sFuture);
        final CompletableFuture<String> jFuture =
(CompletableFuture<String>) cs;
```

We first convert the Scala future with `scala.compat.java8.FutureConverters.toJava`, which gives us a `CompletionStage`. The `CompletionStage` is the interface for the `CompletableFuture`—specifically it is a read-only interface. In this case, we cast the future to gain access to the get method. You won't need to cast the `CompletionStage` outside of test cases.

Note that we're placing a String type on the future. Actors are untyped and return an Object, so you may find the unchecked casting a little iffy. Certainly, some care is needed when talking to Actors from outside of the `ActorSystem` in this regard. We know that the Actor will always return a String on this message, though, so it's a safe assertion that the type of the future is a String.

Finally, we call the `get()` method to block the thread in the tests and get the result. In the failure test, the get method will throw an exception—it will throw the `akka.status.Failure` message's exception, which is sent from the actor.

You now have an example of a successful and failing future to experiment with!

Scala example

Next, we'll cover the Scala example. Akka gives Scala futures, so the test is a bit simpler.

Test case

The following is the complete Scala test case. Next, we'll cover the test in detail:

```
package pong
//[...imports]
import akka.pattern.ask
import scala.concurrent.duration._
class ScalaAskExamplesTest extends FunSpecLike with Matchers {
  val system = ActorSystem()
  implicit val timeout = Timeout(5 seconds)
  val pongActor = system.actorOf(Props(classOf[ScalaPongActor]))
  describe("Pong actor") {
```

```
      it("should respond with Pong") {
        val future = pongActor ? "Ping" //uses the implicit timeout
        val result = Await.result(future.mapTo[String], 1 second)
        assert(result == "Pong")
      }
      it("should fail on unknown message") {
        val future = pongActor ? "unknown"
        intercept[Exception]{
          Await.result(future.mapTo[String], 1 second)
        }
      }
    }
  }
}
```

Actor creation

We begin by creating an ActorSystem and then creating an actor in that actor system with actorOf, as previously covered.

We also create an implicit Timeout for the future creation (note that the import of scala.concurrent.duration is needed for the duration passed in to the Timeout):

```
implicit val system = ActorSystem()
implicit val timeout = Timeout(5 seconds)
val pongActor = system.actorOf(Props(classOf[ScalaPongActor]))
```

Now, we ask the actor for a response to a message:

```
val future = pongActor ? "Ping"
```

 We need to import akka.pattern.ask for this to work.

The call to ask references:

- The actor ref to send the message to pongActor
- The message we want to send the actor
- Implicitly, the timeout for the future—how long to wait for a result before considering it a failure

This gives us back a placeholder—a Future—that represents the actor's reply. In the actor code, the actor will send a message back to sender(), which we will receive as the response to this future.

Finally, we want to block the test until we have the result available. We use `Await.result` on the future with a timeout value:

```
val result = Await.result(future.mapTo[String], 1 second)
```

The Actor is untyped, so we get back a `Future[AnyRef]`. We call `future.mapTo[String]` to change the future's type to the expected type of the result.

You can build on this example now—play around with the Future API as we continue through the next sections of this chapter.

Blocking threads in tests

Asking an actor for a response demonstrates how to talk to an actor from outside the actor system by getting a response via a future. In this test case, we sleep/block the test thread by calling get `Await.result` in order to get the result out of the future synchronously.

This is fine in test cases—it's actually necessary or the test will complete before the result is available—however, blocking is a bad practice anywhere other than in test cases. You should only have non-blocking code outside of the test context.

 Don't sleep or block outside tests.

In tests, the preferred way to block with the Java8 completable future is to call the get() method on the Future. The get() method will block the thread until the result is available:

```
jFuture.get().equals("Pong")
```

While `get()` will sleep forever if you don't specify a timeout, the Scala future requires a timeout (specified in the ask method), so the future will fail if the timeout is violated.

Getting the result from the Scala Future can be accomplished by using `scala.concurrent.Await.result`:

```
import scala.concurrent.duration._
val result: String = Await.result(future.mapTo[String], 1 second)
```

Here the timeout is required—it's redundant as the ask method has already placed a timeout on the future.

In both the Java and Scala examples, if the future fails, blocking will result in the exception that the future failed with being thrown. The Java8 CompletableFuture will throw an ExecutionException caused by the Throwable the future fails with. The Scala API will throw the actual Throwable. (Scala has no checked exceptions, so the API can do this—Java throws an unchecked exception type here.)

You now have an example of a future that you can work with and mechanisms to build test cases to examine the results. We will begin to cover the future APIs in depth now as they are crucial to understand when working with asynchronous code. It is highly recommended you explore the future API inside these test cases. To save some typing, the examples are available in the *Chapter 2, Actors and Concurrency* code bundle available online.

Understanding futures and promises

Modern futures make two effects implicit: failure and latency. To see how we can move from blocking IO to non-blocking IO, we must learn some abstractions that express handling with failure and latency in different ways. It may seem difficult at first, but most developers find they take to the paradigm once they begin to understand it.

Future – expressing failure and latency in types

An asynchronous API, such as the ask pattern, will return one of the placeholder future types mentioned previously. We can try to demonstrate how the code becomes clearer by looking at different ways in which we can work with our PongActor in the test case. It's very strongly advised that you do follow along in this section with the test case we built previously.

Preparing for the Java example

First, for the Java8 examples, we'll simplify the ask by placing it into a method to eliminate duplication. This now looks like a real asynchronous API:

```
public CompletionStage<String> askPong(String message){
    Future sFuture = ask(actorRef, "Ping", 1000);
    CompletionStage<String> cs = toJava(sFuture);
    return cs;
}
```

Then we'll build simple test cases:

```
@Test public void printToConsole() throws Exception {
    askPong("Ping").
        thenAccept(x -> System.out.println("replied with: " + x));
    Thread.sleep(100);
}
```

Preparing for Scala examples

We'll start by defining a simple method to remove any redundancy and make the examples a bit easier to read:

```
def askPong(message: String): Future[String] = (pongActor ? message).
mapTo[String]
```

We're going to look at asynchronous work running on multiple threads, so you'll need to import an implicit ExecutionContext now.

We can make a test case like the following to play around in:

```
describe("FutureExamples"){
  import scala.concurrent.ExecutionContext.Implicits.global
  it("should print to console"){
    (pongActor ? "Ping").onSuccess({
      case x: String => println("replied with: " + x)
    })
    Thread.sleep(100)
  }
}
```

Note on sleeping

This test doesn't yet make any assertions, but shows a test with real asynchronous behavior now. This test isn't helpful, but we can see if it works by looking for the effects (we expect to print to the console in this case). If you want events to occur asynchronously, you may occasionally need to sleep tests. As with blocking, sleeping is OK in tests but should never be done in real code.

While these tests don't actually test anything, they're useful for experimenting to see the effects occur asynchronously. We'll look at how to make assertions in asynchronous code after taking some time to understand futures.

Anatomy of a future

A `Future[T]`/`CompletableFuture<T>` can either be successful with a value of type T or a failure of type `Throwable`. We'll look at how to handle each case—success and failure—and how to transform the future's value to be able to do useful things with the result.

Handling success cases

As we saw in our test, the `PongActor` will reply with "Pong" if it receives "Ping." We'll work with this example to demonstrate different ways we can interact with the future.

Executing code with the result

Sometimes we need to simply "do something" with the result. Maybe we want to log the event or maybe we want to send a response over the network. We can "register" events to occur once the result becomes available.

As demonstrated, we can use `thenAccept` to consume the value in Java8:

```
askPong("Ping").thenAccept(x -> System.out.println("replied with: " +
x));
```

And, in Scala, we can use onSuccess:

```
(pongActor ? "Ping").onSuccess(){
     case x: String => println("replied with: " + x)
    })
```

> Note that onSuccess takes a partial function, so it fits well with the Akka untyped responses—pattern matching takes care of determining the type of the result.

Transforming the result

The most common use case is the need to transform a response asynchronously before doing something with it. For example, we may need to get data from a database and then transform that into an HTTP response to give back to a client.

Transformation of a value is done with map in most APIs, as it is with Scala's Future:

```
askPong("Ping").map(x => x.charAt(0))
```

In Java8, we call `thenApply`:

```
askPong("Ping").thenApply(x -> x.charAt(0))
```

These will give you back new Futures of type `Char`. You can transform the result and then pass the modified future on to other methods for further processing.

Transforming the result asynchronously

If we need to make an asynchronous call, and then make another asynchronous call with the result of the first, it could start to look a little bit messy:

```
//Java
CompletionStage<CompletionStage<String>> futureFuture =
askPong("Ping").thenApply(x -> askPong(x));
//Scala
val futureFuture: Future[Future[String]] =
        askPong("Ping").map(x => {
        askPong(x)
    })
```

Very often you'll need to make an asynchronous call, and then make another asynchronous call as we have done in this example. However, right now, our result is buried inside a future inside another future! This is very difficult to work with—what we want to do instead is to flatten that out so the result is inside of a single future, we want a `Future[String]`/`CompletionStage[String]`.

There are ways to compose our futures to make these chained asynchronous operations. using `thenCompose` in Java:

```
CompletionStage<String> cs = askPong("Ping").thenCompose(x ->
askPong("Ping"));

Orpredictably, flatMap in Scala:

val f: Future[String] = askPong("Ping").flatMap(x => askPong("Ping"))
```

Once the first "Ping" is responded to, then we send a second "Ping" and return the response as the value of the future.

Note you can continue to string together asynchronous computation like this. This is a very powerful way of handling pipelines of data processing. You can make a call to a remote service and then make a call to a second service with the result.

A failure on either call will cause the entire future to fail. We'll look at failure cases next.

Handling failure cases

Failures can occur and we need to handle those failures as well. Failures always have a cause represented by a `Throwable`. Similar to the success cases, there are methods that allow us to handle the failure or even recover from it.

Executing code in the failure case

Very often you will want to do something with a failure. The most basic case is to log something in the case of failure.

In Scala, there is a simple way to do this—`onFailure`. This method accepts a partial function accepting a `Throwable`:

```
askPong("causeError").onFailure{
    case e: Exception => println("Got exception")
  }
}
```

Unfortunately, in Java8, there is no consumer-based method for failure, so we will introduce `handle()` here for this case:

```
askPong("cause error").handle((x, t) -> {
            if(t!=null){
                System.out.println("Error: " + t);
            }
            return null;
        });
```

Handle takes a `BiFunction` that transforms either the success or failure case. The function in handle will provide you with either the successful result or the `Throwable`, so we have to check to see if the `Throwable` is present (only the result or the `Throwable` will be not null). If the `Throwable` is present, then we log the statement. We have to return a value on the function, so we simply return null as we're not doing anything with the value in the failure case.

Recovering from failure

Often we want to use a value if there is an error. If you want to recover from failure, you transform the future to have a successful value.

In Java, we can use exceptionally to take the `Throwable` and transform it into a usable value:

```
        CompletionStage<String> cs = askPong("cause error").
  exceptionally(t -> {
            return "default";
        });
```

In Scala, there is a recover method that is the equivalent. Again, this takes a PartialFunction, so we can pattern match on the exception type:

```
val f = askPong("causeError").recover{
  case t: Exception => "default"
}
```

Recovering from failure asynchronously

Often we'll need to recover from failure with another asynchronous operation. A few use cases could be:

- Retrying a failed operation
- A cold hit to a cache requires making an operation to another service

We'll demonstrate a retry as follows:

```
askPong("cause error")
        .handle( (pong, ex) -> ex == null
                ? CompletableFuture.completedFuture(pong)
                : askPong("Ping")
).thenCompose(x -> x);
```

We have to do this in two steps. First, we check if the exception is not null and return either a future of the result or the new retry future. Then we call thenCompose to flatten the CompletionState[CompletionStage[String]].

In Scala, recoverWith is the function we want to invoke—this is like flatMap for the error case, so is considerably more readable and succinct than the Java equivalent:

```
askPong("causeError").recoverWith({
    case t: Exception => askPong("Ping")
})
```

Composing futures

Often we'll have multiple operations we need to do and maybe we'll want to do them in different places in the codebase. Each call to the methods covered returns a new future that can have additional operations applied to it.

Chaining operations together

We've covered the basics of working with futures. One of the benefits of working with latency and failure in a functional style is that it's easy to compose together multiple operations without having to handle exceptions along the way. We can focus on the happy path and then collect errors at the end of the chain of operations.

Each of the methods that transforms a value covered returns a new future that can then be dealt with and chained into more operations.

Putting it all together, we may have several operations and then one recovery function at the end to deal with any errors that may have occurred. It's possible to combine these functions (aka combinators) in any order you can dream up to accomplish the work you need to get done.

In Java:

```
askPong("Ping").
    thenCompose(x -> askPong("Ping" + x)).
    handle((x, t) -> {
            if(t != null){
                return "default";
            }else{
                return x;
            }
        });
```

In Scala:

```
val f = askPong("Ping").
    flatMap(x => askPong("Ping" + x)).
    recover({ case Exception => "There was an error" })
```

In these examples, we get a future, then call `thenCompose`/`flatMap` to asynchronously make a call when the first completes, and then, in the case of an error, we recover with a String value to ensure the future is successful.

Any failure along the way becomes the failure at the end of the chain. This leaves us with an elegant pipeline of operations where exceptions are handled at the end regardless of which operation caused the failure. We can focus on describing the happy path without extraneous error checking throughout the pipeline. At the end, failure as an effect is described separately.

Combining futures

You'll often have multiple futures executing that you need to get access to. There are facilities for handling these cases as well. In Java, the `thenCombine` method on `CompletableFuture` will let you access the values of two futures once they are available:

```
askPong("Ping").
    thenCombine(askPong("Ping"), (a,b) -> {
            return a + b; //"PongPong"
        });
```

In Scala, for comprehensions offer an alternative syntax for composing together several futures. We're able to extract the results of two futures and handle them together like we would with any other collection. (Note that this is syntactic sugar for flatMap—I prefer this notation over flatMap.):

```
val f1 = Future{4}
    val f2 = Future{5}

    val futureAddition: Future[Int] =
      for(
        res1 <- f1;
        res2 <- f2
      ) yield res1 + res2
```

These examples yield simple mechanisms for handling multiple futures of varying types. In this way, we can parallelize work, making multiple requests at the same time to get responses back to users faster. This use of parallelization can help us improve system responsiveness.

Dealing with lists of futures

If you have a collection and you execute an asynchronous method on each element, you'll end up with a list of Futures.

For example, in Scala, if we take a list of messages, and ask the Pong actor to reply to each method, we end up with a list of futures like the following:

```
val listOfFutures = List[Future[String]] = List("Pong", "Pong",
"failed").map(x => askPong(x))
```

If you try to work with that, you'll see it's not easy. What we want is to get at the list of results—really, we want to flip the types so the List[Future] becomes Future[List]. This is a job for sequence, which is a member of Future:

```
val futureOfList: Future[List[String]] = Future.
sequence(listOfFutures)
```

Now we have a usable type. If we call map on futureOfList, for example, we get a List[String], which is what we want to work with. There is a problem here though. The future generated by sequence will fail if any of the futures in the list fail. We can recover each future before sequencing if we want to get any successful values instead of failing everything:

```
Future.sequence(listOfFutures.map(future => future.recover{case
Exception => ""}))
```

There is no equivalent in the Java8 core library, but there are gists around that cover the functionality for sequencing futures in the same manner.

Future cheat-sheet

The following is a small chart outlining the basic operations covered:

Operation	Scala Future	Java CompletableFuture
Transform Value	.map(x => y)	.thenApply(x -> y)
Transform Value Async	.flatMap(x => futureOfY)	.thenCompose(x -> futureOfY)
Return Value if Error	.recover(t => y)	.exceptionally(t -> y)
Return Value Async if Error	.recoverWith(t => futureOfY)	.handle(t,x -> futureOfY). thenCompose(x->x)

This section gives a good overview of the future and promises APIs. It's necessary to understand this abstraction, so it's recommended that you work with some asynchronous code and futures to get a better grasp on this. In the next section, we will introduce how to interact with actors by getting futures back—you should take some time to practice this to see how to handle multiple future results to ensure you have a good foundation to build on.

Composing a Distributed System – AkkademyDb and client

The purpose of this book is to teach you how to build distributed applications, so we're going to put everything we've covered in this chapter together into a small distributed application. While the code is fairly simple, this example is a bit advanced in its structure in that it jumps right in to showing you how two remote systems can use Akka to talk, but I think it's important to see the power of Akka right away to keep you interested in the material. If you get a taste for what Akka can do for you now, you'll want to keep going through the remaining chapters.

We'll be building a client and a service—our database—and then a database client to talk to it. In order to send messages over the wire between the client and service, we need to share messages between the projects.

We could put the messages in their own project, but to keep the examples shorter, we'll put the messages in the server project and import the server project (and, hence, the messages) into the client project.

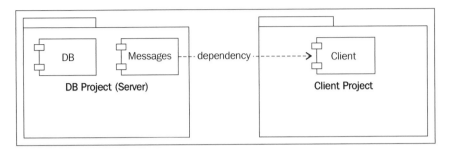

We'll start by extending the server project from the first chapter and producing all of the messages we want the database to expose. Then we'll implement the features for those messages in the database.

After building these basic operations, we'll produce a `main()` to make the store runnable. We'll start the application by producing an `ActorSystem` and the Actor in the `ActorSystem`, creating our first Akka "micro-service."

To consume the service and demonstrate how we can get futures from our remote actors, we'll create the database client to use the service. We'll expose the service in the client by returning futures. At this point, we'll have built a usable key-value datastore, much like redis, and a remote client to consume it.

Preparing the DB and messages

We want to expose a few messages to start with.

- Get message: Return a key if it exists
- Key Not Found exception: If a key isn't found, return this failure
- Set message: Sets a value and reply with a status

In the server, we'll implement these messages, their behavior, and a main so that the datastore can run. Note, we'll use the project from *Chapter 1, Starting Life as an Actor,* adding features introduced in this chapter such as replying and replying with failure.

The messages

As we'll be using remoting to send messages between separate networked applications, we need all of the messages to be serializable so that Akka can turn them into representations of the objects as they transfer over the networks between the applications. We'll implement SetRequest, GetRequest, and KeyNotFoundException.

The Java messages:

```java
public class SetRequest implements Serializable {
    public final String key;
    public final Object value;
    public SetRequest(String key, Object value) {
        this.key = key;
        this.value = value;
    }
}
public class GetRequest implements Serializable {
    public final String key;
    public GetRequest(String key) {
        this.key = key;
    }
}
public class KeyNotFoundException extends Exception implements
Serializable {
    public final String key;
    public KeyNotFoundException(String key) {
        this.key = key;
    }
}
```

The Scala messages:

```scala
case class SetRequest(key: String, value: Object)
case class GetRequest(key: String)
case class KeyNotFoundException(key: String) extends Exception
```

These are simple objects. We omit the Java getter as the message is immutable anyway—you can include one if you like.

 Messages should always be immutable.

(The Scala case class is serializable.)

Implementing the DB functionality

We've covered how to reply to messages with `sender() tell/!`. We also covered how to reply with `Status.Failure(Exception)`. We'll implement replies to all messages and we'll also add failure responses if the `GetRequest` encounters a miss in the key/value store.

The Java code's receive statements:

```
receive(ReceiveBuilder.
                match(SetRequest.class, message -> {
                    log.info("Received Set request: {}",
message);
                    map.put(message.key, message.value);
                    sender().tell(new Status.Success(message.
key), self());
                }).
                match(GetRequest.class, message -> {
                    log.info("Received Get request: {}",
message);

                    String value = map.get(message.key);
                    Object response = (value != null)
                            ? value
                            : new Status.Failure(new
KeyNotFoundException(message.key));
                    sender().tell(response, self());
                }).
                matchAny(o ->
                        sender().tell(new Status.Failure(new
ClassNotFoundException()), self())
                ).build()
        );
```

The Scala code's `receive` method:

```
override def receive = {
  case SetRequest(key, value) =>
    log.info("received SetRequest - key: {} value: {}", key, value)
    map.put(key, value)
    sender() ! Status.Success
  case GetRequest(key) =>
    log.info("received GetRequest - key: {}", key)
    val response: Option[String] = map.get(key)
    response match{
      case Some(x) => sender() ! x
      case None => sender() ! Status.Failure(new
KeyNotFoundException(key))
    }
  case o => Status.Failure(new ClassNotFoundException)
}
```

These are both roughly equivalent, languages aside. If the actor receives a `SetRequest`, the actor stores the value in the map. The behavior has been updated from the first chapter to send back a Success message. For the `GetRequest`, the actor tries to retrieve the value from the map. If it's found, it sends back the value. If it's not found, the actor sends back a Failure containing the `KeyNotFoundException`. Finally, we've changed the behavior for unknown messages to reply with a failure—we stuck a `ClassNotFound` exception in, but you could make a custom one for greater clarity.

Enabling remoting

We need to enable remote access to the actor from a remote application over the network. This is a trivial task fortunately. We need to add the remoting dependency to the `build.sbt` file:

```
"com.typesafe.akka" %% "akka-remote" % "2.3.6"
```

Then we simply add configuration to enable remote access to our actor. Add a new file in the `src/main/resources` file called `application.conf` and put the following configuration in the file with the interface and port to listen on. The `application.conf` file is recognized by Akka. It is a `typesafe-config` HOCON file, which is a JSON like format that is quite usable relative to other configuration formats—you'll see the configuration file referenced in the Akka documentation often and I personally find the HOCON format is quite a nice alternative to properties files if more than a few properties are needed. Note that properties files are usable as well if desired simply by naming the file `application.properties` and using the properties format (for example, `keypath.key=value`).Here is the application.conf::

```
akka {
  actor {
    provider = "akka.remote.RemoteActorRefProvider"
  }
  remote {
    enabled-transports = ["akka.remote.netty.tcp"]
    netty.tcp {
      hostname = "127.0.0.1"
      port = 2552
    }
  }
}
```

Main

Finally, for the datastore, we need to add a main method to start the actor system and create the actor.

In Java, we'll add a class: `com.akkademy.Main`:

```
public class Main {
    public static void main(String... args) {
        ActorSystem system = ActorSystem.create("akkademy");
        system.actorOf(Props.create(AkkademyDb.class), "akkademy-db");
    }
}
```

In Scala, we can put a Main object in the `com.akkademy.AkkademyDb.scala` file:

```
object Main extends App {
  val system = ActorSystem("akkademy")
  system.actorOf(Props[AkkademyDb], name = "akkademy-db")
}
```

We simply need to create an `ActorSystem`, and then create the actor in it. Note we give the actor a name — `akkademy-db` — we use a name to be able to easily look up the actor in the client, and also to ease debugging as Akka will log the Actor's name in error scenarios.

Publishing the messages

We need to publish the messages locally now so that we can use them in the client project. To publish to Nexus or Artifactory, we would set up the repository information in the `build.sbt`, but we'll simply publish them locally.

We need to add an organization and version to the `build.sbt` file like the following:

```
name := "akkademy-db"
organization := "com.akkademy-db"
version := "0.0.1-SNAPSHOT"
```

'-SNAPSHOT' indicates that the version is unstable and can change. As we will probably republish the server, we should add this tag to the version. If we were to release the code, then we would remove the '-SNAPSHOT' tag from the version to indicate that it will not (and cannot) change again.

Lastly, we need to exclude the `application.conf` file so that the client doesn't try to start a remote server. Again, it's better to put the messages in a standalone library—we're cutting corners for brevity. Put this in your `build.sbt` file to exclude the application.conf when publishing:

```
mappings in (Compile, packageBin) ~= { _.filterNot { case (_, name) =>
  Seq("application.conf").contains(name)
}}
```

If we put the messages in a separate library (and you certainly can), we wouldn't have needed to exclude the configuration from the build. We're done with the build configuration. From the command line, in the root of our project, we simply run the activator `publish-local` target to publish the project:

```
$activator publish-local
```

Starting the DB

We're going to build the client next, and to demonstrate integration, we're going to write some integration tests, so we need the server to be running. We can start the database now:

```
$activator run
```

Akka will log that it is listening for remote connections and tells us the address (which we will use shortly in the client):

```
[Remoting] Remoting now listens on addresses: [akka.tcp://
akkademy@127.0.0.1:2552]
```

Producing the client

We've published our messages, and have the key-value store running. We're ready to wrap up our first distributed application by consuming the service with a client.

Scaffolding the project

The first thing we need to do is create a project for the client and have it import the server project for the messages. We'll scaffold the project as we did in *Chapter 1, Starting Life as an Actor* —you can review the material if needed. Run activator-new and choose minimal-java or minimal-akka project. Call the project `akkademy-db-client`.

Modifying build.sbt

We need to add the dependency for our project into the `build.sbt` file. In the new project, add the following dependencies for our messages in `build.sbt`:

```
"com.akkademy-db"   %% "akkademy-db"      % "0.0.1-SNAPSHOT"
```

Apart from the testing frameworks included in the scaffolding, this dependency includes the dependencies we need to get going with the Scala project.

In the Java project, we need to also add the scala-java8-compat library to be able to convert the futures the actor will produce:

```
"org.scala-lang.modules" %% "scala-java8-compat" % "0.6.0"
```

Building the client

In this section, we'll build the client to connect to the remote actor, and then implement methods for the `SetRequest` and `GetRequest` messages.

First, the Java code can be placed in `com.akkademy.JClient`:

```java
public class JClient {
    private final ActorSystem system = ActorSystem.
create("LocalSystem");
    private final ActorSelection remoteDb;
    public JClient(String remoteAddress){
        remoteDb = system.actorSelection("akka.tcp://akkademy@" +
remoteAddress + "/user/akkademy-db");
    }
    public CompletionStage set(String key, Object value) {
        return toJava(ask(remoteDb, new SetRequest(key, value),
2000));
    }
    public CompletionStage<Object> get(String key){
        return toJava(ask(remoteDb, new GetRequest(key), 2000));
    }
}
```

The Scala code can be placed in `com.akkademy.SClient`:

```scala
class SClient(remoteAddress: String){
  private implicit val timeout = Timeout(2 seconds)
  private implicit val system = ActorSystem("LocalSystem")
  private val remoteDb = system.actorSelection(s"akka.tcp://
akkademy@$remoteAddress/user/akkademy-db")
  def set(key: String, value: Object) = {
    remoteDb ? SetRequest(key, value)
  }
```

```
    def get(key: String) = {
      remoteDb ? GetRequest(key)
    }
}
```

The code is fairly simple. First, we create a local `ActorSystem`, and then get a reference to the remote actor at the address provided in the constructor. Next, we create a method for each of the behaviors—get and set. We ask the actor using the messages we imported into our project, and then we return the future. Note we're using an arbitrary timeout value in the asks. Ideally, the timeout should be configurable.

For the Java code, we convert the `scala.concurrent.Future` to `CompletionStage` and return that. This gives us a better Java API for the consumer of our library to work with.

Next, to test that it all fits together, we'll write a small test case.

Testing

We need to make sure the db is running as these are integration tests. Here we'll simply create and then retrieve a record from the remote database.

The Java example:

```
public class JClientIntegrationTest {
    JClient client = new JClient("127.0.0.1:2552");
    @Test
    public void itShouldSetRecord() throws Exception {
        client.set("123", 123);
        Integer result = (Integer) ((CompletableFuture) client.
get("123")).get();
        assert(result == 123);
    }
}
```

And the Scala example:

```
class SClientIntegrationSpec extends FunSpecLike with Matchers {
  val client = new SClient("127.0.0.1:2552")
  describe("akkademyDbClient") {
    it("should set a value"){
      client.set("123", new Integer(123))
      val futureResult = client.get("123")
      val result = Await.result(futureResult, 10 seconds)
      result should equal(123)
    }
  }
}
```

This takes the knowledge we gained about working with Futures to be able to test our API. We use Awaits/get as it's just a test case, but we now have definitive proof that building distributed applications is feasible with Akka. And we're only on *Chapter2, Actors and Concurrency*

Homework

Doing the homework is very important in this chapter as it covers the core skill set needed. The example had fairly simple code, but was a touch advanced in introducing remoting—in the next few chapters we will only work on local Actor systems, so the examples will be simpler. Running the example outlined here will give some insight into exactly what problems Akka tries to solve, though, so I would recommend you take a few minutes to study them. This chapter—in particular the future API—is the foundation for everything that follows. We need to have a solid base to build on in the topics covered in this chapter.

General learning

Here are some tasks you should complete to ensure you understand how to work with the information presented in this chapter.

- Build a small service that has an actor that reverses a string. Have it fail if an unknown message type is sent.

- Build a service for the actor that exposes the functionality through a plain Java/ScalaAPI, returning a future.

- Build test cases for success and failure cases.

- Write a test that will send a list of strings to the actor, and validate all of the results. You should use sequence—a Java8 sequence implementation can be found at
  `http://www.nurkiewicz.com/2013/05/java-8-completablefuture-in-action.html`.

Project homework

Expand on the example code:

- Add an atomic `SetIfNotExists` and Delete messages to the `Akkademy DB` App.

- If you need some `sbt` experience, move the messages to their own project and publish it.

- Complete Tests for the Client—we don't have tests for the failure cases such as getting a missing message. You should complete this.

- Start building your own project:

- Build an actor that delivers some piece of functionality from your project—have the actor reply to messages with the work done.

- Write unit tests to cover success and failure cases it by asking the actor.

Summary

This chapter laid down the foundation for building applications with Akka. All of the prerequisites are now covered for us to begin doing real work with distributed applications. We looked in depth at actor code—creating an instance of an actor, looking up an actor, responding to a message in an actor, getting a response from an actors from outside the `ActorSystem`—and working with futures.

We have enough knowledge now to give our asynchronous event-driven Akka applications to the rest of the world—we can build libraries and services with Akka and expose them with the core Scala and Java8 future APIs. This is what we will be doing in the next chapter.

Getting the Message Across

In this chapter, we will cover all of the details of message delivery mechanisms in Akka. We'll look at different messaging patterns—different ways in which we can get messages between Actors to get work done. We'll look at scheduling message delivery as well—a way of delaying or repeating delivery of messages. We'll cover how these messaging patterns can be used to compose Actors together to get work done in this chapter.

To demonstrate all the ways in which we can get messages between Actors, a new example service will be introduced as a consumer of `Akkademy-DB` as well—a simple article parsing component.

This chapter will cover some of the essential mechanics around handling Messages:

- Making Messages Immutable
- Asking an Actor for a Reply
- Forwarding Messages
- Piping Futures

Setting the stage with an example problem

Imagine you are on a team asked to create a mobile news reader. Someone will produce the application that runs on the device. It will comb RSS feeds from major news sites, presenting the new articles on the feeds to the user. When the user selects an article that they would like to read, they will be shown a simple representation of the text optimized for consumption on a mobile device.

You need to produce a service that will accept the URL of an article and will return back the article's body text. It should contain only the body text and no HTML tags. Because many people will be reading new articles, it should cache all parsed articles so that they can be returned quickly to the user. The articles should be cached in an Akkademy-DB instance running on another machine.

Requirement Overview:

* Expose an HTTP Endpoint that accepts the URL of an article
* Return the main body of text from the article
* Cache the article in `Akkademy DB`

Sketching the project

We will use Activator again to create another project. Refer to *Chapter 1, Starting Life as an Actor* if you need more details.

Perform the following steps:

1. Run—`Activator run`
2. Select a `minimal-java` or `minimal-scala` project.
3. Call the `akkademaid` project.
4. Add the `akkademy-db` and `boilerpipe` dependencies to `build.sbt`:

   ```
   libraryDependencies ++= Seq(
   "com.syncthemall" % "boilerpipe" % "1.2.2",
   "com.akkademy-db" %% "akkademy-db-scala" % "0.0.1-SNAPSHOT",
   "com.syncthemail" % "boilerpipe" % "1.2.2"
   )
   ```

`Akkademy-DB` is added as a dependency for Akka and the messages needed to communicate with it. We add the `boilerpipe` Java library to help with our requirement of getting the body text from a web page. Test frameworks will be included in `build.sbt` by default.

Core functionality

The `boilerpipe` library takes care of the article parsing for us. We simply need to call `ArticleExtractor.getInstance.getText(input)` where input is a Stream or String.

We'll revisit the example and `Akkademy-DB` as we work through different approaches to solving the problem.

Messaging delivery

In this next section, we're going to look at ways of getting messages to an Actor. We're going to cover core messaging patterns, and we'll also introduce scheduling along the way.

There are four core Actor messaging patterns: tell, ask, forward, and pipe. We have looked at `tell` and `ask` where the sender is not an Actor. We will introduce all message passing concepts here from the perspective of an Actor sending messages to another Actor:

- **Ask**: Send a message to an Actor, and get a response back via a future. When the Actor replies, it completes the future. No messages are sent to the sender's mailbox

- **Tell**: Send a message to an Actor. Any replies to `sender()` are sent back to the sending Actor

- **Forward**: Take a message that has been received and send it to another Actor. Any replies to `sender()` are delivered back to the sender of the original message

- **Pipe**: This is used to send the result of a future back to `sender()` or another Actor. If using Ask or handling a future, using Pipe is the correct way to reply with the result of the future

We'll cover these patterns and the basic principles of messages in Akka in the following section.

Messages should be immutable

As mentioned earlier, messages should be immutable. Because Akka is built on the JVM, where Java and Scala have mutable types, it's possible to send mutable messages but you may lose many of the advantages Akka gives in eliminating shared state. By having messages that are mutable, you introduce the risk that a developer may one day start mutating messages in ways that can break the application. It's certainly possible to use mutable messages safely by not changing state, but it's better to use immutable messages to ensure that no errors are introduced in future changes.

There are two ways in which messages can be mutable—references and types. I saw Jamie Allen present recently and he demonstrated a matrix of mutable references and types in relation to a message like so:

References	Mutable Type	Immutable Type
Mutable Reference	☹☹	☹
Immutable Reference	☹	☺

If both your references and types are mutable, then that's the worst case scenario. The following is an example:

```
public class Message{
public StringBuffer mutableBuffer;
public Message(StringBuffer: mutableBuffer){
this.mutableBuffer = mutableBuffer;
}
}
class Message(var mutableBuffer: StringBuffer = new StringBuffer);
```

Here, both the objects are referenced, and the object's state can also change, which is the worst case in our grid.

Variables referenced in the message (for example, fields) can either be mutable or immutable. In Scala, field members marked `val` are immutable references and field members marked `var` are mutable—the reference can be changed to point to a new object/primitive. In Java, members marked with final are immutable references and those without are mutable. All fields in messages should be of the immutable variety. The field members should be passed in via constructor arguments to be able to fulfill the immutability contract.

We can demonstrate how the references can change:

```
Messagemessage=newMessage(newStringBuffer("original"));
message.mutableBuffer=newStringBuffer("new");

valmessage=newMessage(newStringBuffer("original"))
message.mutableBuffer=newStringBuffer("new")
```

Here we create a new message, and then we change the `StringBuffer` reference to point to a new `StringBuffer`. The message is created with `StringBuffer(original)` but is mutated to `StringBuffer`(new). This shows how the message can be changed because of the change in its reference.

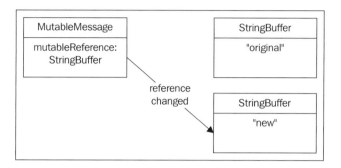

We want to eliminate the possibility of someone changing the reference in the message, so we need to make the references `val`/`final`. The following is an example of immutable references in the message, improving on our previous example:

```
public class Message {

        public final StringBuffer mutableBuffer;


    Message(StringBuffer mutableBuffer) {

            this.mutableBuffer = mutableBuffer;


        }
}
```

In Scala, if no access modifiers are supplied in the declaration, the field reference will be an immutable `val`. In Java, we use the final modifier to make the reference immutable. Now we can't change the `mutableBuffer` reference to point at a new object—we can be sure the message will always point toward the same `StringBuffer`. There is still a problem with this though—we can change the `StringBuffer` object itself as it is a mutable type. We can append new characters to a reference. If multiple Actors have a reference to that message, then it's possible that concurrency errors can occur. The following is an example of us changing the `StringBuffer`:

```
Message message = new Message(new StringBuffer())
message.mutableBuffer.append("appended");
val message = new Message(StringBuffer("original"))
message.mutableBuffer.append("appended")
```

This demonstrates that even though the message's `mutableBuffer` reference is immutable, the `StringBuffer` in memory can still be modified as it is a mutable type as shown in the following figure:

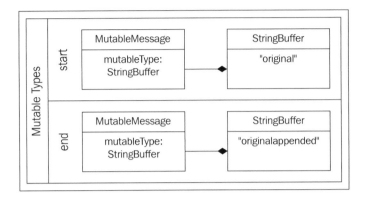

For a message to truly be immutable, it needs to have both immutable references and use immutable types. String is an immutable type, so we can make this message immutable by using String instead of `StringBuffer`. An example of the ideal immutable message is as follows:

```
public class ImmutableMessage{
    public final String immutableType;
public ImmutableMessage(String immutableType) {
    this.immutableType = immutableType;
    }
}
class ImmutableMessage(immutableType: String)
```

Now we cannot change the message in any way—it's thread safe and can be sent across threads or machines without any risk of that message changing in any way in its life:

```
new ImmutableMessage("can't be changed");
```

There is one more improvement we can make—use a case class instead of a class in Scala. Case classes are preferred as they give useful members like a default `toString()` and `copy()` method. They can be serialized for use in Akka remoting as well. In Java, we will often declare our messages as Serializable as well in case we want to send them over the wire:

```
public class ImmutableMessage implements Serializable {
public final String string;
public ImmutableMessage(String string) {
```

```
this.string = string;
    }
}
case class ImmutableMessage(String: String)
```

Understanding immutability is essential not only in Akka messages but also in safe and concurrent computing in general. Any time data is to be shared between threads, therefore, aim for immutability first. Now that we know how to make immutable messages, we can look at how to compose actors together with various messaging patterns.

Ask message pattern

The Ask pattern produces a future that represents the reply from an Actor. This is often used to talk to Actors from plain objects outside of an Actor system. We looked at Ask, we get a future back that represents the response, but it may not be obvious exactly how Akka knows which message fulfills the future.

When you ask an Actor, Akka actually creates a temporary Actor in the Actor system. The sender() reference that the Actor replies to becomes this temporary Actor. When an Actor replies to the message it receives from an ask, this temporary Actor completes the future with the response as shown in the following figure:

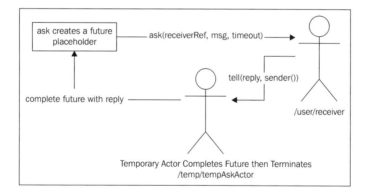

Akka knows which message fulfills the future because the sender() reference becomes that temporary Actor's path. It's important to know this so we can compose together multiple Actors and ensure we're replying to the correct place to fulfill any asks.

Asks always require a timeout be defined and if the ask is not replied to, then the future will fail with the timeout. The ask/? method requires a timeout to be supplied to it—either a long one in milliseconds or an akka.util.Timeout, which offers some more expressive descriptions of time.

In Java, you can Ask with a `Timeout` constructed with a `TimeUnit` like the following:

```
static import akka.pattern.Patterns.ask; Timeout timeout = new akka.
util.Timeout(1,
java.util.concurrent.TimeUnit.SECONDS);
Future future = ask(actor, message, timeout);
```

In Scala, you can use `scala.concurrent.duration` for defining a timeout with the attractive scala duration **Domain Specific Languages(DSL)**, which lets you describe a duration as, for example, 1 second. In Scala, the timeout supplied to the ask is implicit, which helps to simplify the ask semantics to a concise statement:

```
actorRef ? message
```

For example, with the timeout and imports, your code would look like the following:

```
import scala.concurrent.duration._
import akka.pattern.ask
implicit val timeout = akka.util.Timeout(1 second)
val future = actorRef ? "message"
```

We'll look at an example of a design using ask to demonstrate how we can compose together asks. Because Ask gives Futures, this is essentially composing together Futures that the Actors produce with Ask.

Designing with Ask

We'll demonstrate our example application design using the Ask pattern first. This is the most naive approach. The example we'll show here is for the article parse service using ask that will check the cache, and, if the parsed article is not in the cache, it will ask an `HttpClientActor` and then have the result parsed by an `ArtcileParserActor`. After retrieving the results, it will attempt to cache the article and then return the article to the user as shown the following figure:

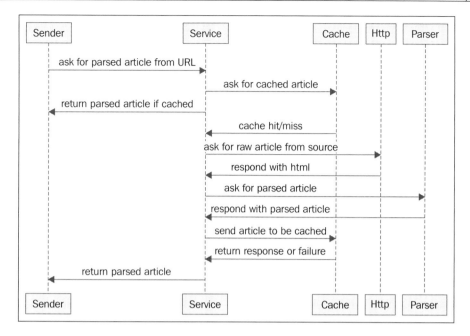

This is a useful example to look at but it's not an optimal design. This is very much how we would have done this using a synchronous API, so it's a good starting point to build on. We'll examine some code before proceeding.

For brevity, we'll omit the Actor code except for the service Actor. The full code examples are in the GitHub examples in the folder in this chapter. For the context of reading the code, each of the Actors sends back either a failure or a success—a String representing the article (raw or parsed).

The following is the Scala source:

```
packagecom.akkademy.askdemo
class AskDemoArticleParser(cacheActorPath: String,
httpClientActorPath: String, acticleParserActorPath: String,implicit
val timeout: Timeout
)
extends Actor {
  val cacheActor = context.actorSelection(cacheActorPath)
  val httpClientActor = context.actorSelection(httpClientActorPath)
  val articleParserActor = context.actorSelection(
    acticleParserActorpath)
```

```
      import scala.concurrent.ExecutionContext.Implicits.global

   override def receive: Receive = {
     case ParseArticle(uri) =>
       val senderRef = sender() //sender ref needed for closure

       val cacheResult = cacheActor ? GetRequest(uri) //ask cache actor

       val result = cacheResult.recoverWith { //if request fails, then
ask the articleParseActor
          case _: Exception =>
            val fRawResult = httpClientActor ? uri

            fRawResult flatMap {
              case HttpResponse(rawArticle) =>
                articleParserActor ? ParseHtmlArticle(uri, rawArticle)
              case x =>
                Future.failed(new Exception("unknown response"))
            }
       }

       result onComplete { //could use Pipe (covered later)
         case scala.util.Success(x: String) =>
           println("cached result!")
           senderRef ! x //cached result
         case scala.util.Success(x: ArticleBody) =>
           cacheActor ! SetRequest(uri, x.body)
           senderRef ! x
         case scala.util.Failure(t) =>
           senderRef ! akka.actor.Status.Failure(t)
         case x =>
           println("unknown message! " + x)
       }
   }
 }
}
```

The following is the equivalent Java8 code:

```
public class AskDemoArticleParser extends AbstractActor {

    private final ActorSelection cacheActor;
    private final ActorSelection httpClientActor;
    private final ActorSelection artcileParseActor;
    private final Timeout timeout;

    public AskDemoArticleParser(String cacheActorPath, String
httpClientActorPath, String artcileParseActorPath, Timeout timeout) {
        this.cacheActor = context().actorSelection(cacheActorPath);
        this.httpClientActor = context().actorSelection(httpClientAct
orPath);
```

```
        this.artcileParseActor = context().actorSelection(artcilePars
eActorPath);
        this.timeout = timeout;
    }

public PartialFunction receive() {
        return ReceiveBuilder.
                match(ParseArticle.class, msg -> {
                    final CompletionStage cacheResult =
toJava(ask(cacheActor, new GetRequest(msg.url), timeout));
                    final CompletionStage result = cacheResult.
handle((x, t) -> {
                        return (x != null)
                                ? CompletableFuture.completedFuture(x)
                                : toJava(ask(httpClientActor, msg.url,
timeout)).
                        thenCompose(rawArticle -> toJava(
                                        ask(artcileParseActor,
                                            new
ParseHtmlArticle(msg.url,

((HttpResponse) rawArticle).body), timeout))
                                );
                    }).thenCompose(x -> x);

                    final ActorRef senderRef = sender();
                    result.handle((x,t) -> {
                        if(x != null){
                            if(x instanceof ArticleBody){
                                String body = ((ArticleBody) x).body;
//parsed article
                                cacheActor.tell(body, self()); //cache
it
                                senderRef.tell(body, self()); //reply
                            } else if(x instanceof String) //cached
article
                                senderRef.tell(x, self());
                        } else if( x == null )
                                senderRef.tell(new akka.actor.Status.
Failure((Throwable)t), self());
                        return null;
                    });

                }).build();
    }
}
```

Both the Scala and Java8 examples have the same functionality—the Actor constructor takes strings with the Actor paths and looks up each of the Actors with `actorSelection` as we have done previously. Injecting the paths are dependencies. This lets us configure where our actors are. For example, the cached b would be local in test and on a remote machine in production.

Once we receive a message, we try to get a cached article. If the `cacheResult` misses or fails for any reason, we compose together two more asks in a recover/exceptionally block:

- Ask the HTTP client Actor for the raw article
- Ask the article parser to parse the raw article from the HTTP Actor

If the cache request fails, we don't care what the issue is with the cache result—we can still give the user a result if the cache is offline for example. We would, however, log the unexpected error or capture the cause of the error in a metric.

Finally, we register what to do when we have the result or error at the end of processing—we either send back the success or send a failure with the cause of the error.

The use of ask is a simple solution, but there are a few "gotchas" and issues to look out for when using ask as the primary message patterns in Actors. Ask is a good place to start with for building simple solutions, but it can sometimes be better to design with tell as we'll look at shortly. Let's look at a few of the elements of using ask that we need to be aware of.

Callbacks execute in another execution context

Note that in the preceding example, a local `ActorRef` variable is created to store the `sender()` method's result. This is very important: this is necessary here and you will no doubt bump into this at least once when you start working with Akka. Because the lambdas are executed somewhere else, in another execution context on another thread, the `sender()` method will return an unexpected value when the code block in the lambda is running. This is a non-obvious issue to beginners. In older Scala Akka examples, `sender()` was often written without the brackets. It's recommended that `sender()` always be expressed with the brackets in Scala as it does not have referential transparency (it doesn't return the same value every time it's called)—it's clearer that this is a method call when you add the brackets. In order for the correct `ActorRef` to be referred to, `sender()` must be called in the main thread and the reference stored into a variable. That variable will correctly be passed into the lambda's closure when it is executed. There is a better way to handle the reply called Pipe, which we'll look at shortly, but this is an important quality of closures to understand.

Timeouts are required

Note that the example uses a single timeout and passes it to several asks. You cannot ask an Actor for a reply without creating a bounded timeout. If the Actor that is asked does not reply to the future before the timeout ends, the future will be failed.

Selecting the correct timeout value can be difficult without real data from production systems under load. Setting the timeout too low will cause failures to be reported for operations that would have succeeded. Setting the timeout too high will force users to wait too long when operations might have failed due to anomalies. To set timeouts, you'll want to have statistics on the operations in production. You can't control the performance of systems you depend on, so it can be difficult to get this correct.

Because every ask requires a timeout, if Actors are asking Actors that are asking Actors, it's not easy to enforce a single timeout. If an error occurs at some point, it's possible you'll see several timeouts in your logs, which can make debugging quite difficult as shown in the following figure:

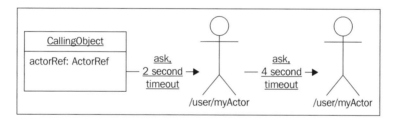

In the preceding image, it's possible that the 2-second timeout causes the future to fail, even if all of the code is working correctly and all systems are responding.

It may seem like a good idea to place a large timeout to avoid errors from occurring. Placing arbitrary and large timeouts should be considered an anti-pattern as it violates the responsive tenet of reactive design we try to adhere to when building our applications. A 30-second timeout offers very little value in reality as a user waiting for data has likely given up by the time the timeout has occurred. In most use cases, if your users legitimately need to wait for more than 10 seconds for an operation, it's possible your users won't be using your software for long. Obviously, there are exceptions, but studies from Microsoft and Google have shown that user behavior is impacted negatively if they have to wait for more than 2 seconds for a page to appear in web applications.

Timeout stacktraces aren't useful

Each ask you use has a timeout. In our example, the operation spans multiple asks, so there are multiple places where timeouts can occur. The ask timeouts will throw exceptions from Akka's scheduler thread rather than a thread local to the Actor, so you won't be able to tell from printing the `AskTimeoutExceptions` stacktrace specifically which ask operation timed out. It can be difficult to debug an application when all you have is an exception like the following:

```
akka.pattern.AskTimeoutException: Ask timed out on [Actor[akka://
system/user/actor#778114812]] after [2000 ms]
        at akka.pattern.PromiseActorRef$$anonfun$1.
apply$mcV$sp(AskSupport.scala:335)
        at akka.actor.Scheduler$$anon$7.run(Scheduler.scala:117)
```

One more thing to watch out for is if your actor throws an unexpected exception and doesn't reply with the failure. It may appear that the error occurred due to the timeout, but the cause might be elsewhere.

The lesson here is that when using ask, you should always reply to messages with failures when errors are encountered in your code. If an Actor throws an exception, the Actor will not reply with a message. In an Actor, you're responsible for implementing all message handling behavior—if an actor expects a reply, Akka will not implicitly handle any replies for you—you must always reply to messages yourself when a reply is expected.

Ask is a pattern built on top of Akka—it's a useful helper, but there is no mechanism in Akka to automatically reply to messages or fail Futures generated by the Ask pattern. The Ask pattern creates a Scala Promise and a temporary (extra) Actor to receive a reply that it uses to fulfill the Promise. There is no mechanism to make the temporary Actor aware of an exception encountered in another Actor, so if you don't reply to the temporary Actor the Ask creates, it will not fulfill the Promise, and the timeout will fail the corresponding Future as in the following figure:

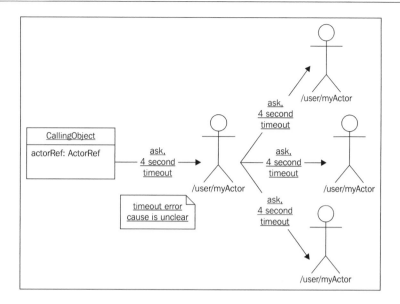

Ask has overhead

The ask pattern may seem simple but it has some `hidden` overhead. First, Ask causes Akka to create a new temporary Actor in the`/temp` path. That Actor awaits the response from the Actor that receives the Ask message. Next, there is also the overhead of the future. Ask creates a future that the temporary Actor completes. It's not a huge overhead, but it is worth considering if your ask operations occur with extremely high frequency. Ask can be simpler, but there are more efficient solutions using only tell where performance matters.

Complexity of Actors and Ask

If you're simply asking your Actors, and they don't contain state, then you may be better off using Futures alone. In the preceding examples Actors are used as an asynchronous API by invoking them with ask. We could replace the Actors with methods that give back Futures and our code would be equivalent and simpler to read.

For quite a while, I was of the opinion that it's better to not use Actors if you don't have either:

- State and concurrency; or
- Distribution

If you aren't using Akka for remoting or you aren't using Akka for concurrent access to state by encapsulating state in Actors, then it may not be obvious what the benefits are compared to stateless classes that are asynchronous and non-blocking.

However, I believe this is because I was writing Actor code with poor designs. It is true that if you have no state, an asynchronous API is simpler than using Ask with Actors. However, if you are designing with the "Tell Don't Ask" principle, then you can have code that is simpler, better performing, and can be easier to debug when using Actors. We'll look at tell next.

Tell

Tell is the simplest messaging pattern—however, it can take some time to learn how to use it best, which is why it is being presented here after Ask. It is often viewed as a "fire and forget" message delivery mechanism as no sender is specified; however, request/reply style messaging can be completed with tell when a little ingenuity is applied.

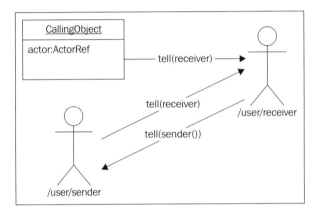

Tell is a method of the `ActorRef`/`ActorSelection` classes. It can take a reply to as an argument as well which becomes `sender()` in the Actor that receives the Message. By default, in Scala, the sender is implicitly defined as the Actor that sent the message. If there is no sender—for example, invoking ask from outside of an Actor—then the response address default is no mailbox (called `DeadLetters`).

In Java, there are no implicits or default values, so you have to supply the sender. If you don't want to supply any specific sender to reply to, you should use the following convention:

- Use `self()` if sending from an actor:

  ```
  actor.tell(message, self());
  ```

- Use `noSender` if sending from outside of the actor system:

  ```
  actor.tell("message", akka.actor.ActorRef.noSender());
  ```

- As covered in Scala, this is all default/implicit, so you get this for free implicitly with the simple syntax:

```
actor ! "message"
```

This is the expected behavior with tell—the reply reference should be the Actor sending the message or it should be none if it's not an Actor sending the message. However, using a different sender can be quite important when using tell—we can actually eliminate asks through some creative use of reply addresses and storing state in Actors, as we'll see soon:

Designing with Tell

It may seem odd to have put ask before tell, as, theoretically, tell is a much simpler message delivery mechanism. In building applications, it may seem natural to ask several Actors and compose the Futures similar to what we did in the ask design example. We covered several of the problems with ask, as well as the timeouts and overhead associated with it, so there is motivation to look at other solutions. We can do better by using tell.

Tell is often viewed as a fire-and-forget messaging pattern, but when designing, changing how you think about objects and actors and how they interact can yield better designs. If you're coming from Scala, you might find your designs become simpler if you store a bit of state in Actors and if you create some temporary Actors to handle certain tasks. This is counter-intuitive for the functional programmer who avoids state. Object-oriented languages were originally message-driven and so we can get a few hints about the lessons learned in design by reviewing some of the good practices from SmallTalk culture.

Handling replies with Tell

Because the sender reference is available to send back a message, it's easy to reply to a message. However, to handle a reply, we need to have the ability to recall which message the Actor is replying to. If we store some state in the Actor about messages that it expects a response to, then we can effectively "ask" an Actor without the pitfalls of ask described earlier.

For a very simple example of designing with tell, we can store some context in an Actor with a map with a key and send the key in the message. Then, when a message comes back with that key, we can restore that context and complete handling the message. This allows us to use semantics similar to ask without the overhead of ask.

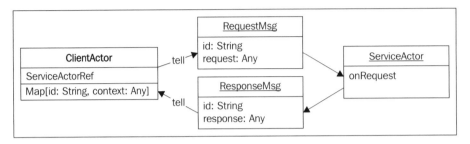

This may seem like a lot of overhead when you can use ask, but if you're trying to compose together many Actors, it removes the timeouts and extra Actor creation that ask incurs. This lets us control where the timeout occurs.

Because there is no timeout with tell, we generally want to produce our own timeout at some point in time.

Scheduling a Tell Timeout

We'll introduce the scheduler here as a minor element. The scheduler is capable of repeating messages at an interval; however, it is most commonly used as a way of deferring a tell. For example, if an Actor wants to send itself a "check-for-timeout" message after 3 seconds, the scheduler is the mechanism that can be used to accomplish that.

Very often in our Actors, we expect some event to occur before a certain period of time elapses, and if that event has not occurred, then we want to fail in some manner. The scheduler can be used to schedule such an event (for example, a timeout). The following is an example of sending an Actor a timeout message after 3 seconds:

```Java
//Java
context().system().scheduler().scheduleOnce(Duration.create(3,
TimeUnit.SECONDS), actor, "timeout");
```

```Scala
//Scala
context.system.scheduler.scheduleOnce(3 seconds, actor, "timeout")
```

We'll see how this comes into play shortly.

Tell Don't Ask–*Procedural code gets information then makes decisions. Object-oriented code tells objects to do things*—Alec Sharp, SmallTalk by Example.

The OO designers who worked in `SmallTalk` delivered a very important principle in Object-oriented design, which translates quite well into the Actor paradigm—Tell, Don't Ask.

This is saying that messages should be commands and that your Actors should be combinations of state and behavior instead of invocations of procedures—just like good object-oriented design. When you're designing, I'd recommend you take that a step farther and consider avoiding ask between Actors to see what your designs look like. This is a heuristic, so evaluate your designs, and the costs and benefits. You'll often find tell will produce simpler, leaner flows.

Tell Don't Ask is actually more of an object-oriented design heuristic, but given some of the pitfalls of the ask pattern covered, we may want consider this rule of thumb in designing with Actors as well. Ask can be simple, so evaluate it when working with Akka, but be aware of the alternative solutions as well.

Avoiding Ask with an Anonymous Actor

If you're invoking tell from outside of an Actor in plain objects, there is no immediately obvious way to receive and handle a response apart from ask. As we've looked at, between Actors, you can handle a response by capturing some state specific to the current message in an Actor (for example, an ID). There is another option for handling a reply as well—by using a new temporary Actor, we can describe the response to a single message.

We'll cover using tell instead of ask in an example. In this example, we'll create a temporary Actor to handle the response to a message. Note that this is very similar to how Akka handles ask under the hood—it creates a temporary Actor to handle the response sent to the sender to complete the future.

We'll demonstrate the receive block only (Java and then Scala):

```
//Java
public PartialFunction receive() {
        return ReceiveBuilder.
                match(ParseArticle.class, msg -> {
                    ActorRef extraActor = buildExtraActor(sender(),
msg.url);
                    cacheActor.tell(new GetRequest(msg.url),
extraActor);
                    httpClientActor.tell(msg.url, extraActor);
                    context().system().scheduler().
scheduleOnce(timeout.duration(),
                            extraActor, "timeout", context().system().
dispatcher(), ActorRef.noSender());
                }).build();
```

```
    }

//Scala
  override def receive: Receive = {
    case msg @ ParseArticle(uri) =>

      val extraActor = buildExtraActor(sender(), uri)

      cacheActor.tell(GetRequest(uri), extraActor)
      httpClientActor.tell("test", extraActor)

      context.system.scheduler.scheduleOnce(timeout.duration,
  extraActor, "timeout")
    }
```

This looks a bit simpler because we're not composing any Futures, but there is an extra actor that is created in the `buildExtraActor` method.

We'll demonstrate the `buildExtraActor` method in a moment, but we'll walk through this first. The block gets the `ParseArticle` message and begins by creating the `extraActor`. The term extra is a term attributed to Jamie Allen in his book *Effective Akka* from *O'Reilly* publications where he demonstrates a similar pattern which he refers to as the Extra Pattern.

After creating the `extraActor`, the receive block continues to send three messages:

- Send a message to the cache actor requesting the cached article that causes a String to be sent back to the sender. Here, sender is supplied to the tell as the `extraActor`

- Send a message to the `httpClientActor` requesting the raw article that causes an `HttpResponse` to be sent to the `extraActor`

- Schedule a `timeout` message to be sent to the `extraActor`

This is different than the ask example because we don't wait for the cache to respond in this particular example. It's possible to compose the requests in the extra Actor's behavior, but for simplicity, here we'll send them both off and have the extra Actor respond to whichever message is received first.

The `extraActor` is an anonymous Actor that describes the response to the three possible messages above:

- If it gets a response from the cache, respond with that to the `originalSender`
- If it gets an HTTP response, send that to the `ArticleParser` to parse and have the article parser reply back with the `ArticleBody`
- If it gets an `ArticleBody`, the `HttpResponse` has been parsed, so we want to cache the result and reply to the `originalSender`
- If it gets a timeout, send a failure back to the `originalSender`

The `extraActor` describes the response to the three messages, including how to get the raw HTML article and then how to parse it. By putting all of this behavior into a single anonymous Actor, which can only handle one of each type of the messages, we can describe the response to the behavior in each case.

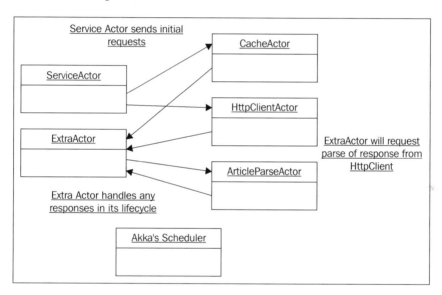

Here is the code for the factory method for the extra Actor:

```java
//Java
private ActorRef buildExtraActor(ActorRef senderRef, String uri){

    class MyActor extends AbstractActor {
        public MyActor() {
        receive(ReceiveBuilder
                    .matchEquals(String.class, x ->
x.equals("timeout"), x -> { //if we get timeout, then fail
```

```
                            senderRef.tell(new Status.Failure(new
TimeoutException("timeout!")), self());
                              context().stop(self());
                      })
                      .match(HttpResponse.class, httpResponse -> {
//If we get the cache response first, then we handle it and shut down.
                            //The cache response will come back before
the HTTP response so we never parse in this case.
                            artcileParseActor.tell(new
ParseHtmlArticle(uri, httpResponse.body), self());
                      })
                      .match(String.class, body -> { //If we get the
cache response first, then we handle it and shut down.
                            //The cache response will come back before
the HTTP response so we never parse in this case.
                            senderRef.tell(body, self());
                            context().stop(self());
                      })
                      .match(ArticleBody.class, articleBody -> {//If
we get the parsed article back, then we've just parsed it
                            cacheActor.tell(new
SetRequest(articleBody.uri, articleBody.body), self());
                            senderRef.tell(articleBody.body, self());
                            context().stop(self());
                      })
                      .matchAny(t -> { //We can get a cache miss
                            System.out.println("ignoring msg: " +
t.getClass());
                      })
                      .build());
               }
          }

          return context().actorOf(Props.create(MyActor.class, () -> new
MyActor()));
      }

//Scala
  private def buildExtraActor(senderRef: ActorRef, uri: String):
ActorRef = {
     return context.actorOf(Props(new Actor{
        override def receive = {
          case "timeout" => //if we get timeout, then fail
             senderRef ! Failure(new TimeoutException("timeout!"))
             context.stop(self)
```

```
        case HttpResponse(body) => //If we get the http response
first, we pass it to be parsed.
            articleParserActor ! ParseHtmlArticle(uri, body)

        case body: String => //If we get the cache response first,
then we handle it and shut down.
            //The cache response will come back before the HTTP response
so we never parse in this case.
            senderRef ! body
            context.stop(self)

        case ArticleBody(uri, body) => //If we get the parsed article
back, then we've just parsed it
            cacheActor ! SetRequest(uri, body) //Cache it as we just
parsed it
            senderRef ! body
            context.stop(self)

        case t => //We can get a cache miss
            println("ignoring msg: " + t.getClass)
      }
    }))
  }
```

Note that there are three possible outcomes:

- The cache responds with the body
- The http article comes back, is parsed and then cached
- Neither of these events occur before the timeout message

All three of these outcomes cause the `extraActor` to be stopped by executing `context().stop(self())`; this Actor is short lived, then – it will not live more than 3 seconds.

There is the case where the cache fails and the article comes back – this is a special case because we need to parse the article still, so we send this message to the article parser and then handle the response.

This looks like a bit more code, and it is, but it's actually lighter than the ask example believe it or not:

- The ask example causes a future to be created for each ask
- The ask example causes a temporary Actor to be created for each ask

Our example has no Futures and only one extra Actor. It's also simpler to analyze errors:

- The ask example has three separate timeouts that can fail

Our example has only one timeout which we control - the timeout is either encountered or else the success case occurs. In this approach, we can also log any state in the temporary Actor when the timeout is encountered to understand exactly what occurred. Future timeouts are not very helpful in comparison.

At the expense of a bit more code than the ask example, we're taking control over the behavior instead of relying on Akka's ask implementation details, and in turn, we're able to construct the solution to fit the exact use case. I've worked in teams that prefer simple terse code so which solution you choose – tell or ask – will be up to you and your team to decide. Explore both and understand their pros and cons. For any performance critical areas of your code, tell can be more performant.

A good exercise here would be to change the extra Actor code only request or only parse the article if the cache request fails to return a result. Don't be afraid to keep state in the extra Actor to understand where it is in its lifecycle.

This demonstrates how a design can be changed from composing asks to a design that avoids ask completely by using an extra Actor to deal with responses and control the flow of messages between Actors. There are no panaceas, but you should try to evaluate a few different designs when building and see which works best in your use case.

Forward

While tell semantically sends a message to another Actor with the reply address being the current Actor, forward is much like the case in forwarding mail—the original sender stays the same but there is a new recipient.

Where tell lets you specify the reply address and it is implicit that the Actor that sends the message, forward delivers a message with the reply address equal to sender.

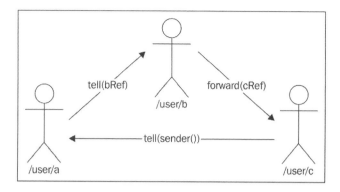

This is useful where a message received will be delegated to another actor to fulfill, and the product of that Actor is needed by the original requester.

The intermediate Actor hands off the message, or possibly a new one, but the original sender is passed with the new message. An example use case could be getting a history from a bank account. There may be one History Actor who then delegates the request for account history to either a `ChequingAccount` or `CreditCardAccount` Actor. The message requesting the account history would be forwarded to the more specific Actor to complete.

There is nothing special about forward, and you can accomplish the same thing with `ActorRef.tell` (message, sender) by supplying the sender. It is semantically clearer to use forward where it makes sense (especially in Scala where the `!` method is generally used):

```
//Java
actor.forward(result, getContext());

//Scala
actor forward message
```

Note that the context is implicit in Scala.

Pipe

Very often you will have a future in your Actor that you want to send back to the sender. We've covered that sender() is a method, so you have to store a reference to sender when using callbacks in Futures:

```
//Java
final ActorRef senderRef = sender();
future.map(x -> {senderRef.tell(x, ActorRef.noSender()})));
```

```
//Scala
val senderRef = sender();
future.map(x => senderRef ! ActorRef.noSender);
```

Callbacks registered on a future, such as map in this example, will execute in another thread, so they don't have access to the correct value from sender(). It's very unclear why the sender is stored and it is hard to understand code like this. It likely won't make sense to anyone who hasn't encountered this issue on their own. Quite possibly, as you read this, you may wonder why you don't just call sender() in the lambda. Try it out and you'll see unexpected results as sender() returns something different when it's called from the lambda.

We can skirt around this entire confusing mess by using the Pipe pattern. Pipe will take the result of a future and reply to the sender with the result of the future, whether success or failure, which is exactly what we want:

```
//Java
pipe(future, system.dispatcher()).to(sender());
```

```
//Scala
future pipeTo sender()
pipe(future) to sender()
```

Again, pipe takes the result of the future and pipes it to the Actor ref provided. In these examples, we show sender(), and because sender() is executed on the current thread, it all behaves as expected without doing anything strange like storing a reference in a variable. Much better!

If this is at all unclear, trust me you will run into this problem sooner or later and ask yourself what is wrong once you start seeing dead-letter messages in your logs. Once you've gone through this once, you can pat yourself on the back and welcome yourself to the async club. This is an important lesson and you will learn it as you work with the APIs, especially when using ask.

Homework

A short recap on what was discussed in the chapter.

General learning

Before looking at the supplied source on GitHub, take the examples in this chapter and try building them.

Using Ask designs, produce some Actors that do work and a cache for the results:

- Improve upon the design using pipe.
- Using Tell Don't Ask Principles, eliminate asks, and do the same work.
- Try to use Tell Don't Ask principles to compose requests to multiple Actors from the extra Actor.

You'll likely need an anonymous Actor:

- In the previous design, schedule a timeout.
- Do the preceding but with the caching actor set up as a remote Actor.

Project homework

You'll have the ability to handle many types of data flows now.

Pick one piece of functionality and try implementing with ask:

- Try changing the behavior to avoid asking.
- Was the design better or worse? Hit the forums such as `http://www.codereview.stackexchange.com` and discuss!

Summary

This chapter covered relatively basic messaging concepts in Akka but has given enough heuristics to help you grow into a competent designer overtime.

You should now have a basic understanding of the messaging patterns:

- Ask
- Tell
- Forward
- Pipe

Some of the more advanced pieces that have been included, include how Ask works, and a few of the pitfalls you might encounter when using Ask, how to simplify working with Futures with Pipe, and how to simplify redirecting messages with Forward. In the next chapter, we'll look at different ways we can handle state in Actors.

4
Actor Lifecycle – Handling State and Failure

In this chapter, we're going to cover the actor's life cycle—what happens when an actor encounters an exceptional state and how we can change its state to modify its behavior. We've looked at fault tolerance as a reactive tenet and covered how to store state in an actor—we're going to expand on those topics here.

Before we get into failure and state, we're going to introduce what is known as The Fallacies of Distributed Computing—a list of common misconceptions that developers hold about systems communicating over the network.

This chapter will cover the following topics:

- The Fallacies of Distributed Computing
- What happens to an actor when it fails
- How an Actor can be supervised to handle failure
- How an Actor can change behavior with `become()` and as Finite State Machines

The 8 Fallacies of Distributed Computing

Before we look at the examples, we'll have a quick look at the Fallacies of Distributed Computing. The Fallacies of Distributed Computing are a set of incorrect assumptions that a team from Sun Microsystems asserted inexperienced developers make about systems working over a network. Let us have a look at the eight fallacies in detail.

The network is reliable

The fallacy we hear is most often cited, and that seems to come into play the most in systems today, is that the network is reliable. It is not. It's easy to think of a remote system in the same way we would think of a local one—Akka further helps us with this false assumption through location transparency by raising the level of abstraction when talking over the network—and we interact with remote actors exactly as we would with local ones.

We can reason that a service may be up or down, but what really constitutes a service being available? Even if a service is running, traffic has to be able to make it to the service. If you have two servers on a small network, it's very easy to think that they will be connected and talking successfully all of the time. But something will eventually fail between them. A router can crash and restart, the power can fail, someone can unplug the wrong cable in the datacenter, and so on. When you start to scale up, and you're talking about a thousand or ten thousand servers, the chance of things being unavailable become more common and more likely. In **Amazon Web Server** (**AWS**), it's actually extremely common for temporary network failures to occur. In the system we are working on today, in AWS, we see disconnects and periods of network failure daily.

Latency is zero

It takes time for messages to travel over the network and it takes time for responses to come back. A remote Actor will incur a lot more latency overhead than one in local memory. Before any data begins to be sent over the network, there are several things that happen.

Hostnames are resolved to IPs (via DNS), IP addresses are resolved to their receiver's MAC address (via ARP), a TCP connection is established by a handshake, and then data starts to move. Data transferred over TCP is sent in sequenced packets, which receive an acknowledgment back. With this complexity, you can imagine that making a request to Google search takes some time just to leave your machine and to get to Google.

Given the overhead of network communication, we can make an assumption that it is better to make less calls with larger messages than it is to make more requests with smaller messages. To put this into practice in our example database, we may want to add a feature to send multiple SetRequests or multiple GetRequests in a single message.

Remember that testing with components in memory on your local machine is fine in development, but you always need to consider the latency that the network introduces and the impact that it has on the user's experience. This refers back to one of the reactive tenets: responsiveness. It's not only real-time systems that this is important for—the responsiveness of web applications is just as important as it is in first-person shooters and stock-trading systems.

Bandwidth is infinite

Bandwidth is increasing quite steadily in our networking technology today, so this is a bit less of a concern. Still, we don't want to send more over the network than we have to. A network has a capacity as well, which must be considered. The more traffic on a network, the more that communication is impacted by the noise. Also, the more you have to move over the network, the longer it will take.

For latency, we discussed how our database should handle multiple `SetRequests` and `GetRequests` in a single message to eliminate the number of requests made over the network. For bandwidth, we strive to reduce the size of the messages sent over the network. Gzip is often used in HTTP communication to reduce how much data is sent on each request. In large-scale distributed systems, compression algorithms that are easy on CPU (fast) are often used such as Snappy and LZO (for example, Cassandra uses LZO for intra-node communication).

For our database to take this fallacy's consideration into effect, we would want to reduce the size of the messages by using compression. Compression isn't free—it has a cost on CPU resources. There are some specialized algorithms that focus on performance rather than compression ratio—we could use one of these, such as Snappy, to deflate the serialized messages before they are sent to the remote actor and then inflate them again before de-serializing them.

The network is secure

It's easy to forget that the networks we operate on are not secure.

In a public space like a shared Wi-Fi network, any HTTP traffic can be intercepted and read with minimal technical knowledge. The MySpace sign-on page used to be sent over un-encrypted HTTP, so it was very common for people to sit in cafes on Wi-Fi and steal your credentials. Even HTTPS can be intercepted and read via a Man-In-The-Middle attack using ARP Spoofing—you'll get a certificate error still, so humans are the weak point in the system.

Just remember people can always read what you're sending on the network, so you need to ensure that if it's sensitive information in transit, it's protected with secure encryption such as AES-256 and that the keys are handled very carefully.

To apply this to our database, we'd want to allow encrypted communications to occur and we would want to validate the identity of the sender.

Network topology doesn't change

When you build an application and deploy it into your company's infrastructure or on the cloud, today your IPs looks one way but it is out of your control. Depending on specific IPs asserts that the network will never change. This problem is exacerbated when you move to the cloud, where stopping and starting your machine means it gets a new IP.

You can work to reduce this impact by using DNS or service registries built with technologies like Zookeeper, but it's important to assume your network will change.

There is one administrator

I've been in trusted positions with access to production systems for major brands on a few occasions—often because I needed to do work in them. You, as the developer, may not realize how many people will walk in and out of your network and machines. It's possible you work with an external datacenter or in cloud infrastructure—remember people can leave the company and different disciplines require multiple people access the box, and so on.

Why would you care? The other day I deployed some software in test and immediately found it was broken after the application started. I was not aware that someone had logged into the system and changed some configuration. While managing your software, you should try to eliminate as many touch points as you can—especially around configuration. Not everyone will have the tools or the understanding of the impacts that changes can incur. A simple change to one component can have unexpected outcomes for other systems.

Transport cost is zero

There are costs in pushing data down to the transport layer. There is a resource cost in serialization of data, compression of that data, pushing it to TCP buffers, and to establish connections. No chatter over the network is free.

Both in networks and in cloud infrastructure, there is an actual money cost to use the network as well. There is a cost in maintenance in infrastructure, and there is a cost incurred in use in the cloud.

The network is homogeneous

In your mind, imagine a network. It has communications coming into a firewall from the Internet, which is forwarded to a load balancer. That traffic is then forwarded to your application running on a **Virtual Machine** (**VM**). Now imagine you build and deploy the exact same application in another environment.

Is the second network the same? Likely, every last component is different. Your firewall might be from Cisco or it might be a home router. Your load balancer might be from F5 or it might be a copy of nginx running on a VM. Your application may be running on an IBM P595 or it may be running on a VMare ESXi host. The VM might be running Ubuntu for an OS or it might be running IBM AIX Unix.

Does the load balancer round robin or does it sticky sessions? Does the load balancer even support sticky sessions? These are all important questions to ask. I've seen an application deployed into production where a load balancer in an early cloud provider didn't support sticky sessions. A stateful application was deployed without state replication. This was unplanned for as we assumed the network was homogeneous; we assumed all load balancers were the same—they do NOT all have the same feature sets.

Failure

The first fallacy of distributed computing is that the network is reliable. It is not. It can and will fail. So all of our code has to correctly assume things will fail: that the network will glitch; that a message will drop.

Remember the Reactive Manifesto? One of the tenets is that we *React to Failure*. That is, we have to assume error cases will be encountered. A secondary benefit of using Akka is fault tolerance. In this section, we will take a good look at how Akka helps us handle failure.

For the example in this section, we will look at different ways we can react to failure with our database.

Isolating failure

Before we look at how Akka responds to failure, we'll look at some strategies we should generally try to adhere to in our distributed applications: isolation of failures.

If every component was a ticking time bomb, you would want to ensure that if one exploded, it didn't blow up, causing a chain reaction with other components going down in the explosion. You might say, then, that we want to isolate the failure or compartmentalize the component that can fail.

I think a better analogy is bulk-heading, which I first saw used as an example in *Reactive Design Patterns* by Jamie Allen and Roland Khun. Ships and planes are often compartmentalized in their hulls—they have many individual vertical walls in the body of the ship. If there is a breach of the hull, only that one compartment is compromised, so even if a ship hits a rock or ice, it may stay afloat as all of the other compartments will not fill with water. This is an excellent example of how we want to design our systems to respond to failure.

Redundancy

One of the ways we can keep a system up in the face of failure is to make components redundant and ensuring that there is no single point of failure. If we have a service, there are a few ways in which we can design the service for high availability with redundancy.

One example is by using a broker. A broker is often used to allow new service nodes to come online or to allow a service node to go offline without taking down the system. Services will connect to the broker and pick up messages from the queue and process them. JMS or RabbitMQ might be examples of a broker. Databases can be used to broker messages. Note that a single broker is itself a single point of failure and can also be a bottleneck. We'll look at clustering services without a broker later in this book.

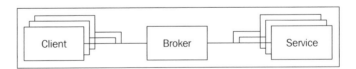

Supervision

Erlang introduced fault tolerance into the Actor Model through a concept known as supervision. At its core, the idea is to separate the response to failure from the thing that can fail and to organize things that can fail into hierarchies that can be managed.

Supervision hierarchies

Supervision is described in terms of Actor hierarchies—when Actors are created, they are created as children of another actor that supervises them. The actor hierarchies are shown as path structures and the hierarchies can be thought of much like folders in a filesystem.

At the very top of the actor hierarchy is the root Actor at /. There is then an actor called the guardian whose path is /user. Any actor created with `actorSystem.actorOf()` function will be created as a child of this guardian actor (`/user/yourActor`).

If you create an actor from inside of an actor, you can create the actor as a child of the actor by calling `context().actorOf`, which would make this actor in the next leaf of the tree (`/user/yourActor/newChild`)

There are other actor hierarchies under the root as well. Supporting system actors go under the system guardian at `/system`. There is a temporary actor hierarchy under `/temp` where actors that complete futures go. You won't need to worry about these too much—they are mostly transparent to the developer as used by Akka's internals.

Remember the sushi restaurant example? Assuming that the restaurant has an owner who oversees a manager and a manager who oversees the line staff (chefs and waiters), then, we may have a hierarchy that looks like the following:

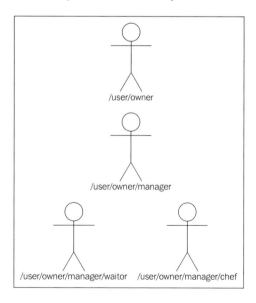

Each actor that oversees other actors can then define its supervision strategy. We will look at supervision strategies next.

Supervision strategies and the drunken sushi chef

To understand supervision strategies, we'll look at an example. We have a sushi chef who likes to drink a lot. His drinking often gets himself in trouble, and his manager has to take action. There are a few different actions the manager can take. We'll look at each in the following.

- **Resume**: The actor will continue with the next message
- **Stop**: Will stop the actor and take no further action
- **Restart**: Will create a new actor to replace the old one
- **Escalate**: Will pass the exception up to the next supervisor

To demonstrate these, imagine our sushi chef actor has to make sushi. He is very skilled and to celebrate his beautiful dishes, he takes a drink every time he makes a plate. The waiting staff pile up menu chits for the sushi chef to fill and he keeps making sushi and drinking. If the sushi chef works all day, eventually he will get into a bad state (to put it lightly).

If the actor makes a mistake—if he cuts his finger or drops a plate—this is probably acceptable. The actor will be told to `resume()` in this case.

If the chef gets tired and makes an error indicating he may need to take a break, then the supervisor may tell the actor to stop processing messages and let the actor take a break. It's often up to the supervisor to take necessary actions in this case, for example, the supervisor would need to tell the actor when to go back to work.

Once the sushi chef is drunk, he makes a really bad looking plate and starts hitting on some customers. The manager—who is the supervisor of the chef—responds to the exception. The manager declares the chef drunk and sends him home for the day. The supervisor calls in another chef who picks up the next ticket and continues with the orders. Retiring the old chef and bringing on a new one is the equivalent to restart.

This next chef is young and can't handle his liquor. He gets particularly intoxicated and knocks over a candle and sets fire to the place. The manager can't handle the error—the roaring flame can't be fixed by sending this chef home drunk and putting another chef in the burning kitchen! The manager calls his supervisor—the owner— who tells him to shut down the restaurant and call the police immediately. This is escalate, where the manager's boss (the owner) makes the decision. If an throwable is escalated through the hierarchy to the guardian, then the application will shutdown.

Defining supervisor strategies

Actors have a default supervisor strategy. If an actor is supervised without changing the supervision strategy, the behavior will roughly be the same as in the drunken chef example:

- Exception in a running actor: `restart()`
- Error in a running actor: `escalate()`
- Exception in an actor during initialization: `stop()`

There is one other case defined in the default behavior—`ActorKilledException`. If an actor is killed, its supervisor will receive an `ActorKilledException`—the behavior when receiving this exception is to `stop()`.

Remember that `/system` path? All of the supervision events actually happen in actors over there—the exception events are not your normal messages—it's important to understand this if you're trying to reason about message delivery order.

We'll look at how we would define the manager's supervision strategy if we wanted to describe the behavior.

In Java:

Following code denotes manager's supervision strategy in Java:

```
@Override
    public akka.actor.SupervisorStrategy supervisorStrategy() {
        return new OneForOneStrategy(5, Duration.create("1 minute"),
                akka.japi.pf.DeciderBuilder.
                    match(BrokenPlateException.class,
                            e -> SupervisorStrategy.resume()).
                    match(DrunkenFoolException.class,
                            e -> SupervisorStrategy.restart()).
                    match(RestaurantFireError.class,
                            e -> SupervisorStrategy.escalate()).
                    match(TiredChefException.class,
                            e -> SupervisorStrategy.stop()).
                    matchAny(e -> SupervisorStrategy.escalate()).
                    build()
        );
    }
```

We override the supervisorStrategy method in an actor returning a new strategy (OneForOneStrategy, which we'll look at more closely shortly.) In Java8, we use a DeciderBuilder to create a Scala PartialFunction for the strategy similar to how we use the ReceiveBuilder for the PartialFunction for the receive block. While Java lacks the pattern matching semantics that Scala has for producing Scala PartialFunctions, the DeciderBuilder alleviates this, giving us a nice API for pattern matching in Java8. We describe each case outlined in the scenarios in our Sushi restaurant example and we also include a matchAny case at the end—if an unknown Throwable is received, we have the manager call his boss.

Scala has pattern matching so it needs less boilerplate to express the same:

```
override def supervisorStrategy = {
    OneForOneStrategy(){
        case BrokenPlateException => Resume
        case DrunkenFoolException => Restart
        case RestaurantFireError =>Escalate
        case TiredChefException => Stop
        case _ => Escalate
    }
}
```

In the Scala example, we override the supervisorStrategy method of the actor again, and then define a PartialFunction matching on Throwables and returning Directives. Here we describe all of the scenarios outlined in the example and any unknown cases, we escalate.

In both Scala and Java, we describe how to handle each of the different Throwable cases if they are thrown by the actor: if the chef breaks a plate, we tell them to resume the next plate; if a chef is a drunken fool, we tell them to go home and bring on a new chef; if the chef lights the restaurant on fire, we have the manager call his boss; if the chef is tired, we tell him to take a break.

Note that the default behavior is generally suitable—if a running actor throws an exception, we will restart the actor, and if it throws an error, we will escalate and stop the application. If your actor can throw exceptions in the constructor, however, this will cause the ActorInitializationException, which causes the Actor to stop. Special care must be taken in these cases as your application will not resume.

Actor lifecycle

We introduced restart, which is like sending a worker home and replacing him with a new one. We'll look at what happens through the actor's lifecycle now.

There are a few methods/hooks that are called through an actor's lifecycle, which you can override as needed.

- `preStart()`: After constructor
- `postStop()`: Before restart
- `preRestart(reason,message)`: Calls `postStop` by default
- `postRestart()`: Calls `preStart` by default

The order of events in an Actor's lifecycle is as given in the following image:

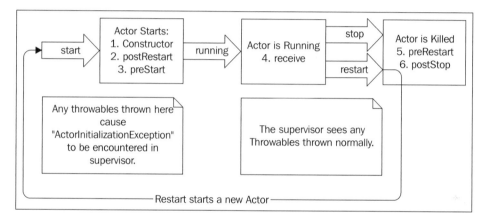

Note that the `preRestart` and `postRestart` are only called on restart. And they are called instead of the `preStart` and `postStop` methods but by default call `preStart` and `postStop`. This lets you decide whether you want to call the `preStart` and `postStop` methods only once (when an actor starts or stops) or every time an actor restarts.

This can be very helpful when designing. Imagine a chat application where each user is represented by an actor that sends messages to an actor representing the chat. When a user joins the room, an actor starts and sends a message so that the list of users in the room can be updated. When an actor stops, it sends another message so that the user can be removed from the list of users displayed as currently active in the chat. With the default implementation, if the actor encounters an exception and restarts, it will unpublish and republish the user in the chat window. We can override `preRestart` and `postRestart` so that the user will only add itself to the list and remove itself from the list when the user actually joins and leaves the chat.

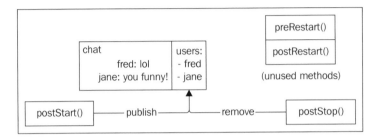

Messages in restart, stop

It's important to understand what happens to a message when an exception is encountered and to take an appropriate position depending on your application. Supervision strategies can be defined to retry failed messages any number of times before raising the exception to the supervision strategy. You can also time bound the failures so that you can retry up to 10 times or retry for 1 minute — whichever comes first:

```
new OneForOneStrategy(2,
     Duration.create("1 minute"), PartialFunction)

OneForOneStrategy(
        maxNrOfRetries = 2) {
      case _: IOException   Restart
      })
```

Once a message raises an exception, it will be dropped. It will not be tried again — the Supervisor will execute the supervision strategy, and in the case of resume or restart, the next message will be processed.

In the case of a worker queue, you likely want to retry the job a few times and then have it fail completely.

Terminating or killing an Actor

Actors can be stopped in a few different ways. You can stop an actor by doing any of the following:

- Call `ActorSystem.stop(actorRef)`
- Call `ActorContext.stop(actorRef)`
- Send a `PoisonPill` message to the actor, which will stop the actor when processed.
- Send a Kill message to the actor, which will stop the actor when processed.

Calling `context.stop` or `system.stop` will cause the actor to stop immediately. `PoisonPill` will cause the actor to stop when the message is processed. By contrast, Kill will not stop the actor directly, but will cause the actor to throw an `ActorKilledException` which is handled by the supervision behavior—you can decide how you want to respond in those cases.

Lifecycle monitoring and DeathWatch

Supervision describes a mechanism for responding to a child actor's states—it's also possible for an actor to monitor any other actor. Calling `context.watch(actorRef)` will register an actor for monitoring another actor for termination and calling `context.unwatch(actorRef)` will unregister. If the watched actor stops, a `Terminated(ActorRef)` message will be sent to the watcher.

Safely restarting

When we build reactive systems, we design them anticipating failure. We need to ensure our systems respond to failure correctly. One of the mistakes that I've seen out in the wild is to initialize an actor's state after it has started without handling the failure case. If you send an actor some initialization messages, with information that is important to its state, you have to be very careful because that information may be be lost in a restart.

Let's demonstrate: Imagine if we make a database client actor with no arguments, and then we tell the actor where to connect. This doesn't seem unreasonable—very often in Java, we set fields in objects after creating them. We also know that Actors can safely store state, so nothing seems wrong with this scenario yet:

```
ActorRef db = system.actorOf(DbActor.props());
db ! Connect(host = "10.0.8.14", port = "9001");

val actor = createActor(DbActor.props);
actor.tell(new Connect("10.0.8.14", "9001");
```

Now we have an actor, and, once it processes that first message, it's initialized and connected to a remote database.

We send messages to the actor for a bit, and then the actor encounters an exception caused by network reliability. The actor will restart at this point. When the actor restarts, it will call preRestart(), and then the original actor will stop. All of the state in that actor will go away with it. Then a new object is created for the Actor. That actor's constructor will run, then postRestart will be called, and then the actor will be up and running.

That Connect message is now lost. You can write some extra code to handle this scenario. You could write a supervision strategy or use Akka's lifecycle monitoring (DeathWatch) to respond to these failure conditions. But, the point is, for this simple initialization message, you have to handle this case now and risk making an error in handling the client. A much better implementation is to pass the initialization information into the constructor of the actor via Props:

```
ActorRef db = system.actorOf(DbActor.props(host = "10.0.8.14", port =
"9001"));

val actor = createActor(DbActor.props("10.0.8.14", "9001"));
```

This seems better—the actor now gets all of the information in its constructor and it connects automatically. If we start sending the actor messages and it restarts, it will recover correctly because it has the connection information in its constructor arguments..` But, if the actor encounters an exception during initialization, perhaps trying to connect to the remote database, then the default supervision behavior is to stop. So, we have a scenario where the actor can restart safely if running, but, if it can't initialize, we have to write extra code in supervision behavior to handle the scenario where the actor can't connect to the database on startup.

It is common to have an actor send itself an initialization message and to have it handle changing its state while running, instead of potentially failing during initialization. To do this, on postStart, an actor might send itself a Connect message:

```
public void postStart(){
    self().ask(new Connect(), null);
}

override def postStart = self ! Connect
```

Now that actor can only fail when it's running, and it will restart successfully, continuing to try to connect to the database until it's available.

If you're paying attention, you might reason that you could have the actor send itself the `Connect(host, port)` message on the `preRestart` event. If the actor were to drop that message for any reason, maybe because its mailbox was full or because a restart caused it to be dropped, then that Connect message could be lost—it's simpler and safer to use the constructor for an actor that is critical to the actor's functioning.

This is a quick and dirty look at building an actor that will just continually retry its connection.

It's important to note that there are some missing details and problems with this still. The first is that we have no way to handle the messages the actor will receive before it connects. And the second is that the mailbox will be flooded if the actor can't connect for a large period of time.

We'll cover handing state in this chapter. Mailbox problems are covered in *Chapter 7, Handling Mailbox Problems*.

State

We have looked at how it is safe to store state in an Actor—how Actors give us a lock-free way to deal with state in concurrency. We're going to look at how an actor can change its behavior in the face of different states now.

There are a few mechanisms you can use to change behavior in an actor:

- Conditionals based on an Actor's state
- Hotswap: `become()` and `unbecome()`
- Finite State Machine (FSM)

We'll look at each after introducing the example that builds on our key-value datastore example.

Online/Offline state

Let's revisit the first fallacy of distributed computing. Not only is the network not reliable, but the components that we try to talk to over the network could be down. We want our application to handle network misses gracefully without dropping too many messages.

To continue to develop our database example, we'll improve the remote client so that it deals with network partitions such as temporary failure of network components or database service restarts as gracefully as possible in the case of a client-server model.

What we looked at in *Chapter 2, Actors and Concurrency* was an example where we had a remote key-value datastore, which we connected to from a client. We did an `actorSelection` to get a reference to the remote actor and then started sending it messages. What if the database isn't ready when we start our application? Or, what if the database goes offline for a moment?

Transitioning state

One of the most common examples I have seen of the use of state is to determine if a service is online or offline. We examined this in the section on failure, and looking at what happens to actors when they restart. We'll continue with the example of a database client actor connecting to a remote database.

Stashing messages between states

If the bartender at our sushi restaurant gets a request to pour a beer while the keg is being changed, he won't be able to take care of that order. But he will be able to at a later point in time, once the new keg is ready. The bartender won't simply throw away the order because the keg isn't ready—he will set aside the order for a minute and process other orders that he is able to (like pouring more sake for the chef). Once the keg is ready, then he'll put any beer orders back in his queue to process.

Similar to this example, it's very common for an Actor to be in a state where it can't process certain messages. If the database client is offline, it isn't going to be able to handle any messages until it is online. We could have the client connection continue to restart until it connects, in which case it will drop every message it encounters until it's able to connect successfully. Or we could have the client set the messages it cannot handle aside while waiting for the client to enter a connected state.

Akka has a mechanism called `stash` to do this. Stashing messages puts the message off to the side in a separate queue that it cannot currently handle:

```
if(cantHandleMessage){
    stash();
}else{
    handleMessage(message);
}
```

Unstash puts the messages that were set aside back into the mailbox queue for the actor to handle.

```
changeStateToOnline();
 unstash();
```

To use stash in Java, your Actor will extend AbstractActorWithStash:
```
class RemoteActorProxy extends AbstractActorWithStash {
  [...]
}
```
To use stash in Scala, you mix in the stash trait:
```
class RemoteActorProxy extends Actor with Stash {
  [...]
}
```

We'll use this mechanism now to demonstrate how to make a client switch between online and offline states.

 NOTE that stash() and unstash() can be handy when you expect state to change quickly, but states where messages are stashed should always be time-bound or else you risk flooding your mailboxes.

Conditional statements

The most naive approach is to store state in the actor and then have a conditional statement decide what behavior the actor should take.

You can store a Boolean to say if you're connected to the database, and if you're connected, try to handle the message. If you're not, you can fail.

The following is a Java example of storing state and handling behavior with conditional statements:

```
private Boolean online = false;
 public PartialFunction receive() {
     return RecieveBuilder.
     match(GetRequest.class, x -> {
         if(online) {
             processMessage(x);
         } else {
             stash();
         }
     }).
     match(Connected.class, x -> {
         online = true;
         unstash();
     ).
     match(Disconnected.class, x -> online = false).
     build();
```

Here is the Scala equivalent to storing state and changing behavior with conditionals:

```scala
var online = false
def receive = {
  case x: GetRequest =>
    if(online)
      processMessage(x)
    else
      stash()
  case _: Connected =>
    online = true
    unstash()
  case _: Disconnected =>
    online = false
}
```

This conditional statement is the most basic way to express different behavior based on state stored in an actor. We store a Boolean called `online` that represents if the actor is connected or not. If the actor is connected, it processes the message. If it is not connected, it stashes the messages, as covered previously. If it receives a Connected message, then it changes its state to be online and unstashes all of the messages. Because of the use of `stash`/`unstash`, once it comes online, the actor will then process any messages it stashed.

It's very common for an actor to store state and behave differently depending on that state. Using conditionals is a very procedural approach to dealing with behavior and state. Fortunately, Akka gives us a couple of better options.

Hotswap: Become/Unbecome

The code with conditionals was not very pretty. It certainly was not very declarative. Akka gives us `become()` and `unbecome()` to manage behavior that can improve the clarity of the code considerably. In the actor's `context()`, there are a two methods:

- `become(PartialFunction behavior)`: This changes the actor's behavior from the behavior defined in the receive block to a new `PartialFunction`.

- `unbecome()`: This reverts the actor's behavior back to the default behavior.

Let's look at how using this mechanism can improve our previous example:

```
public PartialFunction receive() {
    return RecieveBuilder.
    match(GetRequest.class, x -> stash()).
    match(Connected.class, x -> {
        context().become(online);
        unstash();
    }).
    build();
}

final private PartialFunction<Object, BoxedUnit> online(final
ActorRef another) {
    return RecieveBuilder.
    match(GetRequest.class, x -> processMessage(x)).
    build();
}
```

Here is the Scala equivalent:

```
def receive = {
    case x: GetRequest =>
        stash()
    case _: Connected =>
        become(online)
        unstash()
}

def online: Receive = {
    case x: GetRequest =>
        processMessage(x)
    case _: Disconnected =>
        unbecome()
}
```

This has better readability than conditional statements. Each state's behavior is described in its own `PartialFunction` where pattern matching and behavior are described. This lets us read the behavior of the actor in its different states independently.

The actor starts in the offline state where it will stash messages it is not able to respond to (`GetRequest`). Those messages get set aside until the `Connected` message is received. Once the Connected message is received, then the actor calls become to change its behavior to the online state described in the online method. At this time, the actor also calls `unstash` to put the messages set aside, back into the queue. Now all of the messages will be processed with the new behavior.

If the actor receives a `Disconnected` message, then it calls `unbecome`, which will revert the actor to its default behavior. Note that any number of receive blocks can be defined and swapped between. Hotswap can handle mostly any behavior changes that might need to be handled in an actor as it changes behavior. This is a nice easy abstraction for producing readable actors.

Stash leaks

The examples covered so far using stash have a problem — if the connect message takes too long to be received, or is not received, then messages will continually be stashed until the application runs out of memory or the mailbox starts dropping messages (mailboxes are covered further in a later chapter). Wherever using `stash()`, it's a good idea to put a boundary on how much time can pass or how many messages can be received before taking action.

The most basic way to do this is to schedule a timeout message to be sent to the actor after a certain period of time.

We can schedule one message in the actor's constructor or `postStart` hook, and then when it is received, check that the actor is connected. If it's not connected, then the actor can escalate the problem and have the supervisor take action:

```
system.scheduler().scheduleOnce(Duration.create(1000, TimeUnit.
MILLISECONDS),
    self(), CheckConnected, system.dispatcher(), null);
```

If the actor receives the message and it is online, it will be ignored. If the actor receives the message and it is not online, then it will throw an exception:

```
 .match(CheckConnected.class, msg -> throw new
ConnectTimeoutException())
case _: CheckConnected => throw new ConnectTimeoutException
```

Finite State Machines (FSM)

There is another tool for handling state in actors: **Finite State Machine (FSM)**. Much like hotswap, FSMs have state and behavior that changes based on state. FSM is a bit heavier of an abstraction than hotswap and requires more code and types to get up and running, so hotswap will usually be a simpler and more readable option.

We have a good example for connected/disconnected to use in the client—we'll keep that in place for the basic client and look for other ways we can improve the client/server communication.

The Fallacies of Distributed Computing were introduced earlier in this chapter. One of the points is that there is a cost in latency for every request and response over the network (fallacy: latency is zero). Because there is a cost to every request and response, reducing the number of times messages are sent and responded to can cut down on total time spent waiting. To improve our client and server behavior, we can reduce how many messages are sent over the network by combining them into a smaller number of requests.

Using traditional request/response protocols, an application will make a request over the network and then wait for the response to continue processing messages. In an application where we need to read multiple records from a database, the typical flow may look something like the following:

1. **Client**: Send `GetRequest(user)` over network.
2. **Server**: Reply to client with user data.
3. **Client**: Wait for `Success` response.
4. **Client**: Send `GetRequest`(article) to server.
5. **Server**: Reply to client with article data.
6. **Client**: Wait for Success response.
7. **Client**: Return Success response to create user profile request

The time taken for a signal to be sent plus the acknowledgment to be received is called **Round-trip Delay Time (RTD or RTT)**. One of the Reactive Tenets is to be responsive to our users, so we want to eliminate the amount of time we spend waiting for messages to travel over the network.

One way we can improve our datastore API is to allow the datastore to accept a list. This would let us send multiple operations in a single request:

```
ask(remoteActorSelection,
    Arrays.asList(
        new SetRequest(id, user, sender),
        new SetRequest("profile-" + id, profile, sender)),
    timeout);

  remoteActorSelection ? List(
    SetRequest(id, user, sender),
    SetRequest("profile-"+id, profile, sender)
  )
```

Note that on the preceding snippet showing the list, we've included a sender in the messages to allow us to complete futures or reply to Actors.

Trying to create a single list in an application request could prove to be inconvenient to the users of our library. We can improve the client API to handle this concern.

We'll create an actor to use in our datastore client that sends messages to a remote database actor once several messages have accumulated or once a Flush message is received. By doing this, we put the concern of gathering and sending messages in one actor to adhere to single responsibility principle. (Note that this example is similar to the one in the Akka documentation for FSM—you can see the documentation if you need a quick reference or want to see a different implementation.)

The FSM types have two parameters: State and Container. We'll look at defining those and then we'll look at building the FSM.

Defining states

The FSM describes its state a bit differently than other actors we have looked at.

For our FSMs, we will improve on the hotswap example to store messages in the actor instead of stashing them:

- **Disconnected**: Not online and no messages are queued
- **Disconnected and Pending**: Not online and messages are queued
- **Connected**: Online and no messages are queued
- **Connected and Pending**: Online and Messages are Pending

We use an enum in Java for the states:

```
enum State{
    DISCONNECTED,
    CONNECTED,
    CONNECTED_AND_PENDING,
}
```

In Scala, we can use case objects instead:

```
sealed trait State
 case object Disconnected extends State
 case object Connected extends State
 case object ConnectedAndPending extends State
```

Defining the state container

We've described the states, now we need to define the state container for the actor. The state container is where we will store the messages. The FSM allows us to define the state container and change it between states, so our use case maps quite nicely to the FSM as we'll change the state container when we change between states.

For our state container, we'll store a list of requests to be processed on a flush event:

```
public class EventQueue extends LinkedList<Request> {}
```

In Scala, we'll use a type definition for this purpose:

```
object StateContainerTypes {
   type RequestQueue = List[Request]
}
public class Flush {}
case object Flush
```

Now we're ready to build the actor's behavior.

Defining behavior in FSMs

First, FSMs must extend the base traits.

In Java8, we extend `akka.actor.AbstractFSM<S, D>`

```
public class BunchingAkkademyClient extends AbstractFSM<State,
RequestQueue>{
     {//init block
     }
}
```

Note that we create an init block—we describe the behavior in this init block.

In Scala, we extend `akka.actor.FSM[S, D]`:

```
class BunchingAkkademyClient extends FSM[State, RequestQueue]{
   }
```

In the actors, we can now use the FSM API to describe the behavior in different states. First, we call the `startWith` method to describe how the actor starts:

```
{
     startWith(DISCONNECTED, null);

}
   startWith(Disconnected, null) //scala needs no init block!
```

Then we describe how different messages are responded to in different states and how the state changes depending on the message. There are a few ways to describe the behavior. The one that you'll be most comfortable with is calling when (S state, PartialFunction pf). We can build the behavior for each case by calling the when statement several times.

In Java, we can build a partial function again using tools that Akka gives us similar to the ReceiveBuilder.

We'll describe each of the states and the response to Flush, Connected, and Request messages:

```java
        when(DISCONNECTED,
                matchEvent(FlushMsg.class, (msg, container) ->
stay())
                        .event(GetRequest.class, (msg, container) ->
{
                        container.add(msg);
                        return stay();
                        }).event(Tcp.Connected.class, (msg,
container) -> {
                    if(container.getFirst() == null){
                        return goTo(CONNECTED);
                    }else{
                        return goTo(CONNECTED_AND_PENDING);
                    }
                }));

        when(CONNECTED,
                matchEvent(FlushMsg.class, (msg, container) ->
stay())
                        .event(GetRequest.class, (msg, container) ->
{
                        container.add(msg);
                        return goTo(CONNECTED_AND_PENDING);
                        }));


        when(CONNECTED_AND_PENDING,
                matchEvent(FlushMsg.class, (msg, container) -> {
                    container = new EventQueue();
                    return stay();
                })
                        .event(GetRequest.class, (msg, container) ->
{
                        container.add(msg);
                        return goTo(CONNECTED_AND_PENDING);
                        }));
```

```
      scala.PartialFunction pf = ReceiveBuilder.match(String.class,
x -> System.out.println(x)).build();
      when(CONNECTED, pf);
```

And for Scala, we use pattern matching to describe the PartialFunction in each state with when(state):

```
when(Disconnected){
   case (_: Connected, container: RequestQueue) =>
     if (container.headOption.isEmpty)
       goto(Connected)
     else
       goto(ConnectedAndPending)
   case (x: GetRequest, container: RequestQueue) =>
     stay using(container :+ x)
}

when (Connected) {
  case (x: GetRequest, container: RequestQueue) =>
    goto(ConnectedAndPending) using(container :+ x)
}

when (ConnectedAndPending) {
  case (Flush, container) =>
    remoteDb ! container;
    container = Nil
    goto(Connected)
  case (x: GetRequest, container: RequestQueue) =>
    stay using(container :+ x)
}
```

In Both the Java and Scala examples, we describe the three states. The Disconnected state will store messages or go online. It will ignore messages other than Connected or GetRequest.

In the Connected state, we only care about messages that make us transition to the ConnectedAndPending state.

Finally, the ConnectedAndPending state can either flush or add a request to the container. In Scala, the container is an immutable type, so we pass a new container through the state changes.

Note that we ignore messages in some states or process them in others. We'll ignore the Flush command if there are no messages to flush, but we'll process it and move back to the Connected state with no pending messages after a flush.

The actor has to return a description of states that it either stays in or moves to in the FSM, which means that, compared to hotswap, the FSM requires a more descriptive actor. There is some boilerplate to using FSM, but it can produce clearer actor code in some cases. It's possible to use either hotswap or FSM for actor with different behavior in states. You can evaluate which will produce more usable code for your use case. FSM is another tool in your toolbelt—in many cases, hotswap will be enough and simpler, but FSMs might have maintainability benefits in some cases.

The last thing we do in the block is call `initialize()`:

```
initialize();
```

Using restarts to transition through states

Note that the actor does not have any disconnect message or behavior. If we encounter an exception in our actor's state, the easiest way to transition back to disconnected is to simply throw an exception and have the actor restart. Very often this will be the simplest and most reliable way to respond to an exceptional case. Once your actor is running, do not be afraid to restart your actors! You know that the piece of the actor system that is encountering the problem will simply be recreated. The Akka team's blog is called "Let IT Crash" because of the attitude that Akka takes to the reliability of our software. If an exception is thrown, Akka takes care of it for us by recreating the piece of our software that fails.

The best way to handle understanding if the actor is connected is to get a message from the remote actor every couple of seconds. This is called a "heartbeat." We could build a heartbeat that checks that the actor is responding, and, if it is not, then we could restart the actor and log the exception. In our FSM example, if we restarted after a couple of missed heartbeats, the actor would dump any pending messages, which, while it would drop them, would mean that the application wouldn't leak too much memory. When the remote database finally becomes available, then the application will resume behavior as normal.

Homework

- Take the `Akkademy DB` from *Chapter 2*, *Actors and Concurrency* and implement a Connected Message—Have the client send a Ping and respond with Connected

- Returning from the previous chapter, Instead of Ping and Connected messages, use Akka's Identify message using the preStart hook to determine if the remote actor is available. (See documentation.) Use this to acquire an ActorRef for a remote actor and use this instead of the ActorSelection.

- Continuing to use Identity and an ActorRef, implement a connected state in the client using hotswap.

- Every 2 seconds with the Identity message. Have the client restart if it misses 2 response

- Instead of sending a ping and receiving a response, is it possible to have the client subscribe to a heartbeat message that is sent every two seconds?

- Update the client to bunch messages using FSM. Do you think hotswap or FSM is more appropriate for this?

- Implement supervision to have the actor log any restarts it encounters (such as two missed heartbeats)

Summary

We looked at the Fallacies of Distributed Computing to better understand some of the characteristics that the network has and which will affect our application's reliability and performance.

Because our actors can encounter problems — both in the network and in their internal state — we examined how actors move through their lifecycle. We looked at how supervision can be used to build responses to failures and to customize how actors respond when starting, stopping, and restarting.

We also covered different ways in which an actor's behavior can change depending on its state. We covered how Hotswap and FSM can improve the readability of an actor that does have behavior that changes through state instead of simply using conditionals.

At this point, we can build resilient applications that react to errors and can clearly describe behavior in response to state.

In the next chapter, we will cover scaling up an application to better utilize the hardware it is running on.

5
Scaling Up

Scaling up refers to making better use of hardware from a single machine. Akka can help us scale up more easily to make better use of our hardware, with very little effort. In fact, generally, to efficiently utilize your hardware, you will not need to do much, but it's important to understand a few basic techniques.

We will cover the following topics in this chapter:

- The emergence of multicore computing
- Utilizing multiple cores with futures
- Utilizing multiple cores with routers and actors
- Utilizing dispatchers to isolate performance risk

Note that while this chapter does talk about using Akka for distribution problems, it will only cover a single application running on a single node and will not look at how to utilize multiple servers to scale your application. However, the next chapter will cover scaling out, utilizing multiple machines, and will look at how to build clusters of applications that communicate over the network using Akka.

Moore's law

Moore's law states that, every 18 months or so, transistors per square inch in integrated circuits double. This used to be correlated to CPU clock speed doubling every couple of years, but CPU clock speeds are no longer increasing at the same rate that they once were.

What we see today is that processors in environments—for example, servers, computers, and phones—are hitting the market with more and more CPUs and cores. My phone has 6 cores, my workstation at work has 12 virtual cores via a Xeon CPU, and the VMs in AWS can have up to 40 virtual cores. These changes in consumer and server hardware mean that we need to design our software differently—if your application runs on a single thread on an 8 core PC, you'll only be able to utilize one core effectively. Our applications need to be able to utilize these resources—if we're running an application on a single thread, then we're only able to use one of those cores. Today, as software engineers, we need to write concurrent software to be able to take advantage of the hardware our software runs on.

The term "scaling up" means that, when we provide additional resources to a single system—such as additional CPU cores or memory—the application will utilize them. If we have a single server and we give an application more resources, it should be able to utilize those resources running. In cloud services, if we need it to serve more traffic, we might replace the instance with a larger one with more cores. Assuming our application can utilize the resources, we have scaled up our application. (Conversely, when we say scaling out, we mean that we are adding resources to a system by adding more machines or VMs instead of just using bigger machines or bigger VMs.)

Given that most environments we deploy our code to today are going to have several virtual CPUs available, we need to change how we think about writing code to utilize the hardware effectively. It is your duty as a modern engineer to be able to tackle these problems safely and effectively. Given that we are getting more cores instead of more processing speed on a core, we need to design our applications to utilize multiple cores by handling multiple streams of work in parallel.

Multicore architecture as a distribution problem

Utilizing multiple cores in an application can seem like a difficult problem to approach. Traditional thread-based abstractions were very difficult to get right. When threads share access to mutable state, it's easy to build in race conditions that don't present themselves until you've deployed and are running your app at scale. Tim Sweeny has said before that, in a concurrent world, imperative is the wrong default. Fortunately, for us today we have different abstractions that we can use to utilize all of those cores available to us, and they're much easier to build correct concurrent software on than thread abstractions using synchronization and locking.

It turns out that utilizing multicore architecture can be looked at as a distribution problem—we want to take some work and run it somewhere else, either on another CPU or another machine. When working with actors in Akka, the differences between scaling up and scaling out can begin to blur. We can start to ignore the differences between another machine or another core, and instead only think about the problem as sending a message to an actor. We want to send some work somewhere else to be done, and then, at some point in time, we'll receive a response to the request. Looking at scaling up is a great way to begin to understand how you might eventually scale out—if you can do work across 8 cores with Actors, doing work across 8 machines is a small step from there.

The focus of this chapter is on specifically utilizing multiple cores rather than utilizing multiple machines, so we'll highlight the details in that context. The primary mechanism for utilizing multiple cores is parallelism—our applications must do multiple things at the same time. Essentially, we want to separate work into discrete pieces and run the work in different places at the same time to utilize all of the cores that are available.

There are two abstractions in Akka that you can use to do work in parallel across cores: Futures and Actors. We'll look at both of these abstractions in relation to doing heavy computation in parallel at this point. We will still look at how we can better utilize our hardware using both of these abstractions. We'll also talk about when one might be better to use than the other in this context.

Choosing Futures or Actors for concurrency

Both Actors and Futures can be used for concurrency, but which is the correct abstraction to use?

After working with Akka a bit, in the beginning of your journey toward creating highly scalable event-driven systems, you may likely start using Actors everywhere in your design. You may think that the correct way to approach every problem is to use an actor. As the old proverb goes, if you have a hammer, everything can start to look like a nail.

It turns out that deciding whether to use Actors or Futures is actually not a simple question to answer. There is a common rule of thumb I've heard people citing—"Futures for Concurrency, Actors for State."

That is to say that, if you have any state, then you might immediately think of using actors, and if you have no state and only want concurrency, then you can look at futures. While that's a good rule of thumb, it's actually an oversimplification of the problem as there are several use cases where actors can give you designs that are easier to debug and maintain. You'll often want to evaluate both for your use case and consider the design simplicity.

Doing work in parallel

To demonstrate how we can do work in parallel with Actors and Futures, we'll start with a simple use case. We need to do some long-running work and we need to do it many times. Earlier in this book, we looked at an example of parsing article body text from a web page. We'll revisit this example using the `BoilerPipe` library to parse the contents of a page. The article parsing logic might look like the following:

```
public class ArticleParser {
    public static Try<String> apply(String html) {
        return Try.ofFailable(
                () -> de.l3s.boilerpipe.extractors.ArticleExtractor.
INSTANCE.getText(html)
        );
    }
}

object ArticleParser {
def apply(html: String) : String = de.l3s.boilerpipe.extractors.
ArticleExtractor.INSTANCE.getText(html)
}
```

This gives us some work that we can do in parallel to examine how we can scale up to better use a multicore environment using futures and actors.

Doing work In parallel with futures

Futures are highly composable and can be a good fit for parallel processing. Using future function composition techniques examined in *Chapter 2, Actors and Concurrency*, we know that we can do asynchronous work safely and with fairly minimal effort. If we have a collection of items we need to process, we can do it in parallel with futures in very little code.

In the following, we have a List of Strings called `articleList` containing web pages from articles and an HTML page of an article. We want to process the list with Futures for higher concurrency to better utilize system resources. We'll look at how we can do this using Java first:

```
List<ComposableFuture<String>> futures = articleList
        .stream()
        .map(article ->CompletableFuture.supplyAsync(()
->ArticleParser.apply(article)))
        .collect(Collectors.toList());
    Future<List<String>>articlesFuture = com.jasongoodwin.monads.
Futures.sequence(futures).get();
```

Note that we'll use the sequence function from the better-java `monads` library to help us work with multiple futures—it contains a sequence method that will turn a list of futures into a single future containing a list of the results. Include it into your project by adding the following to `build.sbt`:

```
"com.jason-goodwin" % "better-monads" % "0.2.1"
```

In the Java example, we have a list of articles, which we map into futures that will contain the completed article body. This kicks off the processing of all of the articles in the `articleList` in parallel. We use sequence to turn the List of Futures into a Future containing a list of the articles. Using Scala is similar, if more terse. Scala has its own sequence method for transforming the list of futures.

```
    import scala.concurrent.ExecutionContext.Implicits.global
val futures = articleList.map(artlice => {
        Future(ArticleParser.apply(article))
    })
val articlesFuture: Future[List[String]] =
Future.sequence(futures)
```

We take the list of articles and execute the parsing work in parallel by running it in futures. We take the List of Futures and then sequence them into a more usable single future containing the list of our articles. These examples show how simple it is to parallelize with futures.

Doing work in parallel with Actors

We've looked at using futures to do work in parallel. Now we'll look at how we can similarly do work in parallel using actors. Note that, for our example case, the code is very succinct using futures. Depending on your use case, using actors specifically for concurrency can result in more complicated code. We'll look at an equivalent example using actors to do the work.

Using the `ArticleParser` static apply method from the Future's example, we'll first create an actor that will do the work.

The following is the Java actor and message:

```java
public class ParseArticle {
    public final String htmlBody;
    public ParseArticle(String url) {
 this.htmlBody = url;
    }
}
public class ArticleParseActor extends AbstractActor {
   private ArticleParseActor() {
     receive(ReceiveBuilder.
        match(ParseArticle.class, x ->{
               sender().tell(ArticleParser.apply(x.htmlBody),
 self());
               }
        ).
        build());
   }
}
```

The following is the Scala actor and message:

```scala
case class ParseArticle(htmlString: String)
class ArticleParseActor extends Actor{
   override def receive: Receive = {
     case ParseArticle(htmlString) =>
 val body: String = ArticleParser(htmlString)
        sender() ! body
   }
}
```

To do the work in parallel, we need to introduce a "Router" to distribute the work across several actors; we will look at this next.

Introducing Routers

In Akka, a Router is a load-balancing/routing abstraction. When a Router is created, it is given a group of actors or is asked to create a pool of actors.

Note the use of the words group and pool. While creating routers with actors, it's important to understand that there are two ways in which the collection of actors behind the router can be created. Either the router can create the actors (a Pool) or the router can be provided with the list of actors (a Group).

After the creation of the router, if the router receives a message, then it will pass that message on to one or more of the actors in its Group/Pool. There are different strategies that determine the order in which the Router selects an actor to forward its next message to.

In our case, all of our actors are local and we want a router with several actors to allow the CPU's cores to do more of our work in parallel. Routers can also be used to distribute load across clusters of servers if the actors are remote.

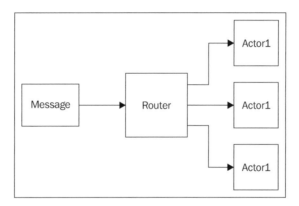

For our use case with local actors, we can create the router as a pool, having the router produce all of the actors for us. It's simple to use routers in this use case—we instantiate an actor as usual, and then call the `withRouter` method, passing in the routing strategy and how many actors we want. This is the same for either Scala or Java:

```
ActorRef workerRouter =
  system.actorOf(
  Props.create(ArticleParseActor.class).
withRouter(new RoundRobinPool(8)));
```

```
val workerRouter: ActorRef =
  system.actorOf(
  Props.create(classOf[ArticleParseActor]).
withRouter(new RoundRobinPool(8)))
```

If we had a list of actors that we wanted to make a router from, then we would create the Router from a group, providing a list of the actor's paths:

```
ActorRef router = system.actorOf(new RoundRobinGroup(actors.map(actor
->actor.path())).props());
  val router = system.actorOf(new RoundRobinGroup(actors.map(actor
=>actor.path).props())
```

At this point, we have the router and actors we need to be able to distribute the load across cores. Taking our list of messages and asking the router to process each of the messages will process them in parallel. We'll continue to look at the more advanced features of routers now to understand how they work in greater detail.

Routing logic

You'll note that we used `RoundRobinPool`/`RoundRobinGroup`—this covers the order in which the messages will be delivered to the routers. There are several routing strategies that Akka comes bundled with—we'll look at a few here. `RoundRobin` or `Random` are fine choices for general purpose.

Routing Strategies	Functioning
Round Robin	Sends a message to each node in the Pool/Group in order and then starts over. Random—sends messages in a random order.
Smallest Mailbox	Sends messages to the actor with the fewest messages. Remote actors have unknown mailbox sizes, so they are assumed to have messages queued—free local Actors will be addressed first.
Scatter Gather	Sends the message to all Actors in the Group/Pool and uses the first response received, dropping any other responses received. If you need to ensure you get a response, and you want to get it as fast as possible, you can use scatter/gather.
Tail Chopping	Similar to Scatter/Gather but, instead of sending a message to all actors in the group/pool at once, the router waits for a small period of time for each subsequent message. Has similar benefits to scatter/gather, but can potentially reduce the load in comparison.

Routing Strategies	Functioning
Consistent Hashing	A key is provided to the router, which is then hashed. The hashed key is used to determine which node to send the data to. Hashing is used when assigning a particular "slice" of data to a particular destination. It's used in working with clusters of servers. We will look at consistent hashing strategies more in the next chapter.
BalancingPool	This is a bit of a unique router. `BalancingPool` can only be used for local actors. The actors share a single mailbox and take work from it in a work-stealing manner. This helps to ensure that all actors stay busy. For local clustering, this will often be the preferred routing mechanism.

You can also roll your own Routing Logic, but it's unlikely you'll need to do so.

Sending Messages to All Actors in a Router Group/Pool

Regardless of the type of Group or Pool you use, you can always send a message to all actors with the broadcast message. For example, if your actors are connecting to a remote database and you need to change the database used in a live system during a failover, you could update all the actors in the pool/group with a broadcast message:

```
router.tell(new akka.routing.Broadcast(msg));
router !akka.routing.Broadcast(msg)
```

Supervising the Routees in a Router Pool

If you're creating a Pool, where the Router creates the actors, the routees will be created as children of the router. While creating the router, you can provide a custom supervision strategy for the router to use.

When building a router, there is a `withSupervisorStrategy` method that you call to create the Pool with your strategy. The Scala and Java API are the same. Assuming we have a SupervisorStrategy instantiated called "strategy", we do the following when creating our router:

```
ActorRefworkerRouter = system.actorOf(Props.create(ArticleParseActor.
class).
 withRouter(new RoundRobinPool(8).
 withSupervisorStrategy(strategy)));
```

```
valworkerRouter: ActorRef =
 system.actorOf(
 Props.create(classOf[ArticleParseActor]).
 withRouter(new RoundRobinPool(8).
 withSupervisorStrategy(strategy)))
```

As Groups are created from pre-existing actors, there is no way to supervise a group using a Router.

Apart from the primary use case of supervising a pool of actors, there is another use case for using routers with a supervision strategy. If you have a top-level actor (created with an `ActorSystem's` `actorOf` method), then it will be supervised by the Gaurdian Actor. If you need to have a custom supervision strategy, you can create an actor to supervise that actor or you could simply create a router and pass it your custom `SupervisorStrategy` to have the router act as the supervisor. As you don't need to define any actor behavior, this is a brief and simple approach to giving a top-level actor custom supervision.

Working with Dispatchers

As we start to try to improve throughput and response times of our applications, we need to understand all bottlenecks and where time is being spent in the request/response cycle. Once we apply load to an application, the threads that are available will be trying to serve all requests—understanding how those resources are used will help you improve how much throughput a service can handle with minimum latency.

Dispatchers explained

A dispatcher decouples a task from how and where the task will be run. Dispatchers will generally contain some threads and will handle scheduling and running events such as actor message handling and future events in those threads. Dispatchers are really what make Akka tick—they are the mechanism that gets the work done.

Any time an actor or a future does work, the resources allocated by an executor/dispatcher are what does that work.

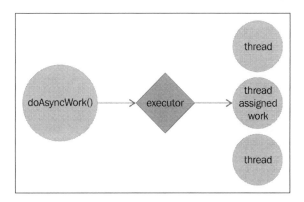

Dispatchers control assigning work to actors. They also can assign resources to handle callbacks on futures. You'll note that future APIs accept Executors/ExecutionContexts as parameters. Because Akka dispatchers extend these APIs, the dispatchers can pull double duty.

In Akka, dispatchers implement the `scala.concurrent.`
`ExecutionContextExecutor` interface, which, in turn, extends `java.util.`
`concurrent.Executor` and `scala.concurrent.ExecutionContext`. Executors can be passed to Java futures and ExecutionContexts can be passed to Scala futures.

For use with futures, dispatchers can be obtained from an `ActorSystem` reference (`ActorSystem.dispatcher`). To get a dispatcher defined in configuration, you can look them up from the actor system by ID:

```
system.dispatcher //actor system's dispatcher
system.dispatchers.lookup("my-dispatcher"); //custom dispatcher
```

Because we can create and obtain these executor-backed dispatchers, we can use them to define thread-pools/fork-join pools to separate, isolate, and run our work in. We'll look at when and why we would want to do this shortly. While you don't need to understand all of the details of the executors to use them effectively, we will visit them in some detail first.

Executors

Dispatchers are backed by executors, so before we look more closely at dispatchers, we'll cover the two main executor types—`ForkJoinPool` and `ThreadPool`.

The thread-pool executor has a queue of work which is assigned to threads. The threads take work as they become free. Threadpools offer a greater efficiency over creating and destroying threads as they allow reuse of threads that are an expensive resource to create and destroy.

The "fork-join-pool" executor uses a divide-and-conquer algorithm to recursively split tasks into smaller pieces and then assigns the work to be run on different threads. The results are then combined. While the tasks we are submitting may not be recursively split as `ForkJoinTasks`, the fork-join-pool executor has a work-stealing algorithm that allows an idle thread to "steal" work scheduled for another thread. Work tends to not distribute and complete evenly, so work stealing will more efficiently utilize hardware.

Fork-join will almost always perform better than the thread-pool executor—it should be your default choice.

Creating Dispatchers

To define a dispatcher in `application.conf`, we need to specify the dispatcher type and the executor. We can also specify any configuration-specific details of the executor such as how many threads to use or how many messages to process for each actor before moving on:

```
my-dispatcher {
    type=Dispatcher
    executor = "fork-join-executor"

    fork-join-executor {
        parallelism-min = 2 #Minimum threads
        parallelism-factor = 2.0 #Maximum threads per core
        parallelism-max = 10 #Maximum total threads
    }
    throughput = 100 #Max messages to process in an actor before moving
on.
}
```

There are four types of dispatchers that can be used which describe how threads are shared among actors.

- **Dispatchers**: Default dispatcher type. The defined executor will be used to process messages in actors. This should provide optimal performance in most cases.

- **PinnedDispatcher**: This gives each actor its own dedicated thread. This executor creates a thread-pool executor for each actor with each executor having exactly one thread. This may sound like a good idea if you want to ensure that an actor always responds immediately, but there are very few use cases where a pinned dispatcher will perform better than sharing resources. You can try this if a single actor has to do a lot of important work; otherwise, pass on this one.

- **CallingThreadDispatcher**: This dispatcher is unique in that it has no executor. Instead, the work is run on the calling thread. Its primary use is in testing, especially in debugging. Because the calling thread does the work, there is a clear stack trace that shows the complete context of the executed method that is useful for understanding exceptions. A lock is still obtained in the actor, so only one thread can execute code in the actor at once, but multiple threads sending messages to an actor will cause all but one thread to wait for a lock. The `CallingThreadDispatcher` is how the `TestActorRef` is able to do work synchronously in tests as demonstrated earlier in this book.

- **BalancingDispatcher**: You will see the `BalancingDispatcher` referenced in some Akka documentation—its direct use has been deprecated and replaced by the `BalancingPool` router mentioned earlier. `BalancingDispatcher` is still used in Akka, but it should only be used indirectly by a router. We will look at the `BalancingPool` in action in the Dispatcher section. The `BalancingDispatcher` is unique in that it shares a mailbox with all actors in the pool and optimally creates one thread per actor in the pool. The `BalancingDispatcher` Actors pull messages from the mailbox so that there is never a queue in one actor while another actor is idle. This is a variation on work stealing as all the actors pull from a shared mailbox—it has a similar beneficial effect on performance.

Actors can be created with dispatchers that have been configured by building Props referencing the dispatcher name configured in `application.conf`:

```
system.actorOf(Props[MyActor].withDispatcher("my-pinned-dispatcher"))
```

Deciding Which Dispatcher to use where

We've now covered how to create dispatchers and executors, but we don't really have a clear picture of what to do with them. The purpose of this chapter is to cover how to best utilize our hardware, so we're now going to look at how we can use dispatchers to produce an application that is more responsive to our users by being more resilient to potential performance problems.

We'll skip back to our example of an application that extracts article bodies from web pages and caches them, and that also serves cached articles to a user. For our example, let's assume that the user profiles are retrieved from an RDBMS requiring thread-blocking JDBC calls. This introduces blocking of our limited threads to aid in highlighting what we're trying to accomplish.

The first step to scaling up is to understand which use cases are most important to serve immediately and where there may be contention for the resources needed to serve those important requests. If we use only the default dispatcher, and 1,000 requests come in consisting of 500 blocking (for example, JDBC) and 500 non-blocking operations, we don't want the blocking operations to tie up all the threads needed to serve the important requests.

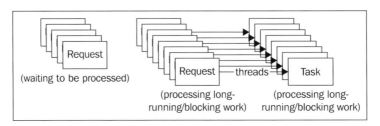

In the preceding diagram, we simplify the scale of this example to show 8 threads being used by longer running tasks such as blocking IO and heavier processing. The diagram shows the impact that it has on other requests that are waiting to be processed because all of the threads available are tied up. The other requests cannot begin processing until those resources are freed. The waiting tasks might just need to do short-lived cache reads, but they will have to wait in line for resources to become free to do the work.

This highlights that having one pool of resources distributed without order can allow riskier areas of the application to tie up resources that we need to give to our important primary use cases.

We can do better than this by isolating the resources in the areas of risk from competing with those that serve the important tasks. If we create new dispatchers and assign any long-running or blocking work to those dispatchers, we can ensure that the rest of our application remains responsive. We want to separate all of the heavy and long-running work into independent dispatchers to ensure that resources are available for other tasks in adverse situations.

By doing this, we can isolate the delays to those areas of the application. If MySQL goes on the fritz and starts taking 30 seconds to respond, at least other paths through the application will remain responsive.

This approach requires us to first examine our application's performance, understanding where the application can block and tie up resources. We need to categorize the work done in the application.

If we look at our example case, we might categorize work it into the following:

- **Article Parsing**: Longer running CPU-intensive tasks (10% of requests)
- **JDBC Profile Reads from MySQL**: Longer running thread-blocking IO (10% of requests)
- **Article Retrieval**: Simple non-blocking requests to get articles from remote in-memory datastore (80% of requests)

Once we have a picture of the types of work that the application is doing, then we want to understand if there are performance risks there — is it possible that something could cause resource utilization to spiral out of control, affecting the rest of the application? Look at both thread blocking and CPU-intensive work and evaluate if it's possible for them to cause some resource starvation in other important areas of the application:

- **Article Parsing**: If someone submits several large books that have been posted online, all threads could be used up in very intensive long-running work. It is of moderate risk and can be mitigated by limiting the size of submissions.
- **JDBC Profile Reads**: If the database starts taking 30 seconds to respond, all threads could be used up waiting. It is of higher risk.
- **Article Retrieval**: Article retrieval does not block and does no heavy work, so it is low-risk. It is also important to serve this traffic fast as it will account for most of the traffic.

Now that we have identified where higher risk activities might be, we want to isolate any portion of work that has risk into its own dispatcher so that if/when those conditions occur, our application will not be negatively affected in other important areas. This is another example of bulkheading to isolate the impact of failure. Just a reminder, never make assumptions and always measure how changes affect your system's performance!

Now that we have categorized our application's work and risk front, we can take any high risk areas, and isolate them into their own dispatcher. The approach we will use will look like the following:

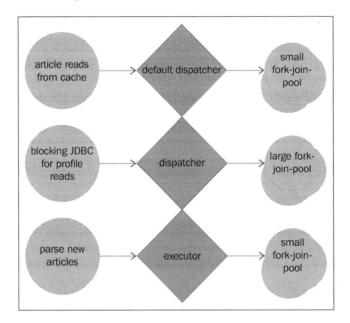

Non-Blocking Article Reads and Akka will be okay to run in the default dispatcher at this point. If we discover other risks, then we can further separate the work later, but this is a good starting point.

Blocking IO—for example, JDBC Profile Reads for profile information—will get its own dispatcher with 50 or 100 threads—work that blocks and waits for IO (that is from a database with JDBC drivers) should be isolated from asynchronous threadpools because the work will halt all other operations in the application if all of the threads get tied up waiting for IO. This is probably the most critical of the changes—we should always try to place blocking IO outside of Akka's dispatcher.

Article Parsing will get its own dispatcher with a small number of threads. We're using the dispatcher for isolation here incase very big jobs are submitted. If big jobs are submitted, then the work will halt any other work in the queue; thus, to protect against those exceptional cases, we can isolate the work. In this case, we can also use the `BalancingPool`/`BalancingDispatcher` to distribute work across a pool of article parsing actors. In addition to giving isolation, using the `BalancingPool` also gives a potential improvement in resource utilization by the `BalancingPool` work-stealing nature.

Default Dispatcher

There are a couple of approaches that we can take with the default dispatcher. We can either separate all work out, leaving it only for Akka to use, or we can check that only async work gets done in the default dispatcher and move any higher-risk work out. Either way, we should never block in the default dispatcher and have to be a bit careful with the work that is run in it to prevent resource starvation.

You don't need to do anything to create or use the default dispatcher/threadpool. We're done. If needed, we can configure the default dispatcher by defining it in the `application.conf` file on the classpath similar to the following:

```
akka {
    actor {
        default-dispatcher {
            # Min number of threads to cap factor-based parallelism
number to
            parallelism-min = 8
            # The parallelism factor is used to determine thread pool size
using the
            # following formula: ceil(available processors * factor).
Resulting size
            # is then bounded by the parallelism-min and parallelism-max
values.
            parallelism-factor = 3.0
            # Max number of threads to cap factor-based parallelism number
to
            parallelism-max = 64
            # Throughput for default Dispatcher, set to 1 for as fair as
possible
            throughput = 10
        }
    }
}
```

You can override default configuration values by defining any values again in your own `application.conf` file:

```
akka {
    actor {
        default-dispatcher {
            # Throughput for default Dispatcher, set to 1 for as fair as
possible
            throughput = 1
        }
    }
}
```

By default, all work done by Actors will execute in this dispatcher. If you need to get the `ExecutionContext` to create futures in, you can access the default threadpool through your ActorSystem, and then supply it to futures:

```
ActorSystem system = ActorSystem.create();
CompletableFuture.runAsync(() ->System.out.println("run in ec"),
system.dispatcher());
val system = ActorSystem()
implicit val ec = system.dispatcher
val future = Future(() =>println("run in ec"))
```

 Note: Be careful about the work you do in futures in the default dispatcher as it will take time away from the actors themselves. We'll look at how to remedy this in the next section.

In Scala, classes extending Actor already have the dispatcher as an implicit val, so you do not have to specify it if working with futures in actors. There are few cases where you want to have futures in your actors — remember that we should prefer `tell` over `ask` so you might want to evaluate your approaches if you're finding you're working with Futures a lot inside your actors.

That covers the default dispatcher and how to use it and tune it. Now, we'll look at how to add and use additional executors.

Blocking IO dispatcher use with futures

If you have any blocking work, you want to get it out of the main dispatcher so that actors can stay lively if your app gets saturated with blocking work.

Consider this use case: a user wants to retrieve a user profile from an RDBMS to see who posted an article. We might have a service interface that looks like the following:

```
import org.springframework.data.repository.CrudRepository;
import java.util.List;
public interface UserProfileRepository extends
CrudRepository<UserProfile, Long> {
    List<UserProfile>findById(Long id);
}
```

For this example, we'll use Spring Data to access a database via JDBC. Spring Data is an arbitrary choice here for use in the example for a blocking API—it lets us demonstrate blocking IO with minimal code, but the approach could be for anything that blocks threads. This interface is actually all the code that you need to query for JPA-annotated `UserProfiles`—Spring supplies the implementations for you by analyzing the method name.

For our example, we have a method called `findById` that accepts an ID and blocks the calling thread while waiting for IO to come back from the database.

If we call this method in an actor, we're tying up a thread in our default dispatcher, not to mention halting the actor from doing any other work:

```
//Java
 sender().tell(userProfileRepository.findById(id), self());
//Scala
sender() ! userProfileRepository.findById(id)
```

Again, if we have several requests that come in and hit that block of code (maybe in a pool of actors), all the threads can be stuck waiting so that no other work is able to move forward until resources are freed.

The simplest solution in these cases is to run the blocking operations in another set of threads in a different dispatcher.

First, in our `application.conf` file we'll create a dispatcher with a bigger pool of resources:

```
blocking-io-dispatcher {
   type = Dispatcher
   executor = "fork-join-executor"
   fork-join-executor {
     parallelism-factor = 50.0
    parallelism-min = 10
    parallelism-max = 100
   }
}
```

That will allow up to 50 threads per core to be created with a minimum of 10 and a maximum of 100 threads. Hundred threads is a large upper limit for a properly factored and indexed database.

For blocking IO to databases, if you have queries that take a long time to run, you should examine the run plans and fix your tables and queries instead of adding more threads. Each thread has a memory overhead, so don't arbitrarily add more threads. Measure, change, and repeat until optimal, adjusting the threadpool only after your queries, tables, and indices are optimized.

Now that we have a dispatcher configured, we need to gain access to it to be able to run the blocking queries in it. We can get a reference to a dispatcher by looking up the dispatcher from the actor system. In an actor, we would call the following:

```
//Java
val ec: ExecutionContext = context.system.dispatchers.
lookup("blocking-io-dispatcher")
//Scala
Executor ex = context().system().dispatchers().lookup("blocking-io-
dispatcher");
```

Once we have the dispatcher references, we can use them with the future APIs to run the work there:

```
//Java
CompletableFuture<UserProfile> future = CompletableFuture.supplyAsync(
    () ->userProfileRepository.findById(id)
    , ex);
//Scala
val future: Future[UserProfile] = Future{
 userProfileRepository.findById(id)
  }(ec)
```

In each of the Scala and Java future APIs, all that we have to do is supply the dispatcher reference as the second parameter of the future and the dispatcher will take care of the rest. Once the result is available, the future will complete.

Having the future reference, we can now use it as we normally would in an actor—likely using `patterns.Pipe` to send the result to another actor asynchronously.

This use of futures is an important technique—blocking IO will very quickly ruin your application's performance. I would recommend that you try to use non-blocking drivers instead of doing this, but if you need to use blocking drivers with chosen technologies, then this is a reasonable approach.

In the same manner as with blocking IO, any heavy computation done with results from futures can also be moved to another dispatcher to help actors stay lively.

Article parsing dispatcher

For our last example, we'll look at how we can assign actors to another dispatcher. This is different than taking only a piece of a task and running it in another dispatcher, like we saw in the JDBC example, because we're actually assigning actors completely to another dispatcher instead of just some work over there. This is well suited for any actors that do heavier processing.

We're going to look at two options:

- Defining a Dispatcher to use with an actor pool
- Using the `BalancingPool` router that uses `BalancingDispatcher`

Using a configured dispatcher with Actors

Here we'll look at configuring a dispatcher in our `application.conf`, and then assigning actors to that dispatcher when we create them. This is fairly straightforward and does not vary much from many of the other activities we've looked at so far.

First, we'll create another dispatcher in our `application.conf` for the article parsing. We'll assign a smaller number of threads this time:

```
article-parsing-dispatcher {
   # Dispatcher is the name of the event-based dispatcher
  type = Dispatcher
  # What kind of ExecutionService to use
  executor = "fork-join-executor"
  # Configuration for the fork join pool
  fork-join-executor {
    # Min number of threads to cap factor-based parallelism number to
    parallelism-min = 2
   # Parallelism (threads) ... ceil(available processors * factor)
    parallelism-factor = 2.0
    # Max number of threads to cap factor-based parallelism number to
    parallelism-max = 8
  }
  throughput = 50
}
```

Now, to create actors assigned to the configured dispatcher, we simply call the `withDispatcher` method while creating the Props. We'll use a range to create a list of actors, and then place them in the dispatcher:

```java
//Java
        List<ActorRef>routees = Arrays.asList(1,2,3,4,5,6,7,8).
stream().map(x ->
 system.actorOf(Props.create(ArticleParseActor.class).
 withDispatcher("article-parsing-dispatcher"))
        ).collect(Collectors.toList());
```

```scala
//Scala
val actors: List[ActorRef] = (0 to 7).map(x => {
 system.actorOf(Props(classOf[ArticleParseActor]).
 withDispatcher("article-parsing-dispatcher"))
     }).toList
```

Now, we can do anything we like with actors created this way. For example, we can produce a router to use the actors so that we can easily do work in parallel with them:

```java
//Java
Iterable<String>routeeAddresses = routees.
                stream().
            map(x ->x.path().toStringWithoutAddress()).
            collect(Collectors.toList());
ActorRefworkerRouter = system.actorOf(new RoundRobinGroup(routeeAddres
ses).props());
```

```scala
//Scala
 valworkerRouter = system.actorOf(RoundRobinGroup(
 actors.map(x =>x.path.toStringWithoutAddress).toList).props(),
     "workerRouter")
workRouter.tell(
     new ParseArticle(TestHelper.file)
     , self());
```

This is a slightly different syntax for creating a router actor than we saw earlier. We saw an example of a pool—where the router creates the routee actors. Here, we are taking pre-existing actors that we created previously and creating a router actor by passing those actors in using a group load-balancing strategy (`RoundRobinGroup`). The router groups take a list of addresses, and then produce the props you need to produce the router actor. This is very similar to what we would do if the actors were remote as well.

Note: The Group can also take the name of a dispatcher if you want the router to be assigned to a dispatcher as well.

Using BalancingPool/BalancingDispatcher

Because the actors are local, we have a better option than using the RoundRobinGroup shown previously. For local actors, we can create a router with a BalancingPool, which was briefly described earlier in this chapter. The BalancingPool will share a single mailbox across all actors in the pool and effectively offer "work-stealing" mechanics to re-distribute load to any idle actors. Using a BalancingPool helps ensure there are no idle actors when there is work to do because all actors pull messages from the same mailbox. Technically, it's not work stealing as the router is not re-assigning work like ForkJoinPool does—it's just that idle actors will pick up the next message from the shared mailbox. The end result is the same—there is no possibility for one actor to have several messages queued while another actor has none. As we can ensure more actors are actively working, this option can often lead to better resource utilization than the other balancing strategies.

The BalancingPool uses a special dispatcher—BalancingDispatcher. In most cases, we want the BalancingDispatcher to have a number of threads equivalent to the number of actors that are used.

First, we'll configure the default BalancingDispatcher executors in the application.conf to have exactly 8 threads:

```
//Dispatcher for BalancingPool
pool-dispatcher {
    fork-join-executor { # force it to allocate exactly 8 threads
       parallelism-min = 8
       parallelism-max = 8
    }
}
```

Then, we make a pool of eight actors—the same number as the number of threads in the pool dispatcher:

```
//Java
 ActorRefworkerRouter = system.actorOf(new BalancingPool(8).
props(Props.create(ArticleParseActor.class)),
                "balancing-pool-router");
//Scala
 valworkerRouter = system.actorOf(BalancingPool(8).props(Props(classOf
[ArticleParseActor])),
       "balancing-pool-router")
```

This is a great way of ensuring work is balanced across all actors when working locally.

Optimal parallelism

There is only one way to determine for certain what the optimal level of parallelism is on your hardware: measuring. You'll almost always make incorrect assumptions about where time is spent and how changes impact systems until you actually measure and adjust.

Using a number of threads far greater than the number of cores in your processor will reduce performance, so don't arbitrarily choose large pools of actors and assume more is better. Akka has to switch processing between actors, and your executors need to balance work between threads. Your OS has to schedule CPU time to the active threads and context-switch by swapping the state of the active thread in and out. Because of the overhead, optimal parallelism for the fastest processing times may actually come in lower than you expect. The only way to know for sure what impact a change has is to measure!

Homework

- Practice doing work in parallel with both Futures and Actors.

- Try moving the work into different dispatchers.

- Write down some assumptions you have about how things will perform with more and less threads.

- Measure the performance under high load. Measure multiple times for each test and average the results. How does raising and lowering the number of threads and actors impact performance?

- How did your expectations compare to your measurements?

- If you were to make general recommendations about optimal parallelism based on your observations, what would it be?

 Note: it's easier to make generalizations if you have more cores. You'll probably find things behave differently than you expect.

- Can you determine how many context switches are occurring and how that impacts performance? On Linux systems, you'll find the info in /proc/ [pid]/status. You may have to look around in ps to find the right Java pid.

- Consider a recent application you have worked on—how would you separate the work into different dispatchers?

- What size of threadpools would you use for the work?

Summary

In this chapter, we looked at two major concepts: scaling up a local application to take advantage of multicore hardware and isolating work into separate dispatchers to protect portions of the isolation from performance risks that may be encountered in other portions of the application.

To scale up, we need to do work concurrently, so we looked at several techniques for parallelizing work. We examined how to parallelize with futures and with actors. Then, we looked at how to examine an application to determine how separate work should be isolated into different dispatchers for different types of work such as computationally heavy work or blocking IO. Because the isolated dispatchers get tied up without impacting other ones, we can ensure that the other areas of the application remain responsive.

In the next chapter, we will build on the concepts here to look at how we can start to distribute load across multiple machines.

6
Successfully Scaling
Out – Clustering

In the previous chapter, we described how to parallelize work to better utilize the hardware of a single physical host. We also looked at how to isolate performance problems to specific dispatchers in a host. In this chapter, we will look at what happens when we reach the limit of a physical host and need to process the work across multiple machines. This may sound like a huge feat, but Akka gives us the tools to get us started quickly.

In this chapter, we will cover the following topics:

- Some of the foundational concepts used in distributed systems
- Introduction to Akka Cluster
- Using Akka Cluster to build distributed systems

Introducing Akka Cluster

We've briefly looked at remoting in earlier chapters in this book. It's helpful to understand remoting a bit to see how Akka communicates over the network, but in this chapter, we're going to use Akka Cluster's mechanics instead of simple peer to peer communication to give us greater resilience and flexibility in our deployments. In this section, we'll review some clustering concepts and learn about how Akka Cluster keeps track of nodes to allow our applications to scale out as needed.

Let's start by giving a definition of what a cluster is. Wikipedia states that *A computer cluster consists of a set of loosely or tightly connected computers that work together so that, in many respects, they can be viewed as a single system.* To be more specific about our definition of a cluster in this chapter, we can say that a cluster is a group of machines (likely VMs), which we will refer to as `nodes` or `members`, that are in agreement about all other nodes who are in the group.

One Giant Monolith or Many Micro Services?

Since I started slinging code, Martin Fowler has been one of my heroes as a developer; so, when I see him reasoning about a problem I'm also pondering, I take notes.

If we're talking about microservices and distributed systems, he has a few articles on his site `http://www.martinfowler.com/`, which you might want to read.

The first valuable point is that in the life of an application, while complexity of an application is low, it can be more efficient for a small team to build a single large application—a monolith—as opposed to trying to build networked services. Start by building one application. Once complexity in the application increases, productivity can fall because teams have to do a lot of coordination of activities to get code merged, and work on features together. At this point, you can start to see productivity benefits of using smaller networked services.

The second valuable point is that building with a monolith-first approach will enable you to understand where services should be separated when you get around to splitting your services into many smaller applications. Fowler argues that you are quite likely to pick the wrong services to represent as discreet applications until you've actually been working on your system for a while.

Once you have some experience and data from running your system in production, it will be clear which pieces will benefit from being separated in terms of both performance and team velocity when adding features. As you start deploying microservices, you can scale up the more loaded services in an asymmetrical manner so that the most used pieces of the application have their own larger cluster of servers.

Luckily, Akka can make deployment decisions more of a configuration item rather than code, but having multiple code bases can greatly ease having large teams work on a codebase. It eliminates the problem of Brooks Law (adding more resources to an already late project makes it later) by eliminating communication channels and isolating code commits to separate repositories (no more merge hell).

Ultimately, you may want to defer considering building a distributed system until you have a system that is too complex to manage as a monolith, or at least until you have good data-backed justifications (performance or team effort related) for deploying in such a manner.

Regardless of whether you decide to build a monolith or services out of the gate, you may want to put different concerns into libraries from day one. You can get the benefits of having teams work on different code bases before you're ready to actually deploy separate applications. Once you want to split your application, it will be much easier to manage sharing code if you've done this from the start.

Definition of a Cluster

A cluster is a group of servers that exist and talk among themselves. Each server in a cluster is referred to as a node or member. A cluster should be able to change size dynamically and survive any failures with minimal impact so that there are two responsibilities that a cluster needs to handle—failure detection and propagating a consistent view of all available members throughout the cluster.

Failure Detection

As we start to add nodes beyond one, it becomes more likely that nodes will fail or that the network will become temporarily partitioned; thus, a cluster is a dynamic entity that can shrink when servers shut down or become unavailable and that can grow when servers are added (for example, to handle more load). Nodes of a cluster do this by sending messages to other members to determine whether those members are available or not. They determine the availability of the members on the basis of the reply or absence thereof.

If every server talked to every other server in the cluster, then a cluster's performance would not scale in a linear manner as the overhead of each additional node would exponentially increase the lines of communication needed. To reduce the complexity of monitoring the heath of other nodes, failure detection in Akka is done by only monitoring a certain number of nodes next to a node. For example, in a cluster ring of six nodes, each node might monitor the two nodes after it for failure. The default maximum for each node to monitor in Akka Cluster is five nodes:

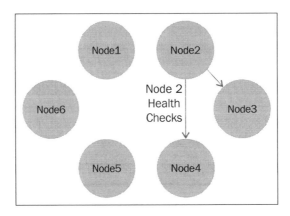

In Akka, the failure detection is accomplished by sending a heartbeat from one node to another, and then accepting a response. Akka will calculate the likelihood that a node is available on the basis of the heartbeat history and current heartbeats. Akka will mark the node as unavailable and available by calculation with these figures and the tolerance thresholds configured.

Gossiping an Eventually Consistent View

Considering handling failure detection, each node in the cluster communicates the known state to its neighbors. Then, those neighbors pass along the known state to their neighbors and so on until the known state of that node is propagated throughout the cluster. Nodes will deliberate and come to conclusions about the members of the cluster.

If a node is inaccessible to one node, it is considered unavailable to all nodes in the cluster.

This mechanism for eventually propagating the state through the cluster is known as gossip protocol or epidemic protocol (as information spreads throughout the cluster like a virus!). Many eventually consistent data-stores, such as Riak and Cassandra, operate in a very similar manner. The Dynamo paper from Amazon was very influential in many of these data-stores.

We don't need to know too much about the inner workings of Akka cluster at this point—we only need to understand that Akka will take care of determining if the state of the cluster changes and will take care of updating everyone in the cluster with any changes that occur.

We're going to cover many of the details of how cluster works as we build our own cluster through the rest of this chapter. If you want to get a bit more background on how Akka Cluster works, there is a document in the Akka documentation called Cluster Specification. At the time of writing, it as available at `http://doc.akka.io/docs/akka/snapshot/scala/cluster-usage.html`.

CAP Theorem

We're going to cover a stateless worker example in this chapter, but we're also going to cover state being stored in a cluster to understand the trade-offs of design choices. Eric Brewer's often cited *CAP Theorem* talks about the compromises of distributed systems and is a helpful model for reasoning about how a system deals with state and exceptional events. CAP Theorem is an acronym for the three qualities of distributed systems, as described in the following, and the compromise of choosing between them.

C – Consistency

Consistency means that a client will return the most recent value for a given record. Consider a bank account—if you try to withdraw $400 immediately after depositing a $400 cheque, you expect the systems to give you the correct balance and allow you to withdraw the $400.

A – Availability

Availability means that a non-failing node is able to give a reasonable response (for example, give an accurate picture of whether a write was a success or failure).

P – Partition Tolerance

Partition Tolerance means that a system continues to operate normally if a node is removed from the network due to a temporary network failure. If data is replicated across three nodes and one of the nodes becomes temporarily unavailable, then the system can be said to be partition tolerant if the other two nodes can come to the same conclusion about the most recent record.

Compromises in CAP Theorem

CAP theorem is often cited as the following statement: of the three—Consistency, Availability, and Partition tolerance—that a distributed system can choose any two. This is a misleading oversimplification, and if you start reading articles, you'll see a lot of conflicting rebuttals.

We'll start by assuming that we want a system that has Partition Tolerance and only talking about the compromises between Availability and Consistency. Why you ask? In a time-bound request, if a node becomes unavailable, you are really deciding between responding with an error (preferring Consistency) or continuing even though there might be inconsistency between servers (preferring Availability). Waiting around too long means the request will be abandoned so time is a factor at play and a system must make a decision. We'll look at this a bit more but Eric Brewer also wrote an article 12 years after his Cap Theorem paper that has further discussion on this point: `http://www.infoq.com/articles/cap-twelve-years-later-how-the-rules-have-changed`:

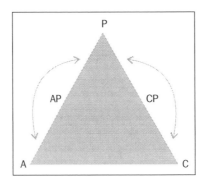

CP System – Preferring Consistency

There are different ways in which a consistent distributed store can be implemented. Perhaps, the simplest example of a strongly consistent data-store would be to have a master node and any number of secondary nodes on which the data is replicated. You always write to the primary node, and to ensure the most recent data is read. Data must always be read from the primary node as well. In the case of the failure of the master node, the system will no longer be available:

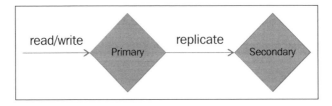

Generally, some sort of failover occurs where a secondary node becomes the new primary node. We give up availability because our system can't be read from or written to in the case of a partition, and instead goes through a failover process to elect the new primary node. Once the failover is complete, availability will be restored. Redis Sentinel, or replicated RDBMSs are great examples of strongly consistent distributed systems.

You would choose a consistent system if you need ATOMIC reads/writes, transactions, and so on.

AP System – Preferring Availability

A system that prefers availability and partition tolerance at the cost of consistency is said to be "eventually consistent." In highly available distributed data-stores such as Cassandra and Riak, this is a very common model.

We'll look at AP systems in more detail in this chapter because they take a bit of work to reason about, but we can look at one example of how we might implement an AP system. Let's assume that there are three replicas of the data on three nodes. When we write data, the data is written to one node and, then, it is later replicated across all three nodes. It doesn't matter which one we write into, that node will coordinate the write across the remaining nodes:

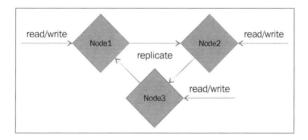

When we read from a node, we only need one node to read the data, so our client may choose a random node to read from. In this example, our system is eventually consistent because when we read from a node, and the data may be a bit out of date (not Consistent), but as we can read and write from any of the nodes, our system is both Partition tolerant and highly Available. If a node becomes unavailable, we can just try another node.

> Note that this is very hard to get correct because the time and ordering of events in systems is challenging to determine. Clocks will never be perfectly synchronized across machines so other approaches are taken for ordering such as Vector clocks.

Consistency as a Sliding Scale

Practically speaking, the choices between the three trade-offs are not toggles but sliders. In an eventually consistent system, for example, if we have three replicas of a record we're looking for, we can have low consistency by requiring any of the nodes to give us the record. We can have greater consistency by having any two of the three return with the data. And we can have the greatest consistency by requiring asking all three nodes to provide back a result. When we get back the data from the nodes, several different mechanisms can be used to order the records, so we'll choose the newest one. However, doing this can sacrifice partition tolerance. If we need all three replicas to be available, then we can't tolerate one of the nodes disappearing. Usually, only requiring a quorum or majority of nodes to be up and give a view is a good trade-off between consistency and partition tolerance.

[

Ordering is its own problem as often clocks are not perfectly synchronized across nodes so other ordering mechanisms are used such as Vector Clocks.
]

Similarly, in a CP system, we can sacrifice some consistency for greater availability by allowing secondary nodes to be read from. If we keep writes on the master, we still have highly consistent writes, but we allow our reads to be eventually consistent, so our database becomes AP on reads.

Based on our use cases, we can "tune" our CAP stance to best meet our use case needs. It is even possible to use blends of these strategies in the same application in the same data-store for different types of data!

Building Systems with Akka Cluster

We will revisit two problems in this chapter — Article Parsing and the key-value store. However, in this chapter, we're going to look at how to distribute them across multiple servers using Akka Cluster. Assuming we have built an application that needs to scale beyond a single node, and that needs higher availability, we will see how we can scale our systems up by adding more nodes.

We might not be able to build Cassandra in a day, but believe it or not, we will be able to produce a horizontally scalable distributed service in this chapter, and we will also demonstrate some of the common techniques that are used in distributed solutions while we're at it.

Creating the Cluster

In this section, we're going to look at how to create a cluster with Akka's Cluster module. We looked at remoting earlier in this book very briefly, but we will look at cluster in much greater detail now. Akka Cluster is built on remoting, but is powerfully useful. If you use Remoting, you'll need to concern yourself with issues such as high availability in your infrastructure or code. Cluster takes care of many of these concerns for you, thus making it a great choice for building your distributed Actor systems.

Configuring the Project

First, we need to configure Akka to be able to create a cluster. We have to do a few things to the project—first, add `Cluster` to the project and, then, add the appropriate entries in `application.conf`. You can start a new project using `activator new` as we'll go over all of the configuration needed in the project. Completed projects are available on GitHub at `https://github.com/jasongoodwin/learning-akka/tree/master/ch6` in both Scala and Java.

In our `build.sbt` file, we first have to add the Akka Cluster dependency:

```
"com.typesafe.akka" %% "akka-cluster" % "2.3.6"
```

We'll also add the `contrib` package. This is a module of contributions from outside the Akka team—there is an Akka Cluster client in the `contrib` package that is a bit simpler to build on. We'll look at the client features a bit later:

```
"com.typesafe.akka" %% "akka-contrib" % "2.3.6",
```

Now that Akka Cluster is in the project, we need to add cluster configuration in `src/main/resources/application.conf`:

```
akka {
    actor {
      provider = "akka.cluster.ClusterActorRefProvider"
    }
  remote {
  netty.tcp {
        hostname = "127.0.0.1"
        port = 2552
      }
    }
  cluster {
      seed-nodes = [
        "akka.tcp://Akkademy@127.0.0.1:2552",
        "akka.tcp://Akkademy@127.0.0.1:2551"]
    }
  extensions = ["akka.contrib.pattern.ClusterReceptionistExtension"]
}
```

There are a few pieces that are significant.

First, configuration for Cluster is very similar to remoting but we change the provider to `ClusterActorRefProvider`.

We specify the host and port. We're using the Akka default of 2552 and specifying the local host IP for testing purposes. To test a cluster on a single machine, you'll need to start instances on different ports, which can be done by passing in arguments to `sbt` on the command line. If you need to pass in any parameters, you can achieve this using the following:

```
activator run -Dakka.remote.netty.tcp.port=0
```

Passing `port=0` will have Akka assign a random port.

We specify seed nodes. We'll look at what exactly seed nodes are in a moment, but please note that the host, port, and `ActorSystem` are described in the configuration lines for the seed-nodes. It's important to ensure that the `ActorSystem` is accurately for the cluster you are trying to join. Multiple `ActorSystems` can run in an instance, so host and port are not enough to connect successfully.

The last line — the extensions line — is to add support for the `contrib` package's cluster client, which we'll look at a bit later.

Seed Nodes

You may be wondering what the `akka.cluster.seed-nodes` configuration is for. Because a cluster can be of any size, you may not know where all the nodes will be located. This is especially true if you're deploying in the cloud, where you can have rapidly changing deployment topology and IPs.

Thanks to the gossip protocol, we can get away with only knowing a couple of nodes. Most technologies such as Cassandra and Akka refer to these nodes as seed nodes. There is nothing special about them apart from the fact that we know where they are accessible.

To understand how this is possible, we'll have a look at how nodes join the cluster. When a new node joins the cluster, it tries to contact the first seed node. If it successfully contacts the node, it will announce its location (port and IP). The seed node will then gossip the new node's location, eventually propagating the change through the cluster. If contact to the first seed node fails, then the node will try the next seed node. As long as one seed node is available, then other nodes can join and leave without requiring any configuration changes:

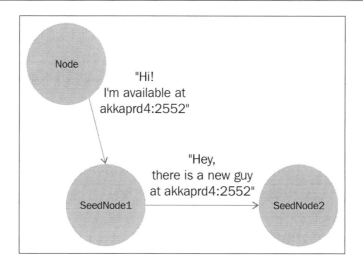

When you deploy to production, you should define at least two seed nodes that will have a constant IP and ensure that at least one of the seed nodes is available all the time. When a node attempts to join the cluster, it will try to sequentially contact each seed node. If no seed nodes are available, then the node will not be able to join the cluster.

 When starting the cluster's seed nodes, the seed nodes can be started in any order, but the first seed node listed must be started to initialize the cluster.

Subscribing to Cluster Events

We have enough configuration now to create a cluster at runtime, thus, we can start building. We'll subscribe to cluster events and log any changes to the cluster ring. After writing the code, we'll test it out and then continue on to look at how we can design a distributed service and a data-store using this base.

We'll produce an actor first, calling it `ClusterController`, and use this as the basis for our other examples. Later, we'll adapt the code to take action on the events. We'll start by creating the actor, and instantiating a logger, and then the cluster object.

In Java, the actor looks like the following:

```
importstatic.akka.cluster.ClusterEvent.*;
public class ClusterController extends AbstractActor {
    protected final LoggingAdapter log = Logging.getLogger(context().
system(), this);
    Cluster cluster = Cluster.get(getContext().system());
    @Override
    public void preStart() {
 cluster.subscribe(self(), initialStateAsEvents(),
 MemberEvent.class, UnreachableMember.class);
    }
    @Override
    public void postStop() {
 cluster.unsubscribe(self());
    }
    private ClusterController(){
        receive(ReceiveBuilder.
 match(MemberEvent.class, message -> {
                        log.info("MemberEvent: {}", message);
                    }).
 match(UnreachableMember.class, message -> {
                        log.info("UnreachableMember: {}",
 message);
                    }).build()
        );
    }
}
```

In Scala, the actor looks the following:

```
class ClusterController extends Actor {
 val log = Logging(context.system, this)
 val cluster = Cluster(context.system)
  override def preStart() {
 cluster.subscribe(self, classOf[MemberEvent],
 classOf[UnreachableMember])
    }
  override def postStop() {
 cluster.unsubscribe(self)
    }
  override def receive = {
     case x: MemberEvent => log.info("MemberEvent: {}", x)
     case x: UnreachableMember => log.info("UnreachableMember {}: ",
 x)
    }
}
```

First, we define the logger. Then, we get a reference to the Cluster object. We'll look at the Cluster object and methods available on it throughout this chapter.

We use the Actor `preStart` and `postStop` hooks to subscribe to events that we're interested in. The unsubscribe in the `postStop` hook is necessary to prevent a leak. We're going to have our actor subscribe to the following two events:

- **MemberEvent**: This tells us when there is a change to the cluster state
- **UnreachableMember**: This tells us when there is a node marked unreachable

Then, we describe the actor's behavior when it receives those events: to simply log them (for now). We'll examine the different events that occur in the cluster shortly.

Starting the Cluster

As a checkpoint to ensure that everything is accurate and configured correctly, we'll try to start up a few nodes now. First, we need to make a `main` where we programmatically start the actor system and create the `ClusterController` actor.

In Java:

```
public class Main {
     public static void main(String... args) {
 ActorSystem system = ActorSystem.create("Akkademy");
 ActorRefclusterController = system.actorOf(Props.
create(ClusterController.class), "clusterController");
     }
}
```

In Scala:

```
object Main extends App {
 val system = ActorSystem("Akkademy")
val clusterController = system.actorOf(Props[ClusterController],
"clusterController")
}
```

Our seed node can be started simply with:

```
activator run
```

However, we're going to enable jmx remote management of the nodes so that we can have them leave the cluster gracefully. Thus, we're going to tack on a few extra parameters — we'll specify the jmx port for the nodes and turn off jmx security features for use in test. We'll see why we want to enable JMX remote management shortly. With the jmx configuration, we will start the node like the following:

```
activator run \
-Dcom.sun.management.jmxremote.port=9552 \
-Dcom.sun.management.jmxremote.authenticate=false \
-Dcom.sun.management.jmxremote.ssl=false
```

It will start a node on the configured port of 2552. You'll see some logging events indicating that the first seed node is up and probably a few dead letters messages as the node attempts to connect to the other configured seed node configured. Eventually, you'll see our log statement for the MemberEvent:

```
[INFO] [06/14/2015 12:22:46.756] [Akkademy-akka.actor.default-
dispatcher-3] [akka://Akkademy/user/clusterController] MemberEvent:
MemberUp(Member(address = akka.tcp://Akkademy@127.0.0.1:2552, status =
Up))
```

In another terminal window, we'll start up the second seed node on port 2551 by specifying the port as a Java argument:

```
activator run \
-Dakka.remote.netty.tcp.port=2551 \
-Dcom.sun.management.jmxremote.port=9551 \
-Dcom.sun.management.jmxremote.authenticate=false \
-Dcom.sun.management.jmxremote.ssl=false
```

The first node running on 2552 should log the status change when the second seed node connects:

```
[INFO] [06/14/2015 12:24:40.745] [Akkademy-akka.actor.default-
dispatcher-18] [akka://Akkademy/user/clusterController] MemberEvent:
MemberUp(Member(address = akka.tcp://Akkademy@127.0.0.1:2551, status =
Up))
```

We'll add one more node now to demonstrate how we might configure nodes beyond the seed node. Because the seed nodes have defined ports, we can have Akka assign a random port by configuring it as 0:

```
activator run -Dakka.remote.netty.tcp.port=0 \
 -Dcom.sun.management.jmxremote.port=9553 \
 -Dcom.sun.management.jmxremote.authenticate=false \
 -Dcom.sun.management.jmxremote.ssl=false
```

After a moment, you'll see the third node connect to the cluster. This is quite exciting—we now have the basis for building a distributed actor system. Akka takes care of numerous things for us that would be quite hard to get right ourselves!

 Again, remember that you need to start the first node in the seed node list for the cluster to initialize.

Leaving the Cluster Gracefully

If you try shutting down one of the nodes by killing the process, you'll notice that Akka marks it unreachable and writes several error messages. In this case, shutting down the node causes it to become unreachable and Akka will eventually mark it down. This is because we did not leave the cluster gracefully. Before removing a node from the cluster, we should announce to the cluster that the node is leaving.

We can do it programmatically by calling `cluster.leave` with the address of the node we want to remove:

```
cluster.leave(self().path().address());
```

However, we don't have any API that we can use to expose this functionality currently. So, instead, we'll use `jmx` and command line tools to remove the node gracefully. We're going to use a tool that comes with the Akka distribution: `akka-cluster`.

You may need to download the Akka distribution first to get the akka-cluster tool. It should be available at `http://akka.io/downloads/`. Unzip the file, and into the `bin` folder.

Now, we can issue commands to the cluster using the tool. Our principle use is to have the node leave the cluster gracefully. We can shut down the seed node on port `2552` that has JMX exposed on `9552` in the following manner:

```
./akka-cluster localhost 9552 leave akka.tcp://Akkademy@127.0.0.1:2552
```

After gracefully removing the node, you'll see it change states from up to exiting and then to removed.

```
[INFO] [06/15/2015 20:05:21.501] [Akkademy-akka.actor.default-
dispatcher-3] [akka://Akkademy/user/clusterController] MemberEvent:
MemberExited(Member(address = akka.tcp://Akkademy@127.0.0.1:2552,
status = Exiting))
 [INFO] [06/15/2015 20:05:26.470] [Akkademy-akka.actor.default-
dispatcher-17] [akka://Akkademy/user/clusterController] MemberEvent:
MemberRemoved(Member(address = akka.tcp://Akkademy@127.0.0.1:2552,
status = Removed),Exiting)
```

Cluster Member States

Nodes that join the cluster can be in one of a few different states. Under the hood, there is a logical leader node that coordinates some of the state changes. The cluster will logically order nodes and everyone will come to a conclusion about that order. The first node in the ordered list of nodes is the leader.

The leader responds to requests to join and leave the cluster by changing a member's state.

When joining the cluster, a joining member announces its state as "Joining." The leader responds by announcing that the member is Up. Similarly, if a node announces that it is "Leaving," then the Leader responds by changing that node's state to "Exiting" and then to "Removed." All these state changes are sent through the cluster as `MemberEvents`, which we subscribed to and logged.

Failure Detection

There is one more path out of the cluster that actors can take—nodes can be detected as unreachable by other members of the cluster that are performing failure detection. When a node is determined to be unreachable for any reason— for example, crashing or temporary network failure—then the state of the node does not change, but it instead is marked with a `MemberUnreachable` flag. We subscribed to this event in our `ClusterController` so that we can become aware of this flag. If the member becomes reachable again within a reasonable period of time, then it will resume. If it stays unreachable for a configurable duration, then the leader will mark the node "Down" and it cannot rejoin the cluster.

From a functional perspective, you can simply watch for the changes in member state, but the implementation of failure detection is actually based on the probability of being unreachable (`phi`) based on data collected from the cluster. If you want to learn more, the Cluster Specification document has a link to information on how failure detection is implemented (`http://doc.akka.io/docs/akka/snapshot/common/cluster.html#failure-detector`).

We're going to leave the values as their default, but in your deployments, you should be sure to read the documentation and adjust depending on your network reliability. **Amazon EC2 instances (AWS)** is notoriously less reliable than a small network sitting on a rack, so you might want to be more reactive to temporary partitions in AWS than you would on your own virtualization infrastructure and network appliances. After working in large deployments in cloud environments, I've found that encountering service interruptions due to temporary network failure are more the norm than the exception in day-to-day operations.

It's worth noting that if a node is marked unreachable, then Akka cluster will not change states—no new members can join until nodes are either marked down after being unable to recover from unavailability or are restored.

If nodes becomes unavailable and are marked down, they can't rejoin the cluster after that point. Two separate clusters can result (forming what is referred to as a "split brain" scenario). Akka does not currently resolve this phenomenon; thus, once a node is downed, it needs to shut down and restart to get a new unique ID and rejoin the cluster.

This wraps up the basics of Akka cluster. We'll look at building out some examples on our cluster now.

Routing Messages to the Cluster

We looked at how to create a cluster. Now we'll look at how to send messages to the cluster. We're going to re-introduce our article parsing problem here and allocate a cluster of nodes to do the work.

Producing a Distributed Article Parse Service

For our first example—a distributed, horizontally scalable service—we're going to produce a cluster of article parsing services and then have a client route messages to random members of the cluster.

We've looked at producing a pool of actors that will parse an article from a web page for us in *Chapter 5, Scaling Up*.

—we're going to re-use all the code and run it on our cluster example. The receive block of the actor that we want to cluster looks like the following:

```
//Java
match(ParseArticle.class, x ->{
 ArticleParser.apply(x.htmlBody).
 onSuccess(body -> sender().tell(body, self())).
 onFailure(t -> sender().tell(new Status.Failure(t), self()));
                 }
         )
//Scala
    override def receive: Receive = {
      case ParseArticle(htmlString) =>
 val body: String = ArticleParser(htmlString)
        sender() ! body
  }
```

You can refer to *Chapter 5, Scaling Up* examples on GitHub for the full example. We're going to put the pool of article parsers in our cluster and start the cluster up. Once that's complete, we'll demonstrate how to talk to the cluster of services from another actor system. All that we need to do to make a cluster of services is add any dependencies missing to our cluster project, and then put the `ArcicleParser`, `ArticleParseActor`, and the `ParseArticle` messages into the application.

Once you've done that, then we can simply start the actor (or pool of actors) as has been demonstrated in the section on starting the cluster. Then, our main could possibly appear as follows:

```
public class Main {
    public static void main(String... args) {
 ActorSystem system = ActorSystem.create("Akkademy");
 ActorRefclusterController = system.actorOf(Props.
create(ClusterController.class), "clusterController");
 ActorRefworkerPool = system.actorOf(new BalancingPool(5).props(Props.
create(ArticleParseActor.class)), "workers");
    }
}
```

We can start up a few nodes now as covered previously in the section on starting the cluster. For brevity, we'll do so without enabling remote management. If you're using Linux, you can do it in one go by backgrounding the tasks:

```
activator run &
 activator run -Dakka.remote.netty.tcp.port=2551 &
 activator run -Dakka.remote.netty.tcp.port=0 &
```

Now, we have a three-node cluster running. We'll move onto the client.

Cluster Client for Clustered Services

Building a client to talk to stateless clustered services is fairly straightforward. Akka Cluster gives some advantages compared with traditional web services with a load-balancer in front—the cluster can be dynamically scaled up and down without changing load-balancer configuration. The client itself can route the messages to random members of the cluster, so the infrastructure requirements are simpler. Because the client is aware of the cluster, it can rebuild the list of services available to send messages to as the cluster increases or decreases in size. The client will internally load-balance requests against all the nodes in the cluster in the following manner:

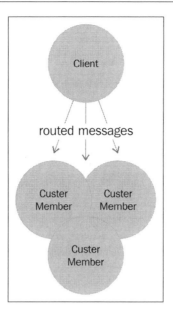

We have a three-node cluster running; thus, we can look at what we need to do to get a client to talk to it:

1. Enable cluster client in the server project.
2. The client must have the message that you want to send to the service.
3. The client must know about the cluster topology without being a member of the cluster itself. For this, we will use the Akka Cluster Client in the `Contrib` library.
4. The client must then know how to find the actors or routers it wants to send to and respond to cluster events.

Setting up the Server Project

In the server project, we added the dependencies necessary to use the cluster client. The Cluster client is in the `contrib` package, which are contributions from outside of the Akka team. We added the following dependency:

```
"com.typesafe.akka" %% "akka-contrib" % "2.3.6"
```

Then, in the configuration (`application.conf`), we added an akka extension for the client:

```
akka.extensions = ["akka.contrib.pattern.
ClusterReceptionistExtension"]
```

This will start the `ClusterReceptionist` on the server, which will handle all the details for our client to be able to talk to the cluster. The cluster receptionist actor is created on the root path in the server–`/user/receptionist`. We'll see how this is used shortly.

After doing that, our main need is to be updated to register the worker with the `ClusterReceptionist`. We'll use the balancing pool introduced in *Chapter 5, Scaling Up* to create a pool of actors on each server.

First, we'll look at the Java code:

```
public class Main {
     public static void main(String... args) {
 ActorSystem system = ActorSystem.create("Akkademy");
 ActorRefclusterController = system.actorOf(Props.
create(ClusterController.class), "clusterController");
         // router at /user/workers
ActorRef workers = system.actorOf(new BalancingPool(5).props(Props.
create(ArticleParseActor.class)), "workers");
         ((ClusterReceptionistExtension) akka.contrib.pattern.
ClusterReceptionistExtension.apply(system)).
 registerService(workers);
     }
}
```

You'll see that we have to cast the `ClusterReceptionistExtension`—we're calling the Scala API's apply method. This works perfectly fine for registering the workers.

The Scala example looks a little simpler:

```
object Main extends App {
 val system = ActorSystem("Akkademy")
 valclusterController = system.actorOf(Props[ClusterController],
"clusterController")
   // router at /user/workers
 val workers =
 system.actorOf(BalancingPool(5).props(Props[ArticleParseActor]),
"workers")
ClusterReceptionistExtension(system).registerService(workers)
 }
```

That's it! If you have nodes running, you'll want to restart them after making the changes.

Setting up the Client Project

We can create a new project for the client. Run `activator new` and select the language template of your choice.

Edit the `build.sbt` file in the new project. You'll need to add the following dependencies:

```
libraryDependencies ++= Seq(
    "com.typesafe.akka" %% "akka-actor" % "2.3.6",
    "com.typesafe.akka" %% "akka-cluster" % "2.3.6",
    "com.typesafe.akka" %% "akka-contrib" % "2.3.6"
)
```

You can add any test dependencies you might like as well, such as `junit` or `scalatest`. There is nothing new in our dependency list here.

Next, we have to make/modify `application.conf` to ensure the provider is correct are correct and set up the mailbox for the Cluster client:

```
akka {
    actor {
      provider = "akka.cluster.ClusterActorRefProvider"
    }
contrib.cluster.client {
      mailbox {
        mailbox-type = "akka.dispatch.UnboundedDequeBasedMailbox"
        stash-capacity = 1000
      }
    }
}
```

Be careful about providing too many messages before letting everything get connected! Messages will be stashed in the Cluster Client.

Sharing the Message Class between Client and Server

There are a few different ways in which you can share messages across client and server applications. You can build them both in the same project, you can include the server project in the client or vice versa, or you can have an extra project that contains the messages that both projects share. In *Chapter 2, Actors and Concurrency* this was demonstrated by publishing a library to the local repository. Nexus or Artifactory can be installed to host the assets as a solution for teams on closed-source projects. Sonatype's OSS Repository and Maven Central can be used for open source projects.

If you're following along, take whichever approach you like—preferably putting the messages in their own project. For the sake of simplicity, in the example, we can change the `ArticleParseActor` to accept and return strings:

```
//Java
match(String.class, x -> {
 ArticleParser.apply(x).
 onSuccess(body -> sender().tell(body, self())).
 onFailure(t -> sender().tell(new Status.Failure(t), self()));
//Scala
    case htmlString: String =>
 val body: String = ArticleParser(htmlString)
     sender() ! body
```

Changing messages over time can break your applications. Google's Protocol Buffers can be used in Akka for message serialization - you may want to learn how to utilize Protocol Buffers to managing changing messages over time.

Sending Messages to the Cluster

Now that we have the cluster configured to talk to the `contrib` package's Cluster Client, we can send messages to the cluster.

We'll take a random article from the Internet, grab the HTML source, and create a String variable called `articleToParse`.

We'll send that to a random member of the cluster, and we should then get back the body of the article from the service. We'll print the result. If you send it a few times, you will see it go to all members of the cluster.

The following is the Java code for the client project:

```
public static void main(String[] args) throws Exception {
        Timeout timeout = new Timeout(Duration.create(5, "seconds"));
ActorSystem system = ActorSystem.create("clientSystem");
        Set<ActorSelection>initialContacts = new
HashSet<ActorSelection>();
        initialContacts.add(system.actorSelection("akka.tcp://
Akkademy@127.0.0.1:2552/user/receptionist"));
```

```
initialContacts.add(system.actorSelection("akka.tcp://
Akkademy@127.0.0.1:2551/user/receptionist"));

  ActorRef receptionist = system.actorOf(ClusterClient.defaultProps(ini
tialContacts));

  ClusterClient.Sendmsg = new ClusterClient.Send("/user/workers",
articleToParse, false);

        Future f = Patterns.ask(receptionist, msg, timeout);
        String result = (String) Await.result(f, timeout.duration());
  System.out.println("result: " + result);
    }
```

And the following is the Scala code for the client project:

```
def main(args: Array[String]) {
  val timeout = new Timeout(Duration.create(5, "seconds"))
  val system = ActorSystem.create("clientSystem")
valinitialContacts: Set[ActorSelection] = Set(
      system.actorSelection("akka.tcp://Akkademy@127.0.0.1:2552/user/
receptionist"),
      system.actorSelection("akka.tcp://Akkademy@127.0.0.1:2551/user/
receptionist")
    )
   import collection.JavaConversions._
  val receptionist = system.actorOf(ClusterClient.
defaultProps(initialContacts))

  valmsg = ClusterClient.Send("/user/workers", articleToParse, false)

  val f = Patterns.ask(receptionist, msg, timeout)
  val result = Await.result(f, timeout.duration).asInstanceOf[String]
  println("result: " + result)
  }
```

We'll look at what is happening in the code step by step.

First, we define a `timeout` variable to use in our test here as we will ask and wait for the result. In real situations, you will likely be using an actual actor to send and receive—this is just for the sake of example. We create the actor system for the client.

Now, we need to produce the client that talks to the receptionist in the cluster. We create the contact list for the receptionists of the seed nodes for our client to talk to. After getting the set of seed node addresses, we can then create the `ClusterClient` actor:

```
system.actorOf(ClusterClient.defaultProps(initialContacts))
```

At this point, our application is able to connect to the cluster and get information about any changes to the cluster topology. The receptionist in the remote actor system will accept a few different messages:

- `ClusterClient.Send`: This sends a message to a random node.
- `ClusterClient.SendToAll`: This sends a message to all actors in the cluster.
- `ClusterClient.Publish`: This sends a message to all actors subscribed to a topic.

We only need to send the message to a random worker; so, `Send` is fine for our case. We make the Send object, describing which actor the message is destined for (the "workers" router running on each node of the cluster) and wrapping our message in it:

```
newClusterClient.Send("/user/workers", articleToParse, false)
```

Finally, we use ask to send the message to the receptionist `ActorRef` to deliver, and to get the result back (shown calling ask method, but in Scala we can also use the '?' operator):

```
Patterns.ask(receptionist, msg, timeout);
```

We take the future that ask gives us and wait for the result—again, this is only for the sake of an example. You never want to block threads by waiting in your code.

If a node becomes unavailable when you try to send it a message, your request will time out and fail. It is your responsibility to handle timeout and retry semantics, or otherwise handle failure cases.

That's all that it takes to use Akka to build distributed workers. Now, there are a lot of things we would want to do to further improve this system. If there are potentially lots of messages, we would likely want to put the messages somewhere other than in the mailbox in memory. Likely, some sort of durable queue or database would be used instead of ephemeral memory. Though, for real-time processing, this isn't a bad start. For a client, we would likely want to build timeout and retry mechanics as well to ensure that we always get the work done that we need done.

Building a Distributed Key Value Store

We've looked at everything that it takes to build on top of Akka cluster and we looked at a small example of a stateless cluster of workers. If state is involved, the problem becomes incredibly difficult to get right.

In the next section, we'll look at the watchouts, tools, and techniques for handling distributed systems that contain state such as a key-value store.

Disclaimer – Distributed Systems are Hard

Before we go on to look at how to build a distributed key-value store, I want to give you a word of warning.

It's not terribly difficult to build distributed systems that appear to work perfectly fine. You might get confident and feel that it's not all that hard after all. You'll tout yourself soon as an expert Distributed Systems Person. But stay humble – in reality, things fail, networks partition, and services become unavailable – and gracefully handling those scenarios without data loss or corruption is an incredibly difficult problem. Perhaps, even an unsolvable one with our network technology today.

How applications respond in those error cases can be more important than their primary functionality because failure is common and, in fact, is inevitable as you scale up.

 Remember that the network is not reliable. In a cluster of 1,000 nodes running in AWS, it's very likely that there will be some service interruption somewhere in your system at any given time.

So, how do all of these new-fangled `NoSql` data-stores actually stack up in their claims of availability and partition tolerance then? There is an interesting series of articles called *Jepsen* or *Call Me Maybe* on `aphyr.com` that tests several distributed system's documented claims about resiliency – you might be surprised by how your favorite technology fairs in some of the tests run in the articles.

This book will not be able to explain all of the techniques or examine all of the solutions to these problems, so all that I can do as the author is to warn you that it's a real can of worms and nobody has done a perfect job at solving the distribution problem yet.

Designing the Cluster

We are going to build a very simple three-node data-store to start demonstrating the techniques that can be used in distributed systems. We are going to look at a couple different designs so that you understand the techniques that are used and what the problems are that distributed systems try to solve.

First, let's begin talking about our cluster and how the client interacts with it. Ideally, we need our multi-node key-value store to offer a few features:

- Mechanisms for replicating data to gracefully handle a node partition
- Mechanism for giving a consistent view of replicated data — to give the most recent update when a client requests it (consistency)
- Mechanism for linear scalability — 20 nodes can handle twice as much throughput as 10 nodes

In terms of design goals in meeting those objectives, we would like to have a database that is highly available, partition tolerant, and able to give a consistent view of the most recent data. Achieving all three perfectly is not likely possible with our technology today, but we can take measures to try. We're lucky that a lot of very smart people have been working on these problems; thus, we have access to their research and publications.

Basic Key-Value Store Design

We've already looked at how a single node can store an object in a map with a key associated with it. Using a `HashMap` gives approximate constant time lookups, so it's a very efficient choice for storing data in memory.

An actor will accept `Get` messages with a key, and Put messages with a key and a value — exactly as demonstrated in *Chapter 2*, *Actors and Concurrency*. To recap, our node will have an actor that looks like the following:

```
//Java
    private AkkademyDb(){
        receive(ReceiveBuilder.
    match(SetRequest.class, message -> {
                        log.info("Received Set request: {}",
    message);
     map.put(message.key, message.value);
                        sender().tell(new Status.Success(message.
    key), self());
                    }).
                    match(GetRequest.class, message -> {
                        log.info("Received Get request: {}",
    message);
                        Object value = map.get(message.key);
                        Object response = (value != null)
                            ? value
                            : new Status.Failure(new
    KeyNotFoundException(message.key));
                        sender().tell(response, self());
                    }).
```

```
matchAny(o ->
                                        sender().tell(new Status.Failure(new
    ClassNotFoundException()), self())
                            ).build()
            );
        }

    //Scala
        override def receive = {
            case SetRequest(key, value) =>
                log.info("received SetRequest - key: {} value: {}", key, value)
    map.put(key, value)
                sender() ! Status.Success
            case GetRequest(key) =>
                log.info("received GetRequest - key: {}", key)
    val response: Option[Object] = map.get(key)
                response match{
                    case Some(x) => sender() ! x
                    case None => sender() ! Status.Failure(new
    KeyNotFoundException(key))
                }
            case o =>Status.Failure(new ClassNotFoundException)
        }
```

I would recommend that you add other messages for common use cases if you're going to attempt to implement this. Semantics like SetIfNotExist, which sends back a failure if the node is already there, is useful for handling concurrency consistently — getting and then setting the value if it does not exist is not at all consistent enough for a distributed workflow. Redis API docs are a good resource to look at if you want to see the types of messages and datatypes that are useful for a key-value store to handle with multiple clients — it's a simple and readable document that will go a long way to ramp you up in the problem space.

Coordinating Node

Now that we have a picture of how we'll store data in a node, we need to look a bit higher level at how we want messages to be handled between a client using the data-store and the cluster.

We have a client example that sends a message to a random node and that's actually quite a good start for most distributed stores because very often such systems will implement the concept of a coordinating node that can be any node in the cluster that will handle talking to other nodes in the cluster to handle the request.

It's probably unclear at this point exactly why we would do this, but let's imagine a coordinating node that needs to talk to three other nodes to get a definitive answer on what a value is.

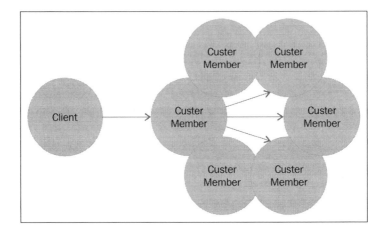

If we implement this logic, a client can send the request to any node in the cluster, and that node becomes the coordinator for the request. That node then goes to the other nodes and requests the data that it needs to make a decision on what the value is that is being retrieved. So, we can continue to use the random delivery mechanism if we implement the coordination logic on the server instead of the client. Because we're not sure where the client is located, it's safer to move this responsibility into the cluster itself — we can be more confident that the nodes we need to talk to have lesser leaps across the network in the majority of circumstances. This is how Cassandra handles requests for example.

We'll look at two models: one for storing a data set across multiple nodes and one for replicating data across multiple nodes.

Sharding for Linear Scalability

The first problem we will look to solve is how to assign a piece of a problem domain to different nodes in a cluster. In the case of storing data in a key-value store, it's easy to see how you might take slices of data (determined by the key) and assign them to different nodes. In Cassandra, a key used to determine which node data goes to is called a partition key.

For our use case of a very simple key-value store, we can take a key and hash it, and then execute modulus on the hash to get an integer value. Let's assume we have three nodes that we want to store data on. A request goes to a node in the cluster to store a key-value pair—for example, `foo` as the key and `bar` as the value. The coordinating node will execute `hashCode()` on the key:

```
"foo".hashCode()
  (101574)
```

Then, it will call the modulus operator on the `hashcode`, giving a result of `0`, `1`, or `2`:

```
101574 % 3
  (0)
```

Now, if we have three nodes that we want to store data on, then we know if we want to set or get a value with the key `foo` that it goes on the first node. This approach of sharding data is used in many distributed data-stores today.

Redundant Nodes

To have high availability and partition tolerance, we have to tolerate a node disappearing from the cluster for both reads and writes. If one node disappears, this should be a non-critical failure and the data-store should continue to operate to meet our goals.

To accomplish this, we can send all writes to three nodes and hope that the majority of them respond with an acknowledgment. If only two respond with an ok, we might be able to handle that on future reads. Now, all the intricacies of this mechanism— and specifically how to determine the ordering of events—cannot be covered here, but you can look at lamport clocks or vector clocks if you're motivated to get this right. We'll look at the mechanics at a high level here using simpler mechanics that are easier to comprehend.

Let's say a client wants to write a value for key `foo` of value `bar`, we want to persist this to three nodes. We'll try to write the value to three nodes from the coordinating node.

We can reference the previous diagram—a client will make a request to write and it goes to three nodes in the cluster. To have a successful write, we might agree that at least two of the nodes need to acknowledge the write, or maybe all three do. Adjusting these values tune how it responds to partitions and node failures.

Now, if we want to retrieve the value, then we can request the data from any of the three nodes as a starting point, but what if one node goes down and misses some writes? In this case, we can request the data from all three nodes, and require the same value from at least two nodes.

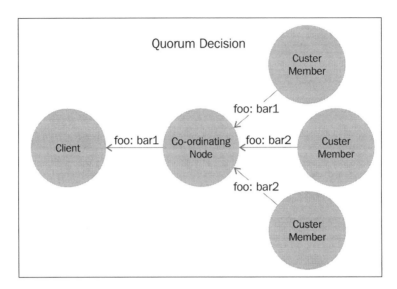

Now, we have some way of determining what the majority of nodes think the value is—we say that two nodes must have the same value to determine which it should be.

But how do we know the order of values? Was bar1 or bar2 written first? Which is more recent? We actually don't have any way of determining the ordering of messages, which it turns out is quite a problem. What happens if one node gets writes in a different order than another node? Cassandra has another read request type called a read repair request, which compares the data stored for a key on all of the replica nodes and tries to propagate the most recent write to the replicas.

The actual ordering of events is an interesting problem. You could start by using a timestamp in the record to determine which records are most recent, but we can't guarantee that all machines have the same clock or that events are occurring infrequently enough to trust the timestamp.

There are a couple of papers and algorithms you can look at that describe the problem and some solutions. Some of the items you may want to look at are Vector Clocks (Used by many distributed technologies such as Akka and Cassandra) and Dotted Version Vectors (used by Basho's Riak in recent versions).

- The Dynamo paper from Amazon describes the use of Vector Clocks in Amazon's Dynamo distributed key-value store—`http://www.allthingsdistributed.com/files/amazon-dynamo-sosp2007.pdf`

- Lamport wrote a paper on the problem of ordering in distributed systems in 1978 that is worth a look as well—`http://research.microsoft.com/en-us/um/people/lamport/pubs/time-clocks.pdf`

Combining Sharding and Replication

Once we have approaches in place for sharding and replication, we will be able to combine the two together by first sharding data into a ring and then replicating the data to the neighboring nodes. Let's say we have five partition keys, and we want to replicate the data across three nodes; with five nodes, we end up with a topology that looks like the following, with the numbers representing the hash of the partition key as demonstrated:

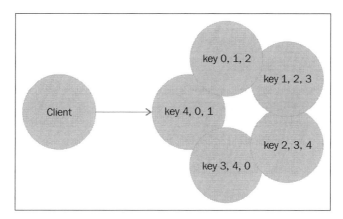

The request goes to a random node that becomes the coordinating node. That node would then calculate key partition key and go to the three nodes that have the data set. The retrieval and handing of the data at that point is no different than what we have looked at.

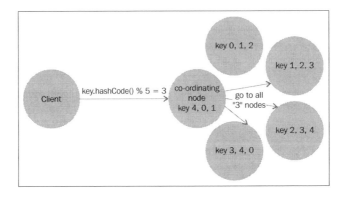

Pre-Sharding And Redistributing Keys to New Nodes

What happens if you want to be able to add new nodes? For example, what if you want to keep your replication factor of 3 and add two new nodes? If our partition key is only 0–4, then we can't move the data across new nodes.

The trick to this problem is to not use five partition keys but to use a much larger number. Cassandra has a concept of a vnode—a virtual node—whereby a cluster has a larger number of shards than nodes out of the gate. If you start by sharding your database into 64 or 128, then you can add new nodes and move a portion of the partition keys to new nodes as they come into the cluster.

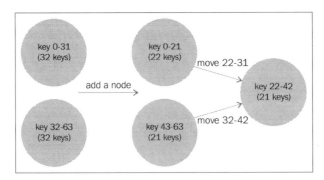

Then the coordinating node can talk to the new node, understanding it has been assigned a new set of partition keys. Note that moving data around to a new node is a one-time operation and likely requires you to stop all operations on all nodes until the re-distribution of partition keys is complete. If your partition is under heavy write through the operation, it might be difficult to ensure no data loss through the operation otherwise.

It will be simpler to assign a fixed size to the cluster until you can eventually get to these features. Akka Cluster has mechanisms to only start a cluster once it reaches a certain size. If you want to try building your own distributed key-value store, you should assume it has a fixed size and a known number of partition keys, and add pre-sharding and re-distributing keys as features later because they are non-trivial problems to solve.

Addressing Remote Actors

We've focused heavily on implementation details, but to round out this chapter, we should have a quick look at Actor Addressing again and how to get references to remote actors.

If we have an `ActorRef`, calling `actorRef.path()` will give us the actors URL—`akka://ActorSystem/user/actor`.

There are two parts to the path:

- **authority**: `akka://ActorSystem`
- **path**: `/user/actor`

Authority can be either local (`akka://ActorSystem`) or remote (`akka.tcp://ActorSystem@127.0.0.7`). The path will be the same for both local and remote actors (`/user/actor` for example).

An `ActorRef` will have an `ActorPath` with a fragment `#123456`, which is what is called the actor's UID. An `ActorPath` will not—it will just have the path.

We looked at `ActorSystem.actorSelection` earlier, which will let us look up an Actor with any path and send it messages:

```
ActorSelectionactorSelection = actorSystem.actorSelection("akka.tcp://
ActorSystem@127.0.0.7/user/my-actor");
valactorSelection = actorSystem.actorSelection("akka.tcp://
ActorSystem@127.0.0.7/user/my-actor")
```

That gives us an actor selection, which we can send messages to. Although, the actor selection does not assume that an actor exists. If we send messages to an `ActorSelection` and the actor does not exist, the message will disappear. Thus, we can look up an actor and get an `ActorRef` for a remote actor.

Using akka.actor.Identify to Find a Remote Actor

All actors by default accept a message — `akka.actor.Identify`. We can create a new Identify message and send it to an actor to get an `ActorRef`:

```
Identify msg = new Identify(messageId)
  Future<ActorIdentity> identity = (Future<ActorIdentity>) Patterns.
ask(actor, msg, timeout);
valmsg = Identify(messageId)
  val identity: Future[ActorIdentity] = (sentinelClient ? msg).
mapTo[ActorIdentity]
```

We will receive a response — `ActorIdentity(messageId, Some(actorRef))`, or `ActorIdentity((path, client), None)` — showing that an actor is either present or absent. This gives us a mechanism for determining if a remote actor exists and obtaining an `ActorRef` for it.

Homework

This chapter is a blend of theory and technique. We covered how to use Akka cluster to run work on and then how to use it to distribute datasets partitioned by key. The problems are too big to cover in an introductory chapter to Cluster, but if you try to approach some of the problems presented in this chapter, you should start to get a good handle on how people solve some of these problems today.

- Build your own worker queue using Cluster.

- Build a distributed key-value store with replication.

- Try to solve the linearization problem — how can you determine ordering? How can you "repair" nodes that fail and then recover?

- Build a distributed key-value store with sharding.

- Can you combine sharding and replication with minimal changes to the code you have now as described?

- In the sharded model, can you develop a way to redistribute data to new nodes? Is it harder to do this with replication? About the same difficulty?

- If you build a project, you should open source it and share your discoveries and learning!

Summary

In this chapter, we covered the basics of how you might design some different distributed systems. This gives you a few models that you can use for various problems—don't simply think of sharding/partitioning when dealing with data—you can use similar techniques for many real-time system problems to be able to scale out.

If you'd like to learn more about the techniques introduced here, you should both continue your learning and try to build the solutions to these problems yourself. In my humble opinion, the best way to learn is to teach and share, so try to start a distributed computing club or otherwise get some presentations together for your peers on how these technologies work—organizing your thoughts will help you get into the details and find your own way in discovering how we're moving to solve these types of distributed computing problems today.

In the next chapter, we'll discuss what happens in mailboxes when our actors get put under heavy load and look at how we can adjust mailbox configuration to adapt to those conditions.

7

Handling Mailbox Problems

Congratulations! You've made it through all of the tough content now. You've learned Akka, you've learned how to scale it, and how to describe your system's behavior in those situations!

In this chapter, we will look at what happens when you start to hit the limits of your actor system and how to describe how your system should behave in those situations.

Let's start by setting the stage for the problem and then look at different approaches we can use to overcome these issues.

Overwhelming your weakest link

To continue our running example, imagine we have an application that extracts articles and stores the body in our key-value store. The extracted articles are then displayed on various devices that have a reader application.

You've launched the application and have a growing user base. Everything is working fine. People can request articles to read from the device on their application; it hits a public REST API, which makes a request to the parse service. The parse service will check the store and, if the article has not been parsed, then it will parse it and then cache it.

The following figure represents the flow of articles as they are parsed and stored:

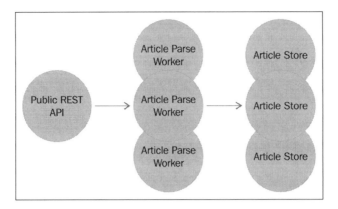

Let's imagine a day when several good events happen. Our app shows up in the number 1 spot, for example on Hacker News, all day and we get 10x more traffic than we have ever seen.

First, we start to see timeouts in the REST API application. Response times balloon when making requests from the API. Eventually, the article parse services crash with out-of-memory errors, so we start to analyze the traffic in the application under load. Because article parsing is the most processing intensive piece of the application, lots of messages will get queued there. This is the slowest service in our data flow.

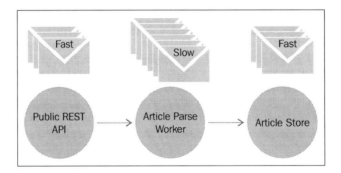

Remember that messages go into a mailbox in memory. If a service is consuming messages slower than the rate at which they are delivered, then mailboxes will become more and more full. Let's look at the events that occurred when we saw the load, in a bit more detail to understand why they occur. We can look at different ways in which we can configure our application to make sure it stays up the next time we're overwhelmed like this.

Ballooning response times

The first thing we'll see when we start overwhelming our slow article parse worker consumer is increasing response times. If our ArticleParser can process 100 articles in a second, and we send it 101 articles a second, then messages will slowly accumulate. After 1,000 seconds, there will be 1,000 messages queued up in the mailbox.

Once there is a queue of messages, any messages that have been received first will need to be processed before any new messages can be processed, so what we will see is response times start to grow.

The more these unhandled messages are queued, the longer it takes to process new messages.

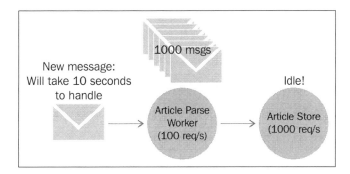

A slow consumer of messages will cause downstream problems as well. If you have a very fast consumer behind a slow consumer, your response times will be primarily affected by your slowest consumer. So we have to focus on the slowest consumer to make our system respond better. One of our goals in a reactive system design is to ensure it is always responsive, so this violates the responsiveness principle.

Crashing

If we continue to try to push more and more messages through the system, we'll eventually have a very large number of messages in the slow message consumer's mailbox, which causes a far worse problem to occur—crashes due to out-of-memory errors.

Once response times get to this point, people trying to use the service are probably going to be hitting retry again and again, piling even more messages into the mailbox of our already overburdened services.

The default mailbox is unbounded, meaning that the service will accumulate messages indefinitely. Resources are limited—the JVM only has so much memory available—so eventually the slow message consumer will have so many messages in memory that the JVM will not have the memory needed to create new objects and will crash.

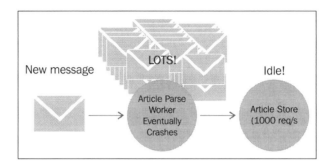

If we have a cluster of workers, as demonstrated in the previous chapter, the crashing of one node in the cluster means that other members of the cluster will suddenly start receiving more messages. The effect is usually a cascading one—more messages go to the other nodes and eventually they will crash as well. When the whole system goes down, then we're completely unavailable.

Resiliency

We've covered the reactive tenets in previous chapters. The behavior of our application violates a couple of the reactive tenets: resiliency and responsiveness.

We'll ignore responsiveness for now and focus on how we can change our application to stay up instead of crashing when it's overwhelmed.

The crashing is caused by an unbounded mailbox, so we can start by changing the mailbox of the actor. An unbounded mailbox is an un-defensive position—we assert that our application will always catch up and handle messages if we don't put a limit on its size.

Mailboxes

Up to this point, we've largely ignored mailboxes. We've simply known that messages get placed there, and then messages are processed. That's a perfectly fine level of abstraction for you until you're facing a reasonably large scale usage. That's why this chapter is at the end of this book—you're introduced to the mailbox very early, but you might not need to tune it until you're handling real traffic.

Configuring mailboxes

Mailboxes are configured in Akka in one of several different ways. You can refer to the Akka Mailboxes documentation (https://doc.akka.io/docs/akka/snapshot/scala/mailboxes.html) if you need more details.

In nearly all cases, actors get their own mailboxes, with the exception being BalancingDispatcher used by BalancingPool, which shares a mailbox between all of its actors as covered in *Chapter 5, Scaling Up*. So there are two areas where an Actor's mailbox is determined — in the actor configuration and in the dispatcher configuration.

We'll cover the different ways in which the mailbox configuration can be set.

Selecting a mailbox in deployment configuration

We've programmatically defined and instantiated actors. Akka's deployment configuration can also be used to configure actors and routers from the configuration file.

You can define an actor's mailbox (by actor path) in the deployment configuration. If this is defined, this will take priority over any other configured mailboxes. In application.conf, you would define an actor's mailbox like the following:

```
akka.actor.deployment {
  /myactor {
     mailbox = default-mailbox
   }
}
```

The actor created at /user/myactor would then have the default mailbox:

```
ActorRefclusterController = system.actorOf(Props.create(MyActor.
class), "myactor");

system.actorOf(Props[MyActor], "myactor")
```

Selecting a mailbox in code

You can also define which mailbox is used in code. Props has a withMailbox method that can be called to assign a mailbox when the actor is created:

```
ActorRefclusterController = system.actorOf(Props.create(MyActor.
class).withMailbox("default-mailbox"));

system.actorOf(Props[MyActor].withMailbox("default-mailbox")
```

Deciding which mailbox to use

The default mailbox will work with all use cases including `BalancingPool/BalancingDispatcher`, where a mailbox is shared between multiple actors.

Unless you're using the `BalancingPool`, you will always have a single consumer of messages from the mailbox.

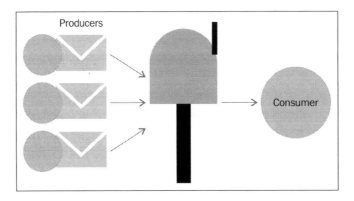

Instead of using the default mailbox, in this case you can use `SingleConsumerOnlyUnboundedMailbox`, which can be more efficient than the default mailbox in most cases (remember to always measure performance related changes). The only time you cannot use this mailbox is with `BalancingPool/BalancingDispatcher`, where multiple actors consume messages from the same mailbox. The queue implementation is single-consumer only.

First we'll define a mailbox in our application.conf:

```
akka.actor.mymailbox{
    mailbox-type = "akka.dispatch.SingleConsumerOnlyUnboundedMailbox"
}
```

Then we can make the actors with the mailbox:

```
ActorRefclusterController = system.actorOf(Props.create(MyActor.class).withMailbox("akka.actor.mymailbox"));

system.actorOf(Props[MyActor].withMailbox("akka.actor.mymailbox")
```

We will often need to decide whether we want to use a bounded or unbounded mailbox. Unbounded mailboxes are preferable in most cases for performance reasons, but what we've set out to do in our example is to use a bounded mailbox to drop messages. We don't want to run out of memory if we get overwhelmed — we would rather drop some messages.

There are two types of bounded mailboxes—blocking and non-blocking. All mailboxes are backed by queues. Blocking versus non-blocking in this case means that the delivery of a message to a full mailbox will either cause the thread to wait until there is room (blocking) or will drop the message (non-blocking.) We've decided to drop the messages so we can settle on the `NonBlockingBoundedMailbox`. We'll add the mailbox in our configuration:

```
akka.actor.boundedmailbox{
   mailbox-type = "akka.dispatch.NonBlockingBoundedMailbox"
   mailbox-capacity = 1000000
 }
```

And then instantiate the actors with it:

```
ActorRefclusterController = system.actorOf(Props.create(MyActor.
class).withMailbox("akka.actor.boundedmailbox"));

 system.actorOf(Props[MyActor].withMailbox("akka.actor.
boundedmailbox")
```

Now, if our system gets overwhelmed, we'll lose some messages, but things will stay up.

What happens if messages get dropped? Well, your systems that communicate with downstream systems should have timeout and retry semantics baked in. You can expect that messages will get dropped occasionally, so if you need at least once processing, you need to build your systems to keep track of requests and retry them if they fail for any reason. In the case of our example application, the client will probably get an error, so the user can choose to retry. In your own systems, timeout and retry mechanisms can easily be built.

Prioritizing messages in mailboxes

There are two other families of mailboxes that you should be aware of: priority mailboxes and control aware mailboxes. They both serve a similar purpose: allowing the ordering of messages.

Priority mailboxes allow messages to be prioritized and sorted after they are delivered to the mailbox. This has a fairly significant performance overhead: the queue that backs the mailbox—java `BlockingPriorityQueue`—has to reorder messages as they come in, which means that both producers and consumers of the queue have to wait around while messages are shuffled around. Fortunately, there aren't many cases where reordering messages is important, so you won't need to use these mailboxes in most use cases.

There is one case, though, that would be common, and that's if you need to give your actor some sort of control message to let them know that something has changed that will affect how they process any queued messages.

Fortunately, there is another mailbox type—a `ControlMessageAware` mailbox—that handles messages with an efficient queue but allows any message that extends `akka.dispatch.Controlmessage` goes to the front of the queue. This is a much better solution than priority mailboxes and should be your preference if you need to get a message to an actor in front of the rest of the queue without more complex ordering.

We don't need to look at these in depth as they are very rarely used, but it's important to understand that they do exist. The Akka documentation covers their use in greater detail.

As one final note, it's worth mentioning that if none of the mailboxes fit your use case, then you can create your own.

Staying responsive under load

We've now looked at how we can drop messages if we get overwhelmed. This lets our application stay up instead of running out of memory if the mailbox gets too full.

Let's take a minute to look at what happens with our application once it gets under a very heavy load now.

The application is humming along, and then some promotion of your app happens again and sends way more traffic to the site than we anticipate or are provisioned to handle. Just as before, more messages start coming in than we have the capacity to handle, so they begin to build up in the mailbox. It starts to take longer to handle a given message because we have to handle the backlog of messages in the mailbox first.

Eventually, under the continued heavy load, the mailbox will reach the bounded limit we configured. At this point, it will start dropping messages. If we had used the blocking bounded mailbox, then the thread would sit and wait until the message could be placed in the mailbox. Either way, now we have a way of ensuring our application doesn't crash.

But is this a good solution? We can look at the bounded mailbox capacity at a few levels and determine how we can expect our applications to behave:

- If we have a very small bounded mailbox, any spikes in traffic will cause messages to be lost, which the application might be able to respond to in a reasonable amount of time

- If we have a very large bounded mailbox, the requests will likely time out before the actor can reply to them

In either case, the user has to wait for the timeout to occur. If the mailbox is very small, the dropped message will simply disappear and, so, anyone waiting on a reply will timeout and fail. If the mailbox is very large or unbounded, even if the message is eventually processed, anyone waiting for a reply will eventually timeout and fail, for example, in their browser or dependent application. You'll have to evaluate your use case to see if either of these are suitable—if you don't care about the response or can tolerate messages being lost during spikes in traffic, then these may be acceptable.

For most cases, in real-time systems, waiting for very long periods of time is not acceptable, especially waiting just to receive an error.

Circuit breakers

With responsiveness as a goal in our systems, any of the situations where we make users wait for failure are not really acceptable. Similarly, with resiliency as a goal, allowing systems to become overwhelmed with messages to the point that a component fails completely is not acceptable either.

Circuit breaker is a pattern where some path through your application is monitored for the latency of the responses or error. Messages pass through the circuit breaker as they normally would, with the response time on the messages being measured. This state is "closed."

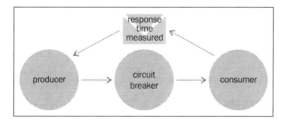

Once a certain latency threshold is reached, the circuit breaker will change states to 'open' and will immediately fail all requests.

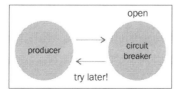

Then, after a period of time, the circuit breaker will change states to "'half-open'" and try sending a request.

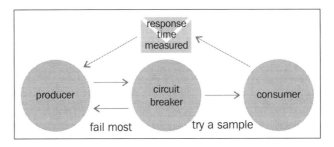

If the request comes back quickly, we can assume that the service has recovered and the circuit breaker can change states back to "open".

It turns out that this is exactly what we want.

If the circuit breaker opens, in this condition this system gains the following:

- **Responsiveness**: The service will respond with failures quickly
- **Resiliency**: Instead of overwhelming downstream services until they crash, the circuit breaker will let them recover

Note that the circuit breaker will also respond to errors the same way as timeouts. If many errors are occurring, it will also cause the circuit breaker to open. The Akka circuit breaker does not discriminate between timeouts and other failures (this is probably what we want!) but you can certainly implement your own if you want to change that behavior. If a downstream system starts failing under heavy load, we can often make similar assumptions—that it needs time to recover from the load—so, often the circuit breaker pattern will be a good idea to implement in order to protect downstream systems.

Circuit breaker listeners

We might not know exactly how and when our circuit breakers will trip when we put them into production. So, what we want to do is to collect data. Remember, we always want to measure any assertions we make about how things actually perform as we're often very, very wrong.

Fortunately, the circuit breaker has hooks that let us add behavior on the different events that occur—onOpen, onClose, and onHalfOpen.

You want to alert, or at least log, on these events so that you can determine how your circuit breakers are behaving.

Circuit breaker examples

Circuit breakers work on futures, not on actors, so they have a use beyond only using them for actors. Even if you're not using Akka in your project, you should consider whether circuit breakers can be used to protect your systems.

We'll have a look at a simple CircuitBreaker example now in front of a service that takes some time to respond. For the example, we'll use a local actor, but we'll add a delay to the response to simulate network time and processing time.

To see the circuit breaker in action, we'll make a producer that produces messages at a slightly faster rate than the target actor can handle. We'll make a producer that produces messages every 50 ms and we'll make the consumer take 70 ms to respond. This way, messages will slowly queue and the response times will get larger and larger until the circuit breaker trips.

We'll use the key-value store example again and introduce the 70 ms delay.

In Java:

```
                          match(GetRequest.class, message -> {
    Thread.sleep(70); //slow down the actor's response
                          Object value = map.get(message.key);
                          Object response = (value != null)
                              ? value
                              : new Status.Failure(new
    KeyNotFoundException(message.key));
                          sender().tell(response, self());
```

In Scala:

```
    case GetRequest(key) =>
  Thread.sleep(70)
  val response: Option[Object] = map.get(key)
        response match {
          case Some(x) => sender() ! x
          case None => sender() ! Status.Failure(new
  KeyNotFoundException(key))
        }
```

In our calling class, we'll create a circuit breaker that will trip when latency becomes greater than one second.

In Java:

```
CircuitBreaker breaker =
                new CircuitBreaker(system.scheduler(),
                    10,
  FiniteDuration.create(1, "second"),
  FiniteDuration.create(1, "second"),
  system.dispatcher()).
  onOpen(() -> {
  System.out.println("circuit breaker opened!");
                        }).
  onClose(() -> {
  System.out.println("circuit breaker opened!");
                        }).
  onHalfOpen(() -> {
  System.out.println("circuit breaker opened!");
                        });
```

In Scala:

```
val breaker =
    new CircuitBreaker(system.scheduler,
  maxFailures = 10,
  callTimeout = 1 seconds,
  resetTimeout = 1 seconds).
  onOpen(println("circuit breaker opened!")).
  onClose(println("circuit breaker closed!")).
  onHalfOpen(println("circuit breaker half-open"))
```

You can see the parameter names in the Scala example — they are equivalent. We build the CircuitBreaker with the following:

- Max number of failures before the breaker trips (either timeout or failure in the future)
- The call timeout (what latency to fail at)
- The reset timeout (how long to wait before changing to half-open and trying a request)

Then, we also register a log event on the circuit breaker opening, changing state to half open and changing the state to close.

Using the circuit breaker is simple — we supply a `0-argument` lambda that returns a future (a `producer` function.) For our example, we'll use `ask`.

We'll make a call every 50 ms, and the actor will respond in 70 ms, so the messages will queue. Then the mailbox will fill, response times will balloon, and eventually the circuit breaker will open.

In Java:

```
Timeout timeout = Timeout.apply(2000);

ActorRefdb = system.actorOf(Props.create(SlowAkkademyDb.class));
Await.result(Patterns.ask(db, new SetRequest("key", "value"),
timeout), timeout.duration());

for(inti=0; i<10000000; i++){
        Future future = breaker.callWithCircuitBreaker(()
->Patterns.ask(db, new GetRequest("key"),  timeout));
toJava(future).handle((x,t) -> {
                if(t != null){
System.out.println("got it: " + x);
                }else{
System.out.println("error: " + t.toString());
                }

            return null;
        });

Thread.sleep(50);
        }
```

In Scala:

```
 implicit val timeout = Timeout(2 seconds)
valdb = system.actorOf(Props[FastSlowAkkademyDb])
Await.result(db ? SetRequest("key", "value"), 2 seconds)

  (1 to 1000000).map(x => {
Thread.sleep(50)
valaskFuture = breaker.withCircuitBreaker(db ? GetRequest("key"))
askFuture.map(x => "got it: " + x).recover({
    case t => "error: " + t.toString
  }).foreach(x =>println(x))
})
```

In some cases, you might want to roll out your own circuit breaker or be careful with what you consider to be a failure in a future. The circuit breaker counts any and all failures and will trip after the maxFailures is reached. If your futures fail in ways that you don't want your circuit breaker to fail, you can wrap the responses in a `Try` instead of failing the future so that the future is successful.

There is one more strategy that you can think about to overcome overwhelming your consumers. If you have a hot producer—something that will endlessly send requests—then you might want to turn the way you supply messages around so that actors ask for messages to process instead of simply receiving endless piles of messages.

Another related concept—"Back-Pressure"—talks about slowing down the flow of messages to what the slowest consumer can handle to avoid overwhelming downstream systems. You can certainly implement something like this yourself but the Reactive Streams proposal deals with this specific problem with a defined standard.

From `https://www.reactive-streams.org/`—Reactive Streams is an initiative to provide a standard for asynchronous stream processing with non-blocking back pressure. This encompasses efforts aimed at runtime environments (JVM and JavaScript) as well as network protocols.

There are now multiple implementations of Reactive Streams, including one from the Akka team (Akka Streams). Reactive Streams is a fairly large topic, so we won't introduce the technologies here, but know that people are working on this problem actively and it might be worth looking at Reactive Streams—in particular if you have "hot" producers that have a nearly endless supply of requests that they can make.

Reactive Streams take a blend of approaches, both receiving requests with a mechanism to slow flow down if a service becomes overwhelmed (back-pressure) and asking for extra work if there is capacity in the pipe line.

Reactive Streams is an exciting topic, but is still in its infancy at the time of writing. Akka Streams is still marked experimental but is nearing GA and Typesafe are spending a lot of time in holding seminars and letting people know about the progress in the space.

You can learn more about Reactive Streams at `http://www.reactive-streams.org/`.

The Akka Streams Reactive Streams implementation documentation can be found at `http://doc.akka.io/docs/akka-stream-and-http-experimental/snapshot/`.

Homework

You should try to build an application that overwhelms a mailbox and then try different approaches to stop the mailbox from being overwhelmed.

- Try overwhelming a mailbox in a local actor system (you can sleep the actor's thread by a few milliseconds to simulate the effect processing has on throughput). See how the application behaves.

- Try overwhelming a mailbox in a distributed application built with cluster. Try sending very large messages instead of implementing delays. What do you observe in the health of the cluster when it is overwhelmed with messages? What happens to the health of the cluster when the network is overwhelmed?

- Can you think of a solution to the observed issue of the network reaching saturation?

- Try to implement reactive streams and see if you can stop any errors from occurring. (It will take some effort to learn reactive streams as the material is not covered here.)

Summary

This chapter is at the end stages of this book because you might not need to think of mailbox too much in your day to day activities. It's important to understand the effects that changes to the mailbox have in your systems. Implementing a bounded mailbox might seem like a good choice to stop you systems from crashing, but we want to respond to the user as fast as possible—even in failure scenarios—so it will often be better to fail quickly instead of drop messages once your systems are at their capacity. This chapter introduced you a few of the tools you can use to adapt your applications once they are running at very high scale and are being pushed to their limit.

In the next chapter, we will be learning about behavior-driven testing and development. We will also take a look at domain modeling with actors and classes.

8
Testing and Design

While both testing and design-related items have been demonstrated throughout this book, they were presented as secondary to the specific details of the toolkit that were being introduced. Now that much of the Akka toolkit has been introduced, we're going to examine some general approaches to design and testing in somewhat greater detail.

Testing and design may seem like unrelated topics, but they have a tendency to affect one another. For code to be testable, it has to be reasonably designed. Also, if code is well designed, it will inherently be easy to make assertions about its behavior and to test them.

On the topic of testing, we will explore the basic concepts in **Behavior Driven Development (BDD)**—and see how we can both document and test our Actors with those approaches. Good testing approaches are one of the most powerful tools for documenting and describing our code. Tests cannot go out of date or deviate from the application's behavior—generally, as soon as they have lost their validity, they will fail and, therefore, force the engineer to change them to reflect the application's behavior.

On the topic of design, we will cover a few basic strategies on the level of code in actors that can help ease the task of testing their behavior. However, we will also examine how we can keep our application flexible and easy to maintain as it grows by creating context boundaries around different pieces of our application. We'll examine how and where we may want to make those boundaries and will look at how it relates to scaling in Akka.

We will cover the following topics in this chapter:

- Domain-driven design and modeling with Actors and Classes
- Behavior-driven testing and development

Example problem

For this chapter, we're going to pick up a new problem from scratch so that we can go over the process of doing some analysis and design and use that work to test and build. For the example in this chapter, we'll look at how we might build pieces of a chatroom application. You work in an organization and have been asked to produce something for use within the office. As it's meant for use inside a private network, the client can talk to the server using `Akka remoting`.

Looking at the macro level, our supported feature set might look something like the following:

- Application will have a lobby where different chatrooms are displayed
- From the lobby, users can join a chatroom or leave a chatroom
- When a user joins a chatroom, they will receive a recent history of the chat
- Obviously, whenever someone posts, everyone will receive the update that who is in the room

The user client will be written by some other team, and then it will interact with our application. As it's a native application, or a swing application, we don't need an HTTP API and we can use actor remoting to interact with the actors.

Approaching application design

There are arguably a couple of approaches that can be taken when writing code—the more traditional waterfall approaches where design and analysis are done upfront, and then code is built, or the Agile, especially Extreme Programming, camps, where you might keep upfront analysis to a minimum, and instead iteratively build and refactor your code to good design as you go.

Realistically, it's never one case or the other as you'll always do some analysis upfront, and you'll always make discoveries as you build that will force you to rethink and redesign your solution until completion. However, looking at some projects a few years after inception I can say that when you're starting a new project, you want to get the application foundation designed correctly or you'll be building on a rickety tower for years to come.

As we're starting a new piece of work here, I think it's prudent to look at the design before we begin. We'll work from the top down to see how we can slice the application into separate components to be able to build and test each one in isolation. By separating pieces of the domain into distinct modules, we can ensure we build simpler pieces. You can assign a developer to work on one piece, and he/she will be able to pick it up and understand it in a few days without needing to understand the entire system from front to back.

To begin designing our chat application, we can look at how we might create a domain model to represent what we're trying to build in a way that is simple and clear. Using object-oriented approaches, we aim to build classes that blend behavior and data while not knowing too much about the pieces it interacts with. Creating classes that have these qualities allows our application to change and grow over time with minimal cost.

Looking at the brief description of requirements, it's easy to identify a few major entities of the domain:

- **Chatroom**: A chatroom has a topic or name that uniquely identifies it.
- **User**: When a user registers, they acquire a username.
- **Lobby**: A lobby contains a list of chatrooms. It may contain a list of active users as well. Likely one lobby exists but, as our application scales, it's possible that we may network together multiple offices or create different lobbies for different teams.

I also find it very helpful to talk about where state may exist in the problem upfront. Because we have an asynchronous environment where several users are interacting with server state at the same time, it will help us decide how to best use Akka to build the application. The following areas could have state:

- **Lobby**: It will contain a list of all chatrooms
- **Chatroom**: It will contain a history of messages and a list of all current users who need to receive updates to the chat

We know that Akka is a very good choice for encapsulating state in concurrent systems, so likely these areas are good targets to implement with actors.

High-Level design

Our chatroom will have a client/server model. We now know that it has a client that is accessed by a user, and then on the server side we have a lobby and a chatroom as distinct elements of the domain. By creating a clear context boundary around those three elements, we can look at any one of them in isolation.

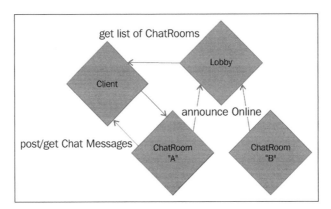

We can look at the interactions of the components of the domain in the following way:

- Client gets a list of chatrooms from the lobby
- When new chatrooms come online, they announce that they are available so that clients can see them
- Clients can join the chatrooms
- Clients can post messages to the chat chatrooms
- Clients will receive updates from the chat chatrooms

We'll look at turning this into specifications shortly, but by listing out basic interactions we can identify the components of the problem. Listing the components, we can draw context boundaries that separate them, allowing us to work on each of these components in isolation from the other elements. We also gain the ability to easily test these components if we don't couple them together.

As one final benefit, with what we know about Akka's location transparency, if we keep the chatroom separate from the lobby we could likely run chatrooms on different servers. One lobby could let everyone know what rooms are available, and then we could scale the chatrooms out as needed. Now that we have a picture of the higher-level components, we can pick one of the components and focus on designing it.

Designing, building, and testing the Domain model

Designing, building, and testing are very much intertwined pieces of the development process. There are numerous approaches that we could take. I'm going to prescribe some upfront analysis describing the domain model and its behaviors, and then use that written analysis to extract the domain model and produce tests. In the following section, we'll look specifically at the chatroom and how users interact with it.

Specifications

I'm going to make the assumption that you have used a chatroom of some sort before, such as Slack, Hipchat, Google Hangouts, or Campfire. If you haven't used any of those tools, you should evaluate introducing one into your development team—group chat can be a real boon for engineering teams. We'll focus on an individual chatroom design for the moment, and we can start by describing our expectations for the behavior of the chatroom. A few simple statements about the application's behavior in different contexts can easily be used as lightweight specifications that can drive our building and testing.

Behavioral specifications can be used for lightweight design documentation and tests. A useful format for writing specifications is the Given When Then format:

- Given the world is in a particular state
- When some event occurs
- Then some observable outcome is expected

In this format, we are describing the context or state of the application, the event that occurs in the application or to the application, and then the consequence or observable outcome of that action. You might be able to see how unit tests are often informally broken up into those three distinct concerns as well—setup, action, and assertion.

For a chatroom actor, we might define the behavior for a few simple scenarios in the following way.

- **Scenario**: User Joins Chatroom:
    - Given a chatroom has no users, when it receives a request from a user to join the chatroom, then it should add the user to its list of joined users
    - Given a chatroom has a chat history, when a user joins the chatroom, then it should receive the last 10 posts to the chatroom from the history

- **Scenario**: Post to chatroom:

  ○ Given a chatroom has a joined user, when the chatroom receives a request to post to the chatroom from a user in the room, then it should update the chat history

  ○ Given a chatroom has a joined user, when the chatroom receives a request to post to the chatroom, then it should notify the joined users

These are basic and incomplete specifications, but there is enough here to demonstrate. We can add more specifications later and change the behavior of the application to accommodate those additions.

Designing the Domain model

Now that we have this written down, we can actually use this to both design and test. The great thing about specifications and the language that we use when talking to each other about the problem domain is that it makes designing and naming quite simple. *Eric Evans*, in his book *Domain Driven Design*, describes the words that we and the users use when talking about the application and calls that the **Ubiquitous Language**. The great thing about the ubiquitous language that we are using is that it hints at both the structure and the names that we may want to use in our domain model.

If we revisit the specifications we just wrote for the chatroom, we can pull out all the pieces of the domain model described with our ubiquitous language and just make a list of those elements:

- Chatroom
- User
- Join chatroom request
- Joined users
- Post to chatroom
- Chat history

Quite incredibly, by writing down the specifications, we've described most of the domain model! We can look at the specifications and pull out everything we can identify with the words that we use to describe the things. The only piece left is deciding how to arrange it all together. We know that, in object-oriented programming, we want to group behavior and data wherever possible, so we'll use that as a heuristic for placing related data and behavior in classes. And we know that Akka helps us deal with state, so we'll also use that heuristic to understand what would benefit from being an actor.

We can deduce the following:

- Chat room has a list of user references called `joinedUsers`, which can change (state)
- Chat room has a list of posts called `chatHistory`, which can change (state)
- Join request contains a user reference

The chatroom itself will probably benefit from being an actor as it contains state. Nothing else needs to have any mutating state, so we can use immutable objects for the other elements we identified. We can get to building and testing now that we have an idea of what our domain model looks like and now that we have specifications describing its behavior.

Testing and building the Domain model

Now that we have identified the elements of the domain, we can proceed with testing and building. Often developer unit testing and building the items to be tested benefit from being done together as one task. It's easier to capture all the small edge cases in tests if you write the tests while building the behavior, so you end up with a nice set of unit tests that describe the behavior you've expressed when all is said and done. If you've never used the Test Driven and Behavior Driven approaches, I would encourage experimenting with these approaches while you work as you are much more likely to end up with a useful set of tests than if you approach testing after you finish building.

The approach that I'll introduce is to take the specification, write a test that translates the specification, and then fill out the code to make that test/specification pass.

First, we know that users exist remotely, so a good place to start is by modeling that remote item. We'll have some sort of user entity representation somewhere else, but the chatroom doesn't need to be concerned with it necessarily. The chatroom only needs to know where to send updates to and information to get the entity information for display. We don't have the user entity modeled at this point, so we'll just use a simple `UserRef` in our case.

In Java:

```java
public class UserRef {
    public final ActorRef actor;
    public final String username;
    public UserRef(ActorRef actor, String username) {
  this.actor = actor;
```

```
this.username = username;
        }
    }
```

In Scala:

```
case class UserRef(actor: ActorRef, name: String)
```

The `UserRef` will have the name to display and then an actor ref that we can send updates to. This is all the user info that the chatroom itself will need at this point in time.

The chatroom has to keep two pieces of data: joined users and chat history. Because these items represent state, and multiple users will be trying to access and change the state, we can guess that the chatroom itself would benefit from being an actor. Because the chatroom will be an actor, we'll model the Post request and Join request as immutable messages. We'll call them starting with a verb name (this may be a small deviation from Java naming conventions but is common with message names). This is expressive of the intent of the message. Then we will have the message include any data relevant to the request.

In Java:

```java
public class Messages {
    static public class JoinChatroom {
        public final UserRefuserRef;
        public JoinChatroom(UserRefuserRef) {
  this.userRef = userRef;
        }
    }
    static public class PostToChatroom{
        public final String line, username;
        public PostToChatroom(String line, String username) {
  this.line = line;
this.username = username;
        }
    }
}
```

In Scala:

```scala
case class JoinChatroom(userRef: UserRef)
case class PostToChatroom(line: String, username: String)
```

Now that we have the messages, we can build the skeleton of the chatroom. We won't implement any logic yet—just create the actor. Because we also know the state, we can add those fields to the actor as well at this point:

- Chatroom has a list of user references called joinedUsers, which can change (state)

- Chatroom has a list of posts called chatHistory, which can change (state)

In Java:

```java
public class Chatroom extends AbstractActor{
    List<Messages.PostToChatroom>chatHistory = new
ArrayList<Messages.PostToChatroom>();
    List<UserRef>joinedUsers = new ArrayList<UserRef>();
    @Override
    public PartialFunction<Object, BoxedUnit> receive() {
        return ReceiveBuilder.
  matchAny(o ->System.out.println("received unknown message")).build();
    }
}
```

In Scala:

```scala
class Chatroom extends Actor {
var joinedUsers: Seq[UserRef] = Seq.empty
var chatHistory: Seq[PostToChatroom] = Seq.empty

override def receive = {
case _ =>
println("received unknown message ")
  }
}
```

Building by specification

Revisiting the specifications we wrote, we can start to build the class and the tests. We'll take one of the specifications here and show how we might build the test. Then, we'll implement the behavior. The class can be built by adding each specification one at a time. After completing one specification here, we'll take a look at different ways of testing Actors.

Scenario: User Joins Chatroom

- Given a chatroom has no users, when it receives a request from a user to join the chatroom, then it should add the user to its list of joined users

In Java, we'll continue to use Junit, but C supports *Given, When, Then* style of specification testing with appropriate annotations—it's worth taking a look if you're starting a new project:

```java
public class ChatroomTest extends TestCase {
    static ActorSystem system = ActorSystem.apply();

    @Test
    public void testShouldAddUserToJoinedUsersWhenJoiningTest() {
        //Given a Chatroom has no users
        Props props = Props.create(Chatroom.class);
 TestActorRef<Chatroom> ref = TestActorRef.create(system, props,
"testA");
        Chatroom chatroom = ref.underlyingActor();
 assertEquals(chatroom.joinedUsers.size(), 0);

        //When it recieves a request from a user to join the chatroom
 UserRefuserRef = new UserRef(system.deadLetters(), "user");
 Messages.JoinChatroom request = new Messages.JoinChatroom(userRef);
 ref.tell(request, system.deadLetters());

        //It should add the UserRef to its list of joined users
 assertEquals(chatroom.joinedUsers.get(0), userRef);
    }
}
```

Note that we can start the test name with the word "should"—as Dan North writes, this helps us write descriptive test names that will print useful information when the tests run. The actual structure of the test reflects our given when the format is as shown in the comments. The comments themselves may not be necessary, but here this demonstrates how the specification relates to the code.

In Scala, we have better DSLs with the common testing tools, so we can more directly structure our test to reflect the specification:

```scala
class ChatroomSpec
    extends FunSpec with Matchers {

 val system = ActorSystem()
```

```
    describe("Given a Chatroom has no users"){
  val props: Props = Props.create(classOf[Chatroom])
  val ref: TestActorRef[Chatroom] = TestActorRef.create(system, props,
  "testA")
  val chatroom: Chatroom = ref.underlyingActor
  chatroom.joinedUsers.size should equal(0)
      describe("when it receives a request from a user to join the
  chatroom"){
  val userRef: UserRef = new UserRef(system.deadLetters, "user")
  val request: JoinChatroom = JoinChatroom(userRef)
        ref ! userRef
        it("should add the UserRef to the list of joined users"){
  chatroom.joinedUsers.head should equal(userRef)
        }
      }
    }
  }
```

This maps more directly to the *Given When Then* format to show how you might use
FunSpec to layer your tests. While this demonstrates the specification quite directly, in
real scenarios I would avoid creating too much nesting and duplicate things instead
so that your tests aren't bleeding—unlike your production code, duplication can be
appropriate in tests. There are several ways in which you can structure tests using
ScalaTest—check out the API and see which suits you best.

At this point, we need to run the test and ensure that it fails with the expected
problem. Running the failing test is an important step as it gives us confidence that
our test is validating the correct thing. Here we can see the test failing because there
are no joined users in the list, as expected. Then, when it passes, we know that the
behavior is correctly implemented to meet the specification:

```
[info]    - should add the UserRef to the list of joined users ***
FAILED ***
[info]      java.util.NoSuchElementException: head of empty list
```

At this point, we've covered the basics of designing and testing a new project. To
recap, we can draw a lot of the design from the way we describe it. We've identified
where state exists, and in any case where we identified state in a concurrent
environment, we can decide to implement it with an actor. Any behavior that doesn't
have mutable state accessed from multiple places at the same time, we can probably
simplify by using plain objects. As an example, maybe we want to represent the
ChatHistory in a class instead of simply a list. As the ChatHistory is only accessed
by the chatroom, the ChatHistory object could be a plain object implementing
getRecentHistory with a simple unsynchronized method as the actor safely
handles only one message at a time.

After checking the test fails, you can implement the behavior, then ensure the test passes in a traditional TDD/BDD manner, and then move on to implement the next specification in the same way—building the test and then implementing the behavior. Each edge case you find and build for should have a corresponding test. In my opinion, this is the most reliable way to build maintainable code.

Next, we'll look at some different aspects of the *akka-testkit* module that we can use to help us build clear and expressive tests.

Testing actors

The *akka-testkit* module is a component of Akka that gives us several tools to test our Actors. We'll extend our chatroom example to look at a couple of tools in the testkit that can improve on our testing.

We'll cover two major concerns here–unit-testing underlying actor behavior and testing Actor responses.

Testing Actor behavior and state

We've looked at synchronous testing previously but, to recap here, using `TestActorRef` gives us a way to test request and response with Actors without needing to await messages. Using Awaits is a more flexible and realistic approach to testing Actors, but for testing Actor behavior in isolation, there are a couple of approaches we can use.

In the previous example, you'll note that we don't wait for the message to be processed. Because we created the actor using Akka Testkit's `TestActorRef`, the Actor will use the calling thread (via `CallingThreadDispatcher`) to process the message, so we immediately get free synchronous testing by creating the actor with `TestActorRef`. This is the first thing that Akka testkit gives us; we've already demonstrated it.

Next, testkit's `TestActorRef` gives us access to the object behind the `ActorRef`, which gives us the ability to inspect it in ways we normally cannot and do not want to use. Without this, we'd have to use messages to check the internal state of the actor for validation in the tests. At this point, then, we might have to add features only for the sake of being able to test the actor accurately, which is not desirable. If we can access the underlying actor, then we can test its state with minimal code and less test-induced design damage.

We'll look at how we can use this feature of testkit to shape how we might write and test actor code when using the TestActorRef. We know that the Akka TestActorRef gives us access to the underlying actor, and that if we can get access to the underlying actor, we can validate any fields and methods exposed in that actor. But if we construct our actors with the behavior in a method instead of in the receive block, then we can actually test an actor like a plain class. This can be a real benefit to creating clear and simple tests of Actor behavior without worrying too much about sending and receiving messages. We want to validate the integration as well, but for scoping in on just the behavior, we can test the underlying object itself. Let's take a look at the test we created previously and see how we can use the access to the underlying actor to our advantage.

First, we'll look at the implementation of the behavior in the last specification:

- **Scenario**: User Joins chatroom

    ○ Given a chatroom has no users, when it receives a request from a user to join the chatroom, then it should add the user to its list of joined users.

We'll write a method in the actor to express the behavior.

In Java:

```java
public class Chatroom extends AbstractActor{
    List<Messages.PostToChatroom>chatHistory = new
ArrayList<Messages.PostToChatroom>();
    List<UserRef>joinedUsers = new ArrayList<UserRef>();

    @Override
    public PartialFunction<Object, BoxedUnit> receive() {
        return ReceiveBuilder.
 match(Messages.JoinChatroom.class, this::joinChatroom).
 matchAny(o ->System.out.println("received unknown message")).build();
    }
    public void joinChatroom(Messages.JoinChatroommsg) {
 joinedUsers.add(msg.userRef);
    }
}
```

In Scala:

```scala
class Chatroom extends Actor {
 varjoinedUsers: Seq[UserRef] = Seq.empty
 varchatHistory: Seq[PostToChatroom] = Seq.empty
   override def receive: Receive = {
     case x: JoinChatroom =>
```

```
joinChatroom(x)
    case _ =>
println("unimplemented")
    }
  def joinChatroom(joinChatroom: JoinChatroom) {
   joinedUsers = joinedUsers :+ joinChatroom.userRef
    }
}
```

Note that the behavior is placed into a method instead of the receive block itself. With the behavior expressed in a method, we can test and change it without worrying about the actual delivery of the message. In the test, then, we can use Akka testkitTestActorRef to get and test the underlying actor behavior.

In Java:

```
@Test
  public void testShouldAddUserToJoinedUsersWhenJoiningTest() {
      Props props = Props.create(Chatroom.class);
TestActorRef<Chatroom> ref = TestActorRef.create(ActorSystem.apply(),
props, "testA");
      Chatroom chatroom = ref.underlyingActor();
UserRefuserRef = new UserRef(system.deadLetters(), "user");
 Messages.JoinChatroom request = new Messages.JoinChatroom(userRef);
chatroom.joinChatroom(request);
assertEquals(chatroom.joinedUsers.get(0), userRef);
    }
```

In Scala:

```
describe("Given a Chatroom has no users (Unit example)"){
 val props: Props = Props.create(classOf[Chatroom])
val ref: TestActorRef[Chatroom] = TestActorRef.create(ActorSystem(),
props, "testA")
val chatroom: Chatroom = ref.underlyingActor
chatroom.joinedUsers.size should equal(0)
    describe("when it receives a request from a user to join the
chatroom"){
 valuserRef: UserRef = new UserRef(system.deadLetters, "user")
 chatroom.joinChatroom(JoinChatroom(userRef))
      it("should add the UserRef to the list of joined users"){
 chatroom.joinedUsers.head should equal(userRef)
       }
     }
   }
```

You can see in this case that it's not much simpler—but instead of sending the message, we just call the method directly instead. If we have several methods we want to test inside an actor, this can greatly help us decompose and test smaller-grained details of its behavior.

Testing Message flow

Being able to test the underlying behavior in an actor is obviously useful, but what if we want to test sending and receiving messages in more complex situations? What happens if we want to mock another actor's behavior to ensure that the integration points are successfully built?

Let's look at a couple of scenarios where other actors are involved, and we'll look at two main approaches: using the test class as an actor and using a mock probe as an actor.

Using the test Itself as an Actor

Now we're going to look at how to have the test class itself receive messages so that we don't need to examine any extra external actors when checking for message flow from an actor under test. First, let's take the following specification.

- Scenario: User joins chatroom

  ◦ Given a chatroom has a chat history, when a user joins the chatroom, then it should receive the last 10 posts to the chatroom from the history.

In this case, we want to ensure that, when a user joins the chatroom, they receive the updates from the history. We have two actors involved then: The chatroom and the User actor that is referenced in the `UserRef`. Because we don't care about any of the details of the user actor, all we want to do is test that a message comes out of the chatroom actor with the appropriate data. The simplest approach for testing interaction between one actor and the subject is to use the test itself as the receiver. Akka testkit lets the test itself receive messages, so where you're testing responses, you can express the assertions with an API that is made for doing so:

```
@Test
public void testShouldSendHistoryWhenUserJoin() {
    new JavaTestKit(system) {{
        //Given
        Props props = Props.create(Chatroom.class);
TestActorRef<Chatroom> ref = TestActorRef.create(system, props);
        Chatroom chatroom = ref.underlyingActor();
 Messages.PostToChatroom msg = new Messages.PostToChatroom("test",
"user");
```

```
chatroom.chatHistory.add(msg);
            //When
UserRef userRef = new UserRef(system.deadLetters(), "user");
 Messages.JoinChatroom request = new Messages.JoinChatroom(userRef);
 ref.tell(request, getRef());


            //Then
 List expected = new ArrayList<Messages.PostToChatroom>();
 expected.add(msg);
 expectMsgEquals(duration("1 second"), expected);
          }};
    }
```

For Java, the points to note here are that we send the message with the test ref as the sender—ref.tell(request, getRef()), and, then, the test itself expects a message with one of the expectMsg* methods. We check for exact equality, but you can test the class type for example.

In Scala, instead of creating an anonymous TestKit object as in Java, the test class itself works, which makes for a nicer syntax.

We have to change the test class definition:

```
classChatroomSpec(_system: ActorSystem) extends TestKit(_system) with
ImplicitSender
  with Matchers with FunSpecLike {
```

Then the class becomes an actor, so the specification can look like the following:

```
    describe("Given a Chatroom has a history"){
  val props = Props.create(classOf[Chatroom])
  val ref = TestActorRef.create(system, props)
  val chatroom: Chatroom = ref.underlyingActor
  valmsg = PostToChatroom("test", "user")
  chatroom.chatHistory = chatroom.chatHistory.+:(msg)

      describe("When a user joins the chatroom"){
  val userRef = UserRef(system.deadLetters, "user")
  val request = JoinChatroom(userRef)
        ref ! request

        it("(the user) should receive the history"){
  expectMsg(1 second, List(msg))
        }
      }
    }
```

That's a bit clearer than the Java syntax—knowing that the test is an actor, then when we call tell, we know that the test itself will implicitly be the sender and, hence, receive the reply. The only point to mention is the `expectMsg` method—this will stop the test and await the noted reply. The test will fail if the expectation is not met in the time passed in the method call.

Using TestProbes as mock Actors

Next, we'll look at the post message specification for the chatroom and look at how we can mock an external actor in a test.

- **Scenario**: Post to chatroom:

    ○ Given a chatroom has a joined user, when the chatroom receives a request to post to the chatroom, then it should notify the joined users

This gives us an opportunity to look at the joined user as a mock that expects a message and see how that might look in code.

Here it is in Java:

```
@Test
public void testShouldSendUpdateWhenUserPosts() {
    //Given
    Props props = Props.create(Chatroom.class);
TestActorRef<Chatroom> ref = TestActorRef.create(system, props);
    Chatroom chatroom = ref.underlyingActor();
    final TestProbe probe = new TestProbe(system);
UserRefuserRef = new UserRef(probe.ref(), "user");
chatroom.joinChatroom(new Messages.JoinChatroom(userRef));

    //When
Messages.PostToChatroommsg = new Messages.PostToChatroom("test",
"user");
ref.tell(msg, probe.ref());
    //Then
probe.expectMsg(msg);
    }
```

In Scala:

```
describe("Given a Chatroom has a joined user"){
 val props = Props.create(classOf[Chatroom])
 val ref = TestActorRef.create(system, props)
 val chatroom: Chatroom = ref.underlyingActor
val probe: TestProbe = new TestProbe(system)
 valuserRef: UserRef = new UserRef(probe.ref, "user")
 chatroom.joinChatroom(JoinChatroom(userRef))
```

```
    describe("when someone posts to the chatroom"){
val msg = PostToChatroom("test", "user")
ref.tell(msg, probe.ref)
    it("(joined user) should get an update"){
probe.expectMsg(msg)
    }
  }
}
```

You'll notice that this looks quite similar to the previous test, except that the test probe is sent as the joined user, and then the assertions are made with the `TestProbe` as well (`probe.expectMsg`). `TestProbes` have additional behavior such as the ability to send messages, so they truly can be used to both mock out any Actor behavior and make assertions about receipt. They're a powerful tool to keep in your toolbox when working with actors.

Testing Advice

We've looked at some techniques to test on different levels. We've looked at how to unit test the code in an actor, then how to test an actor from the perspective of the test sending the actor messages, and, finally, how to create test probes to mock the interaction from an actor to our actor under test. Using test probes, we could certainly test many different integration scenarios.

It can be hard to know what to test and what not to test. The best advice I heard was probably from Kent Beck in a response to a thread on test coverage on Stack Overflow. He said, *I get paid for code that works, not for tests, so my philosophy is to test as little as possible to reach a given level of confidence.* The thread is available at `http://stackoverflow.com/questions/153234/how-deep-are-your-unit-tests`.

What I would take from that in relation to testing your actors is to target the biggest bang for your buck. You don't need to test both the underlying behavior and the integration of an Actor to be confident that it works and that you won't introduce regressions, so test accordingly. Test where you need to be confident that it works.

Because the `TestActorRef` uses the `CallingThreadDispatcher`, you have mechanisms that will let you test your actors synchronously without using `Thread.Sleep`. `expectMsg`on probes or in the test when using the test as a sender gives you another way to wait longer than needed. Using mechanisms like these can be better than putting sleep in your tests because your tests will stay fast-running. It's very important to have a test suite that takes as little time as possible to run—if you let a few suites get into your code that call`Thread.sleep`, the cost in breaking flow or the avoidance of running the whole suite can get higher.

It can be a bit harder to write the tests to be fast, but I'd recommend prioritizing speed when writing your tests because you want your team to really be able to lean on the tests for confidence. Figure out how to get your tests to run without any calls to Thread.sleep—it's almost always possible with the tools Akka gives us.

If you are using mechanisms such as Sleep, the other thing to look out for is flaky tests. It's possible to write tests that usually pass and then intermittently fail. If someone picks up the code after you and they randomly see tests failing, it'll very likely cost them some time trying to understand if they broke something in the code or not. Again, tests where the test thread has to wait for an external event can be the cause of these tests that intermittently fail. It's better to rearrange the test so that the test or a probe is in the middle of the behavior to be able to catch the event when it occurs and make assertions then, instead of waiting an arbitrary period and then validating the outcomes. In complex cases, you can use things such as Java's CountDownLatch to wait for several events to finish.

If you're not experienced with writing tests, I'd just like to note here that the objectives in your production code can be relaxed a bit when testing. Specifically, duplication in your tests is fine. Do not worry about factoring out duplication if having a similar setup over and over documents the API and behavior very clearly in each specification.

Homework

To ensure you can see how to work with the tools provided, I would recommend that you do finish implementing the specifications and some others:

- Ensure when a user posts, it receives back an OK.

- Ensure that, when a user is joined and posts, the user does not receive its own update.

- Continue to design the application. If you were to replace the ChatHistory with its own class instead of a simple list, and were to implement a getRecentHistory function, would a plain class be enough? What would the benefits be of using an actor, if any? What would the drawbacks be?

Summary

Testing and designing with Actors has a bit of a learning curve. The most important thing to realize about Actors is that they are not always the best approach—plain classes should be used when it's simpler to do so. But, in the domain, where is state and concurrency exist together, then Actors are generally a safe bet. Actors can be more involved to build and test than simple classes. There are excellent tools to help us build actors and their tests, though, and this chapter rounds out the end of this book by covering some of those tools, not only in the process of designing and testing, but also in using the technology available to better express our test cases.

In the next chapter, we will look at some extra features in Akka, some items related to deployment and monitoring, and some steps you can take in your continuing journey.

9
A Journey's End

You have made it to the Journey's end. You are now armed with a bit of knowledge about building concurrent and distributed systems with Akka and Scala or Java8.

I expect a wide variety of readers to be here—some with distributed computing experience, and some with none. Either way, the material requires practice to master.

The Akka toolkit is quite large and the documentation is a very thorough and useful reference to all of its parts. This book has hopefully showed you why and when to use many of Akka's different tools. This chapter will highlight a few outstanding features and modules that you may want to be aware of, and some next steps, as follows:

- Other Akka features and modules:
    - Logging
    - Event Bus
    - Agents
    - Akka Persistence
    - Akka I/O
    - Akka Streams and Akka HTTP

- Next steps:
    - Learning about Domain Driven Design
    - Deployment tools
    - Monitoring logs and events

Other Akka Features and Modules

From the outset, this book has said that it will not cover every last corner of the Akka toolkit, but instead focus on helping you learn about distributed computing using Akka. Akka is quite a large tool kit, and all of the most important core pieces have been well covered.

Now that we're at the end of our journey here, it's a good time to highlight a few areas of the toolkit that you might want to take a look at in more depth. I'll give a brief introduction to them here so you're aware of some of the interesting extensions.

Logging in Akka

We briefly introduced logging in Akka early in the book, but we'll review logging again here briefly to show how to use more advanced features. Akka by default will log to the console; however, it offers an event handler for slf4j that is available by importing an slf4j backend into your project such as Logback.

To use the slf4j logger, you'll need to provide the Akka slf4j module (it's not in the Akka core), and you'll also need to provide an slf4j backend such as Logback. You can add these dependencies to your build.sbt file using the following code:

```
"ch.qos.logback" % "logback-classic" % "1.0.0" % "runtime",
"com.typesafe.akka" %% "akka-slf4j" % "2.3.11"
```

Then, in your application configuration (the application.conf file), you can declare the Akka slf4j event handler to be used as follows:

```
akka {
  event-handlers = ["akka.event.slf4j.Slf4jEventHandler"]
loglevel = "DEBUG"
}
```

You can put a logback.xml file into your project's resources folder to enable fine-grained log control and more extended control over appenders. If you wanted to log to both a file (logs/app.log) and the console, a basic configuration will look like this:

```
<configuration>
<appender name="FILE" class="ch.qos.logback.core.FileAppender">
<file>logs/app.log</file>

<encoder>
<pattern>%date %level [%thread] %logger{10} [%file:%line] %msg%n</pattern>
</encoder>
</appender>
```

```
<appender name="STDOUT" class="ch.qos.logback.core.ConsoleAppender">
<encoder>
<pattern>%msg%n</pattern>
</encoder>
</appender>

<root level="debug">
<appender-ref ref="FILE" />
<appender-ref ref="STDOUT" />
</root>
</configuration>
```

To use Akka logging in the application, you can either create a logger explicitly, passing in an `ActorSystem` object:

```
//java
LoggingAdapter log = Logging.getLogger(getContext().system(), this);

//scala
val log = Logging(context.system, this)
```

Or, if using Scala, you can mix in the logging trait into your actor:

```
class MyActor extends Actor with akka.actor.ActorLogging {
   log.info("actor startup: {}", self.toString)
}
```

Note that Akka will accept a variable length argument list as parameters in the messages, where it will replace each pair of brackets,{}, with the parameters in the order they are provided. Exceptions can be logged by passing them as the first argument:

```
#+BEGIN_SRC
//java
log.debug("params {} {} {}", param1, param2, param3);
log.error(e, "exception encountered: "); //exceptions are first arg

//scala
log.debug("params {} {} {}", param1, param2, param3)
log.info(e, "exception encountered: ") //exceptions are first arg
#+END_SRC
```

There are performance benefits to letting logger handle the string interpolation, as it will execute the interpolation only if the log level is set so that the logger will actually log the event. If the event is not logged, then the string interpolation will not occur. Thus, this is generally better than doing something such as this:

```
#+BEGIN_SRC
log.debug("this actor is " + self().toString);
#+END_SRC
```

The preceding code will always create the joined string in memory, even if the message is never logged.

This covers almost everything you'll need to know about logging in Akka. For additional information on configuring logging, you will want to check the Logback documentation. Rolling log files, multiple appenders, and other advanced features can be handled by configuring Logback, especially using logback.xml. For very advanced use cases, Logback also supports configurations written in the groovy programming language.

Message Channels and EventBus

The EventBus object in Akka can be used to publish and subscribe to events to send messages to multiple actors. Pub/Sub approaches can be built with very little code by sending subscribe messages to an actor that will in turn hold a list of actors. However, Akka also describes a mechanism to handle this, where you listen for a topic.

Eventbus is a part of the core Akka library, so no extra imports are required.

Using an event bus requires choosing and extending a classifier that will describe the event type and how to target subscribers. Classifiers are described in the documentation referenced at the end of this section.

IRemember you can always use actor hierarchies to send messages with actorSelection as well. Event Bus should come to mind if you have very specific topic subscription to handle that hierarchies are not suitable for.

To use the event bus, there are three types that we're concerned with foremost and that we'll declare as types in Scala, or define with type arguments in Java, as follows:

- **Classifier Type**: what the topic type is for the message
- **Event Type**: what data type is provided on the publish event:
    - Needs a topic (you'll define the logic for the topic)
    - Optionally needs some other data to publish
- **Subscriber Type**

Multiple Classifiers are available. As a quick example, assume we have a message called `EventBusMessage`, and we want to use the Event Bus to have actors subscribe and publish to them. The event bus doesn't need to use actors—it can implement any pub/sub behavior you require. A simple `LookupClassifier` object will describe the type of the event, the topic/classifier type, and how to lookup the classification of the topic for subscribers. In the case of `LookupClassifier`, the subscribers need to have an ordering.

A simple Java message might look like this:

```java
public class EventBusMessage {
    public final String topic;
    public final String msg;

    public EventBusMessage(String topic, String msg) {
this.topic = topic;
        this.msg = msg;
    }
}
```

The following are the Java and Scala event bus examples:

```java
public class JavaLookupClassifier extends
LookupEventBus<EventBusMessage, ActorRef, String> {

    @Override public String classify(EventBusMessage event) {
        return event.topic;
    }

    @Override public void publish(EventBusMessage event, ActorRef
subscriber) {
subscriber.tell(event.msg, ActorRef.noSender());
    }

    @Override public int compareSubscribers(ActorRef a, ActorRef b) {
        return a.compareTo(b);
    }

    // determines the initial size of the index data structure
    @Override public intmapSize() {
        return 128;
    }
}
```

```
class ScalaLookupClassifier extends EventBus with LookupClassification
{
    type Event = EventBusMessage
    type Classifier = String
    type Subscriber = ActorRef

    override protected def classify(event: Event): Classifier = event.
topic

    override protected def publish(event: Event, subscriber:
Subscriber): Unit = {
        subscriber ! event.msg
    }

    override protected def compareSubscribers(a: Subscriber, b:
Subscriber): Int =
a.compareTo(b)

    //initial size of the index data structure
    override protected defmapSize: Int = 128
}
```

The preceding code implements some pretty basic logic such as how to determine the topic, what to do with a publish event for any relevant subscribers, and a requirement—how to compare subscribers. Also, the beginning size for the map needs to be declared, although it will adjust automatically as needed.

You might use it like this:

```
JavaLookupClassifier lookupBus = new JavaLookupClassifier;
lookupBus.subscribe(myActor, "greetings");
lookupBus.publish(new EventBusMessage("time", System.
currentTimeMillis().toString));
lookupBus.publish(new EventBusMessage("greetings", "hello"));

val lookupBus = new JavaLookupClassifier
lookupBus.subscribe(myActor, "greetings")
lookupBus.publish(new EventBusMessage("time", System.
currentTimeMillis().toString))
lookupBus.publish(new EventBusMessage("greetings", "hello"))
```

In this case, our actor subscribes to the topic greetings. Then, we publish an event with the topic time and the topic greetings. As you can probably guess, the only message that gets to the actor will be the one sent with the topic "greetings."

The Akka documentation has examples and explanation for the classifiers if you want to further explore using Akka's Event Bus features. The Akka documentation can be found here:

- `http://doc.akka.io/docs/akka/snapshot/java/event-bus.html`
- `http://doc.akka.io/docs/akka/snapshot/scala/event-bus.html`

Agents

The Akka Agent module is inspired by Clojure's Agents, which are reactive constructs to help handle shared access to state. A better way to think about the Agent is much like a Java `AtomicInteger`, but for any value or type. It holds that state, and allows you to execute atomic operations on the value stored in a thread-safe manner, while allowing access to read the value safely.

More formally put, Agents provide a single storage location for a single value and allow modification of that value by providing a function. Agents allow safe atomic and transactional access to their value, giving a mechanism for safe concurrent access to state much like an actor would.

The advantage of Agents is that they are a bit lighter weight than using actors to encapsulate state. If you see a single stateful value or object that you need to safely handle, you can consider if an Agent might be a good fit, especially if you're thinking about how to make operations atomic (that is, checking the value, and then setting the value if it meets a certain condition where race conditions would be problematic). Thus, when you need to access a single value from across threads, Agents offer a nice alternative. to Actors.

Agents are not a core feature in Akka, and so they are in a separate module that you need to place in your project's `build.sbt` file:

```
"com.typesafe.akka" %% "akka-agent" % "2.3.6"
```

A fairly standard example is a bank account withdrawal where we first need to check to see if there is enough money in the bank account; and then, if there is, we can withdraw the money. Because two threads could check the account, and then deduct the money from the account, we need the account check-and-set operation to be one atomic operation so that we ensure the value isn't modified after it's read.

If we used an integer shared across threads, it would be possible to do something like this if two people try to withdraw $20 from an account at the same time:

1. Account has $25.
2. Husband and wife try $20 withdrawal simultaneously.
3. Husband checks to see if account has more than $20. Account has $25.
4. Wife checks to see if account has more than $20. Account has $25.
5. Husband withdraws $20, setting account to $5.
6. Wife withdraws $20, setting account to $5 (illegal!.).

Because the account had enough money in it when both threads checked the account, both threads proceeded to try to withdraw the money. However, when the second thread deducted the amount, it didn't see that someone else had already taken the money. The bank has now lost $20 and would not know where it went! The application would generally appear to act normal, but if two transactions happen at the same time, money disappears and nobody notices. If this happened a few hundred thousand times before someone caught the issue, the bank could have potentially lost hundreds of thousands of dollars!

We need the check and set operation to be atomic (one complete unit of work) to provide this functionality safely. Doing this with an actor is certainly possible as the actor will only handle one message at a time, but it's a bit more succinct to do this with an agent.

Agents use actors and threads in their underlying implementation, so we need to provide an execution context for them. We'll create an actor system and use its dispatcher to create the agent with the $25 in the account:

```
import akka.actor.ActorSystem;
import akka.agent.Agent;

//Java
ActorSystem system = ActorSystem.create();
Agent<Integer> account = Agent.create(25, dispatcher);

//Scala
val system = ActorSystem()
implicit valec = system.dispatcher
val account = Agent(25)
```

You can get the value with `Agent.get()` or `Agent.apply`:

```
Integer currentValue = account.get();
valcurrentValue = account()
```

 Note that getting the value will immediately return the value, although operations may be pending.

To update the value with the check-and-set operation, we can provide a function (int =>int) describing the operation using send. For Java, you need to provide a Mapper function:

```
//Java
final Integer ammountToWithdraw = 20;
account.send(new akka.dispatch.Mapper<Integer, Integer>() {
        public Integer apply(Integer i) {
            if(ammountToWithdraw<= i)
                return i - ammountToWithdraw;
            else
                return i;
        }
    });

//Scala
valammmountToWithdraw = 20
account.send { i =>
  if(i>= 20) {
i - 20
  } else i
}
```

These operations are fire-and-forget, and they run in the other thread pool, so you would need to complete a future if you want to get the result of the operation back from the agent. The `alter` method is identical, except it returns the result of the operation in future.

Scala offers us some extra flexibility to be able to complete this operation. In Scala, you can use a transaction block to allow multiple agents to participate in one atomic operation, and return the result of that block. If we want to move money from one account to another, for example, then the transaction block can be used to have multiple agents interact, as shown in the following code:

```
import scala.concurrent.stm._
val wifeAccount = Agent(25)
val husbandAccount = Agent(0)
val wasSuccess = atomic { txn =>
  if(wifeAccount() >= 20) {
wifeAccount.send(_ - 20)
husbandAccount.send(_ + 20)
    true
  } else false
}
```

Agents can be a useful little abstraction to have in your tool belt. Again, think of places you could use `AtomicInteger`. Now, you have an `AtomicAnything` object and it's called an Agent.

Documentation for Agents can be found here:

- `http://doc.akka.io/docs/akka/snapshot/java/agents.html`
- `http://doc.akka.io/docs/akka/snapshot/scala/agents.html`

Akka Persistence

Another module that may be of interest is Akka Persistence. Akka Persistence gives a mechanism to maintain actor state through crashes/JVM restarts or restarts of the actor by a supervisor.

It's common to misunderstand the name of the library to mean that it has a mechanism to use external persistence mechanisms such as databases and key-value stores. You would not use Akka persistence to store user information or account information, for example.

Remember that, by default, when an actor restarts, it loses any internal state and only keeps its constructor arguments. Akka Persistence offers the ability to add a journal of events that an actor has encountered so that an actor can be run through those events again after restarting to restore its state. By re-applying the journal of events, the actor will fast-forward, recollecting any internal state. For instance, if you're building a metrics library, an in-memory counter collecting latency information from an endpoint would be able to more accurately collect data by using persistence. If the actor restarted, it would be able to roll forward through events since its last flush, and then pass that information along successfully.

Note that the Akka Persistence module is marked experimental at the time of writing (Akka 2.4 was released GA a couple weeks before the last editing was completed on this book.) Binary compatibility is not guaranteed across minor versions while modules are marked experimental; thus, it should be added to a project with some caution that understands the state of the component. More information is available on Akka Persistence in the Akka documentation.

Akka I/O

Akka I/O was introduced in Akka 2.2, which was a joint effort from the Akka and Spray teams based on Spray's underlying I/O module. It offers some lower-level TCP and Socket abstractions to build your own network communication. As Akka itself tries to raise the level of abstraction, this book has focused on introducing Akka as a toolkit that takes care of network communication concerns for you. However, if you want to handle TCP communication yourself, then there are tools in Akka that can help you do so.

Handling your own TCP communication is a fairly advanced topic and is beyond the scope of this book, but there are some libraries that you can read, such as the Brando Redis client library, that will give some good examples of how to handle TCP communication using Akka I/O. It can be accessed at `https://github.com/chrisdinn/brando`. Redis communication is a good example for analysis as it is quite simple.

Akka streams and HTTP

Akka Streams have been discussed briefly in the chapter on Mailbox-related items. Streams is one of the more interesting new modules in Akka as a reactive streams implementation. Akka HTTP is built on top of Akka Streams with help from the Spray team.

Akka Streams and Reactive Streams in general are a more advanced topic. If you would like to explore Akka Streams, I would recommend beginning with learning about Reactive Streams. As Akka HTTP is built on Akka Streams, you would likely want to learn about Akka Streams before exploring this topic. Akka HTTP, as the name suggests, offers an abstraction to build HTTP Client or Server applications.

Deployment Tools

One last topic to bring up is the deployment of applications. Because this is a book targeting developers, it does not cover deployment of applications from the infrastructure perspectives.

Because Akka Cluster helps applications talk to each other, your work is basically done once your application is able to build clusters. But building new application nodes at the infrastructure level can be an intensive feat.

At a minimum, I'd recommend you look at tools such as Puppet, Chef, Salt, and Ansibe right out of the gate—don't wait until you deploy to start handling these concerns. Get to deployment automation in your dev and QA environments. The problem with these tools is that they may still be too oriented to server inventories. Thus, tools such as Mesos and ConductR, which abstract away the multiple nodes underneath, might be the right approach. They will help you treat multiple nodes in a datacenter like a pool of resources, rather than distinct entities. Whatever approach you take, as a rule of thumb nobody should ever need to log into your servers once your DevOps concerns are sufficiently mature.

It's a big area to cover and is a specialization on its own more in the field of operations, but you don't need a dedicated DevOps engineer to make this happen—you just need to work beside your operations team as a Developer/Engineer to start to grow the discipline. Start a group that meets for a couple hours a week and tries to nail down how to get your dev and QA environments under automation. Once you've got that covered, you can start to look at how to tie in new nodes to a cluster in your production deployment environment once you see how the general automation practices work. You'll be doing your team a big service if you can plant the seed.

A brief example of what `ConductR` can do is that it will take your infrastructure and "bundle" applications and handle replication of the "bundles" across the infrastructure for you, as shown in following figure:

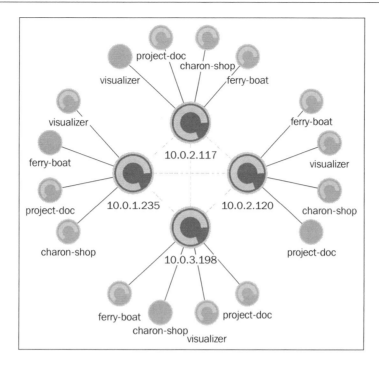

Have a look at the ConductR whitepaper from Typesafe if you'd like to understand the problems with yesterday's approaches in the context of applications today. It's a problem area that has a lot of intense activity, and Typesafe has tools and approaches that integrate with applications on which you build the Typesafe platform.

Monitoring Logs and Events

Finally, after talking about deployment, we need to quickly glance over how to monitor your application. There are probably three major concerns to examine to ensure your application is maintainable:

- **Events and Metrics**: Number of successes, failures, amount of traffic, and latency.

- **Logs**: Internal application behavior and details of failures.

- **Health**: Is it up? Is it healthy? And, is it working as expected?

For general event and metrics, tools like Statsd or Metrics can be used to put internal counters and timers in your app and "ship them" to another service where graphs are produced. AppDynamics and NewRelic are partners of Typesafe and offer SaaS solutions for similar concerns if you don't want to handle these in house.

Logs at scale can be very difficult to handle, and I've seen some big systems be set to Error or even Off. Whatever approach you take, you probably don't want to be scrubbing through multiple files on many different servers to understand what's going on with your application. The ELK stack—Elasticsearch, Logstash, and Kibana—is a very good stack of tools that will allow an agent to send log events to a cluster of Logstash services where events are indexed and then put into Elasticseach for fast queying. Kibana sits in front of Elasticsearch as a very capable frontend to query and analyze log events. I would really recommend this type of solution, even if it's not ELK. You want a centralized log collection in your systems to improve its maintainability.

Being able to "see inside" your running systems is critical to understand the health of your live systems. Being able to interpret the events requires views of the data that are easy to understand. NewRelic is easy to get started with as it's a SaaS model. If you don't mind working with infrastructure more, tools such as Graphite can visualize events collected with statsd to help you recognize trends in your data related to performance or errors, for example. Here is a screenshot from the Graphite

Next Steps

To really grow with the material in this book, you'll need to keep venturing forward on your journey. I have to assume that you want to learn about building distributed things if you're reading this book. In this next section, I'll provide a few more activities and resources outside of the Akka documentation that you might want to check out to help you understand other related concerns.

Writing some Actor Code

At this point, if you have not already, I would strongly advise that you go back over the homework problems in each section and try to accomplish the tasks.

The initial chapters up to *Chapter 4*, *Actor Lifecycle – Handling State and Failure*, in particular, are enough to work from for quite a while. Build a local concurrent application with Akka first. This material, and what you will certainly build on from it, is the most important foundational work.

Chapter 5, *Scaling Up*, and further chapters, while I believe they are the most interesting pieces, are more advanced topics, and I myself have worked on very large systems with Akka that have employed very few of the techniques only because some of the modules, like clusters, are newer, or they may not be needed for some use cases (for example, adjusting the mailbox configuration.)

While I've talked about Akka as a distribution toolkit a lot in this book, it arguably has a use as both a concurrency framework and a distribution toolkit. Understanding when to use each is a fine balancing act, and you should always prefer simplicity until you have a good reason to make a change. Very often, using futures will be enough for concurrency. Thus, it takes a fairly critical examination of the problems to employ Akka's actors in the right places, and I've seen a few cases where Actors were probably a worse decision than simply using futures. It's only through experience that you'll develop the foresight to understand where the right place is to use Actors.

Certainly, though Akka will seldom be a bad choice for distribution problems, I would definitely learn the material in *Chapter 6*, *Successfully Scaling Out – Clustering*, with zeal to be confident enough with Cluster to employ it in your projects. Tools like Zookeeper can coordinate nodes in a cluster, Principles of Reactive Programming. It also covers a rather broad set of concerns as far as systems coordinating and talking; not only understanding who is available and who isn't, but also how to get messages between systems without introducing much complexity to the code that you must yourself maintain.

Coursera Courses

I reviewed some courses on Coursera while reaching the end of writing this book. There are a couple of courses that I thought might be helpful to someone trying to learn a bit more about how Akka works, or to advance their own Distributed Computing skills and knowledge.

The second iteration of the *Principles of Reactive Programming* course on Coursera from École Polytechnique Fédérale de Lausanne wrapped up around the time I was finishing this book. The last couple of weeks cover Akka, Cluster, and related topics. I feel that it would be a good piece of material to review for anyone looking for some more information on Reactive Programming in general, and to have some more homework assigned to them to help them learn. It might reiterate some of the concepts in this book, but will certainly help to re-enforce the topics. It can be found at `https://www.coursera.org/course/reactive`.

The Functional Programming in Scala course is also great for learning about functional programming if you're currently a Java Developer. It can be accessed at `https://www.coursera.org/course/progfun`.

One of the best courses you could take to accompany this book is Cloud Computing Concepts from the University of Illinois at Urbana-Champaign covers. It covers many of the topics that the Akka team used to build Cluster. Concepts such as Gossip Protocol (week 2) and time and ordering concepts such as Vector Clocks, used to achieve a consistent view of the cluster (week 4), are covered in great detail in this course. Understanding these concepts in detail will certainly help you in your journey. This course can be found here:

- **Part 1**: `https://www.coursera.org/course/cloudcomputing`
- **Part 2**: `https://www.coursera.org/course/cloudcomputing2`

Summary

We've had a good look at how to use Akka throughout this book. This book has tried to be a read that shows you how to build distributed systems, and has covered many of the concerns that you should understand once you step into the world of high-scale distributed computing. This last chapter highlighted some areas of Akka that you should be aware of, some deployment concerns, and additional areas of education that you can move on to as the next steps in your personal journey. I hope that this book has been helpful in introducing the concepts that you need to get off the ground using Akka. It's an interesting and powerful toolkit. While the documentation covers how to use Akka, it doesn't always show you where and when you want to use the different portions of the framework. I hope that this book covered the "why" and "when" so that you understand how great these tools are, and how they can help you.

Congratulations on making it to the end and good luck on your journey!

Index

A

Actor
about 3, 4
configured dispatcher, using
with 147, 148
creating 21, 38, 39
killing 111
messaging patterns 73
remote access, enabling to 63
responding, via future 45, 46
selecting, for concurrency 129
terminating 111
testing 216
test, using as 219-221
working in parallel with 130-132
Actor, anatomy
about 34
Java Actor API 34-36
Scala Actor API 37, 38
Actor behavior
testing 216-218
Actor Code
writing 238, 239
Actor Model
about 3-5
examples 6, 7
Actor response, defining to message
about 22
in Java 23, 24
in Scala 24, 25
Actor state
testing 216-219

Actor system
about 4, 5
main method, used for starting 64
Agent module
about 231-234
references 234
Akka
about 3
adding, to build.sbt 20
examples 10, 11
akka.actor.Identify
used, for finding Remote Actor 186
Akka application
creating 19
Akka Cluster
about **9**, 153
creating 161
leaving 167
project, configuring 161
starting 165, 166
systems, building with 160
akka.cluster.seed-nodes
configuration 162, 163
akka-cluster tool
reference link 167
Akka features, and modules
about 226
Agent 231-234
Akka HTTP 235
Akka I/O 235
Akka Persistence 234, 235
Akka Streams 235

Thank you for buying
Learning Akka

About Packt Publishing

Packt, pronounced 'packed', published its first book, *Mastering phpMyAdmin for Effective MySQL Management*, in April 2004, and subsequently continued to specialize in publishing highly focused books on specific technologies and solutions.

Our books and publications share the experiences of your fellow IT professionals in adapting and customizing today's systems, applications, and frameworks. Our solution-based books give you the knowledge and power to customize the software and technologies you're using to get the job done. Packt books are more specific and less general than the IT books you have seen in the past. Our unique business model allows us to bring you more focused information, giving you more of what you need to know, and less of what you don't.

Packt is a modern yet unique publishing company that focuses on producing quality, cutting-edge books for communities of developers, administrators, and newbies alike. For more information, please visit our website at www.packtpub.com.

About Packt Open Source

In 2010, Packt launched two new brands, Packt Open Source and Packt Enterprise, in order to continue its focus on specialization. This book is part of the Packt Open Source brand, home to books published on software built around open source licenses, and offering information to anybody from advanced developers to budding web designers. The Open Source brand also runs Packt's Open Source Royalty Scheme, by which Packt gives a royalty to each open source project about whose software a book is sold.

Writing for Packt

We welcome all inquiries from people who are interested in authoring. Book proposals should be sent to author@packtpub.com. If your book idea is still at an early stage and you would like to discuss it first before writing a formal book proposal, then please contact us; one of our commissioning editors will get in touch with you.

We're not just looking for published authors; if you have strong technical skills but no writing experience, our experienced editors can help you develop a writing career, or simply get some additional reward for your expertise.

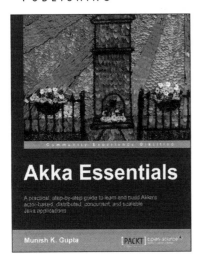

Akka Essentials

ISBN: 978-1-84951-828-4   Paperback: 334 pages

A practical, step-by-step guide to learn and build Akka's actor-based, distributed, concurrent, and scalable Java applications

1. Build large, distributed, concurrent, and scalable applications using the Akka's Actor model.

2. Simple and clear analogy to Java/JEE application development world to explain the concepts.

3. Each chapter will teach you a concept by explaining it with clear and lucid examples– each chapter can be read independently.

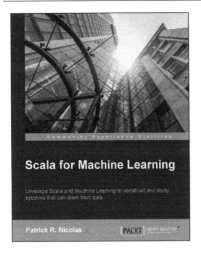

Scala for Machine Learning

ISBN: 978-1-78355-874-2   Paperback: 520 pages

Leverage Scala and Machine Learning to construct and study systems that can learn from data

1. Explore a broad variety of data processing, machine learning, and genetic algorithms through diagrams, mathematical formulation, and source code.

2. Leverage your expertise in Scala programming to create and customize AI applications with your own scalable machine learning algorithms.

3. Experiment with different techniques, and evaluate their benefits and limitations using real-world financial applications, in a tutorial style.

Please check **www.PacktPub.com** for information on our titles

Made in the USA
Middletown, DE
16 August 2016